CW01261460

At Home in Ireland

Mary Leland

At Home in Ireland

ATRIUM

To Peter Levy and Irene Feighan

And in memory of the late Seán Dunne

First published in 2012 by Atrium
Atrium is an imprint of Cork University Press
Youngline Industrial Estate, Pouladuff Road, Togher, Cork, Ireland

Text © Mary Leland
Images © the photographers

All rights reserved. No part of this book may be reprinted or reproduced or utilised in any electronic, mechanical, or other means, now known or heareafter invented, including photocopying or recording or otherwise, without either the prior written permission of the Publishers or a licence permitting restricted copying in Ireland issued by the Irish Copyright Licensing Agency Ltd, The Irish Writers' Centre, 25 Denzille Lane, Dublin 2.
The author has asserted her moral rights in this work.

British Library Cataloguing in Publication Data

A CIP catalogue record for this book is available from the British Library.

ISBN 978-1-85594-223-3

Book design and typesetting, Anú Design, Tara
Printed by Gutenberg Press, Malta

For all Atrium books visit www.corkuniversitypress.com

Contents

Preface ix
Introduction xi

Abbeyknockmoy, County Galway (2000) 1
Adelaide Memorial Church, Myshall, County Carlow (2003) 3
Airfield House, Dundrum, Dublin (2002) 5
Annesbrook, Duleek, County Meath (2001) 7
Ardgillan Castle, Balbriggan, County Dublin (2004) 11
Ardtara Country House, Upperlands, County Derry (2004) 13
Ashley Park House, Nenagh, County Tipperary (2003) 16
Ballaghmore Castle, Borris-in-Ossory, County Laois (2003) 19
Ballaghtobin, Callan, County Kilkenny (2003) 22
Ballinacurra House, Midleton County Cork (2006) 25
Ballinkeele Country House, Ballymurn, Enniscorthy, County Wexford (1996) 27
Ballyboy House, Clogheen, County Tipperary (1998) 30
Ballyduff House, Thomastown, County Kilkenny (2003) 32
Ballyfin Country House Hotel, Mountrath, County Laois (2007) 35
Ballymacmoy House, Kilavullen, County Cork (2008) 39
Ballymote House, Downpatrick, County Down (2004) 42
Ballynatray House, Youghal, County Cork (2010) 45
Ballyteige House, Bruree, County Limerick (1998) 48
Ballyvolane House, Castlelyons, County Cork (2004) 51
Bantry House, Bantry, County Cork (1997) 55
Barberstown Castle, Straffan, County Kildare (2008) 58
Barnabrow Country House, Cloyne, County Cork (1998) 60
Beaufort House, Killarney, County Kerry (1998) 63
Belvedere House, Mullingar, County Westmeath (2001) 66
Blackwater Castle, Castletownroche, County Cork (2006) 68
Blanchville House, Dunbell, Maddoxtown, County Kilkenny (2000) 70
Boherwilliam, Modeligo, County Waterford (2010) 72
Cahernane House, Killarney, County Kerry (2006) 74

Cairbre House, Abbeyside, Dungarvan, County Waterford (2007)	76
Carrig House, Caragh Lake, Killorglin, County Kerry (2000)	78
Cashel Palace Hotel, Cashel, County Tipperary (2001)	81
Castle Durrow, Durrow, County Laois (2002)	84
Castle Oliver, Ardpatrick, County Limerick (2005)	86
Clonalis House, Castlerea, County Roscommon (2001)	88
Coopershill House, Riverstown, County Sligo (2002)	91
Coursetown Country House, Athy, County Kildare (2004)	94
Creagh House, Doneraile, County Cork (1999)	96
Curraclone, St. Peter's Church, County Laois (2004)	100
Delphi Lodge, Leenane, County Galway (1997)	102
Derrynane House, Caherdaniel, County Kerry (2001)	106
Desmond Castle, Adare, County Limerick (2008)	108
Dromana House, Cappoquin, County Waterford (2010)	110
Dún na Séad, Baltimore, County Cork (2010)	113
Dunbrody Country House, Arthurstown, County Wexford (2001)	115
Dysert, Ardmore, County Waterford (2010)	118
Enniscoe House, Castlehill, Ballina, County Mayo (2002)	120
Ennismore, Montenotte, Cork (2008)	124
Fair Green Cottage, Ballymacoda, County Cork (2003)	126
Flemingstown House, Kilmallock, County Limerick (2004)	128
Fortwilliam House, Lismore, County Waterford (2010)	131
Foxmount Country House, Passage East Road, Waterford (2003)	135
Frewin, Ramelton, County Donegal (2002)	137
Gaultier Lodge, Woodstown, County Waterford (2008)	140
Ghan House, Carlingford, County Louth (2007)	143
Glebe House and Gallery, Ballinadee, Bandon, County Cork (2002)	145
Glenlohane, County Cork (1996)	147
Glenville Park, Glenville, County Cork (1996)	149
Glin Castle, County Limerick (1997)	151
Gregan's Castle Hotel, Ballyvaughan, County Clare (2007)	154
Griesemount, Ballitore, County Kildare (2004)	1571
Hilton Park, Clones, County Monaghan (1999)	159
Hollywell, Carrick-on-Shannon, County Leitrim (2002)	162
Hunter's Lodge, Lismore (1996)	164
Inch House, Thurles, County Tipperary (2007)	166
Inchiquin House, Corofin, County Clare (2010)	168
Inis Beg, Baltimore, County Cork (2010)	171
Kilcash, County Tipperary (2000)	174

Kilcolman Rectory, Enniskeane, County Cork (2009)	176
Kilmokea Country Manor and Gardens, Campile, County Wexford (2000)	178
Lisdonagh House, Cahirlistrane, Headford, County Galway (2003)	182
Lismacue House, Bansha, County Tipperary (1997)	184
Lismore Castle Arts, Lismore, County Waterford (2007)	187
Longueville House, Mallow, County Cork (2009)	188
Lorum Old Rectory, Kilgreaney, Bagenalstown, County Carlow (2000)	192
Loughcrew House and Gardens, Oldcastle, County Meath (1999)	196
Mahaffy House, North Great George's Street, Dublin (1997)	198
Martinstown House, The Curragh, County Kildare (1999)	202
Mobarnane House, Fethard, County Tipperary (2001)	205
Mount Rivers, Carrigaline, County Cork (1997)	208
Mount Vernon, Flaggy Shore, New Quay, County Clare (2007)	210
Newbridge House, Donabate, County Dublin (2001)	214
Newman House, St Stephen's Green, Dublin (2009)	218
Newtown House, Kinsalebeg, County Waterford (2011)	220
Rathmullan House, Lough Swilly, County Donegal (2002)	223
Rathsallagh Country House, Dunlavin, County Wicklow (2001)	225
Roundwood House, Mountrath, County Laois (2004)	227
Russborough House, Blessington, County Wicklow (2001)	230
Salterbridge House, Cappoquin, County Waterford (2011)	234
Shankill Castle, Paulstown, County Kilkenny (2004)	236
Shelburne Lodge Country House, Kenmare, County Kerry (2009)	238
Sion Hill House, Ferrybank, Waterford (1999)	240
Springfield Castle, Dromcollogher, County Limerick (2009)	242
Stable Diet Kitchen, Yoletown, County Wexford (2000)	246
Strokestown Park House, Strokestown, County Roscommon (2001)	248
Temple House, Ballymote, County Sligo (1999)	250
The Glebe House, Ballinadee, County Cork (1997)	254
The Glen House, Kilbrittain, County Cork (2007)	256
The Grain Store, Ballymaloe, County Cork (2010)	259
The Old Convent, Clogheen County Tipperary (2006)	261
The Quay House, Clifden, County Galway (1997)	263
The Sprigging School, Rathbarry, County Cork (2007)	267
Tourin House and Gardens, Cappoquin, County Waterford (2008)	269
Ulusker House, Adrigole, County Cork (2008)	272
Woodstock House, Inistioge, County Kilkenny (2003)	275
Eating for Ireland	281

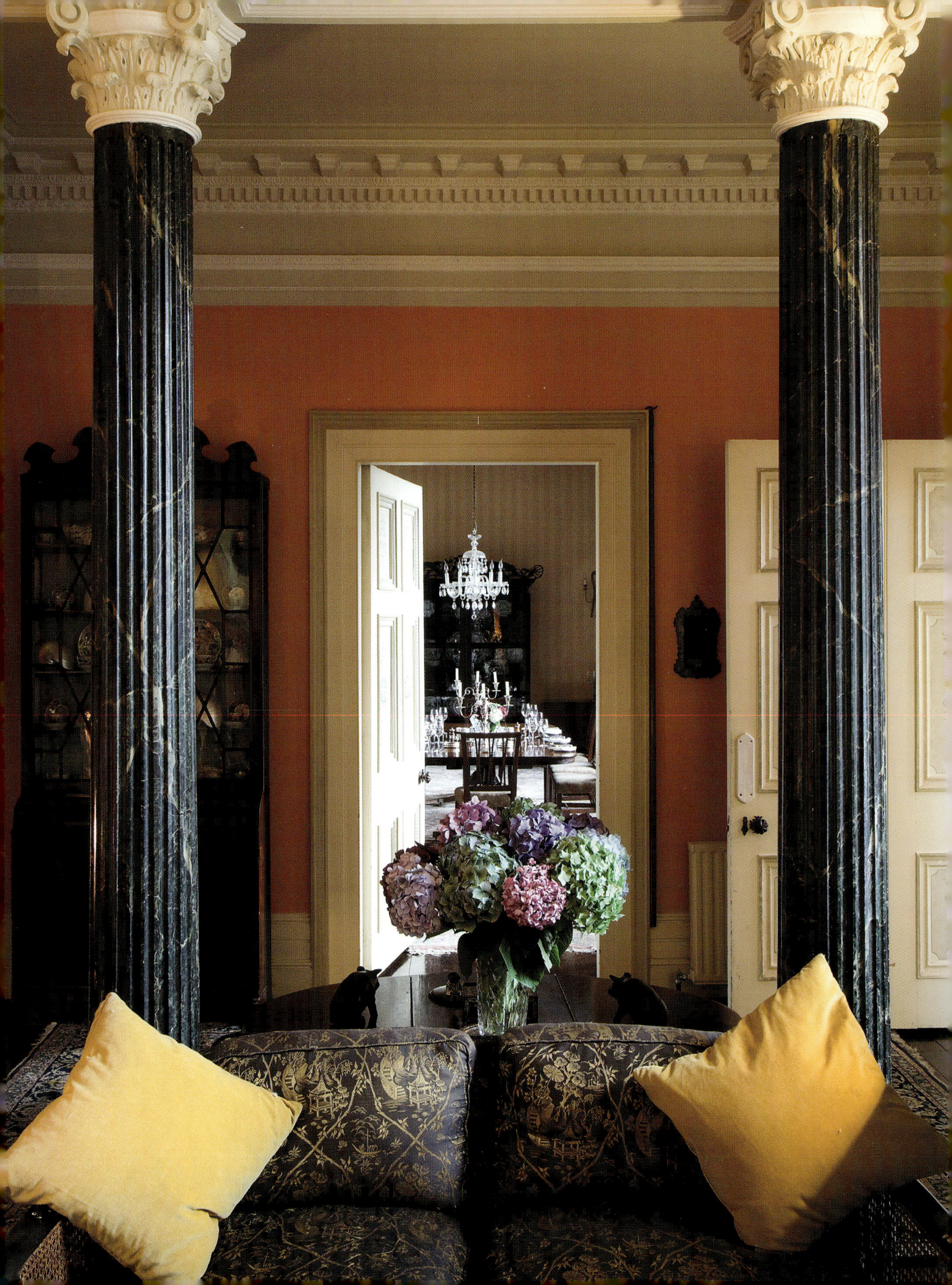

Preface

It was, as they say, a hard job, but someone had to do it. That lucky someone was me, given the gift of regular journeys around Ireland to track and trace the hospitality on offer at our old houses by old and new families. Inevitably the work took on different aspects, not least with the discovery of the new generations revitalising both the old, inherited or acquired properties, the accommodation and food provided within them and the occasional use made of them which has nothing to do with hospitality at all. It was also probably predictable – although I didn't predict it – that these forays into undiscovered landscapes would yield other locations of interest. If I have a regret about this book it is that the majority of these have had to be omitted; if I have a regret about the writing of the articles in the first place it is that I wrote with such surprise, forgetting that territories unknown to me were familiar and treasured sites to those who lived in or near them.

This is not a guide book. The places and people within it are easily found – this is a small country after all – and follow one of the principles directing the original idea for these features, that of choosing the road not taken. The pieces began with the development of the Weekend Supplement at the *Cork* and then the *Irish Examiner* from 1993 to 1995; from restaurant reviews for that publication the brief changed to reviews of country houses and other properties of historic or cultural value so that a wider experience of place, people and atmosphere could be shared with readers of what subsequently became the *Property Supplement*. It is also important to say that the articles have been selected from a range of years, so that they are reproduced here as they were written at the time of their publication. Any up-dating is carried in a footnote.

I have been granted a lot of space over the years, and for the purposes of this collection the features have been reduced to about two-thirds of their original length. I have had the privilege of welcome from people united by their shared love of what they do and by their gritty determination to bloody well keep on doing it. I have also had the privilege of working with the '*Examiner*'s' finest photographers who have always responded with patience and sensitivity to locations as various as medieval towers, thickly-carpeted Victorian drawing-rooms and muddy, bull-haunted fields.

At Home in Ireland is a record of survival; buildings, land and families yes, but also of a tradition of hospitality and a custom of good taste. The builders, designers, crafts workers and artists whose names, for reasons of space, have had to be omitted from this book have all left their mark on our countryside. The Office of Public Works under various guises through the years has made its hugely important contribution, so have the Irish Georgian Society and An Taisce, the Irish Landmark Trust, The Heritage Council and other conservation-based organisations or groups. The keepers of the small forgotten churches whose doors rarely open any more, the seed-savers, the tree-growers, the farming and fishing campaigners, the thatchers, the gardeners and bee-keepers and bird-watchers. Above all there are The Hidden Ireland and Ireland's Blue Book organisations which introduced sophistication to their members without reducing the authenticity with which each property is presented.

There are many people to thank for my explorations, among them all those who understand the crucial relationship between bedside-lamps and beds, who provide china on bedroom trays and breakfast tables, or antique bed-linen and utterly modern showers, or afternoon tea with cakes made at home from family recipes, or a blazing fire even on a fine summer's evening. In many cases proprietors were doing all this anyway (well, maybe not the showers, at first!). But then came Myrtle and Ivan Allen and Ballymaloe House and what, even in terms of the Irish country house, could be called consciousness-raising.

So my first thanks go to the Allens. I would like to express my gratitude and admiration too for the indomitable and innovative home-owners and home-makers who have kept to this arduous path without showing just how arduous it can be. I willingly pay my debt of gratitude to my colleagues at the *Irish Examiner,* especially Dan Buckley, Peter Levy, Tommy Barker and Irene Feighan and to the editors with whom we worked from Tim Vaughan to the late Fergus O'Callaghan. Special thanks are due to Paddy Barker and Anne Kearney of the *Irish Examiner* photographic department. I am very grateful for the help of Caroline Long-Nolan and Kieran Burke of the Local Studies Rooms at Cork City Library, of Ber Murphy at Dowling and Dowling and for the skilful encouragement of Editor Maria O'Donovan and Publications Director Mike Collins at Cork University Press. I should also add an appreciative note to my family who don't seem to have missed me too much.

Finally, as proof of my appreciation of the travels of the last twenty years or so let me add that if I were to be offered a last meal it would have to be breakfast at an Irish country house.

Mary Leland
September 2012

Introduction

I was delighted to be asked to write the introduction for this book and to give the point of view of the new generation taking on an historic property in today's world.

I live at Ballyvolane House in north-east Cork with my wife Jenny and three children Toby, Jamie and Fleur, my father Jeremy, my granny Joyce (aged 101) and my maternal grandparents Wendy and Ian (in their nineties) who live in a house on the place. We took over the running of Ballyvolane from my parents in 2004, which was just after my mother Merrie passed away. Together she and Jeremy had restored most of the house and developed the gardens, parkland and woodlands over the last thirty years and Ballyvolane is in pretty good nick. They first started taking in paying guests, or 'PGs' as we used to call them, in the mid-eighties when the income from the farm was not enough to maintain the house. Luckily they were natural hosts and when we took over, Ballyvolane House was well established in the market place and had earned a great reputation already; it was also one of the founding members of The Hidden Ireland organisation (www.hiddenireland.com).

My father still plays a key role in the running of Ballyvolane and he has given us a master-class in handing over from one generation to the next. Not only does he have endless patience and good grace, he has an encyclopedic knowledge of the workings of the house such as the archaic plumbing systems, drains, chimneys, windows, roof, gutters, as well as the farm. I am slowly getting to grips with all of these myself. He still maintains the gardens and they have never looked better, while providing quantities of vegetables from the walled garden and looking after the pigs, donkeys and poultry, all of which is pretty impressive as he is now pushing eighty. Luckily we all get on really well and we all depend on each other. The guests like to see the different generations living and working here and we can relate to all ages, from my kids playing with guests' children to my father conducting garden tours. Our regular guests love to see a familiar smile too.

I consider myself very fortunate living in such a house, with its idyllic setting located in a beautiful part of the country. I love living here and enjoy seeing the house purr when it's busy and full of people. These old houses were built for lavish entertaining. I see myself as a caretaker dedicated to maintaining the integrity of the house and keeping it in good order until it is passed on. However, it is difficult in these times when we are faced with rising costs, a depressed economy, scarce tourists and increasing regulation. What I mean by integrity is that it remains an authentic, slightly beaten-up Irish country house. A house that is almost 300 years old should show a little wear-and-tear.

I feel saddened when I see so many old houses that were bought-up by developers in the Celtic Tiger Years, which had millions spent on them and has resulted in many cases in the loss of their sense of mystery. We try very hard to preserve this sense of mystery, which is what makes these old houses so appealing. As owners of historic houses, we have to adapt to the current economic climate as unfortunately most of us don't have deep pockets with which to keep up with the high running costs. It requires enormous effort, commitment, energy and passion from all the members of the family and from the staff working here, as in other similar properties.

At Ballyvolane we have adapted successfully and we are now hosting weddings at Ballyvolane House, and we have just launched a glamping option here this summer. We support local businesses and use only local produce as we see this as a way of keeping cash in the local economy. In the summer, we employ over forty people between Ballyvolane House and our restaurant, O'Brien Chop House in Lismore, and we very much appreciate the support of our staff. We host charity events here regularly to raise money for local charities and not only is this a great way of showing what we do, it also keeps us connected to our own neighbourhood.

In my capacity of running the marketing with The Hidden Ireland group I find myself very indebted to Mary Leland as her regular column in the *Irish Examiner* and other print media over many years gave her readers a real picture what it is like to own, live and work in a historic house – 'warts and all'. Not only was she interested in our homes but she was also interested in their families and traditions, and especially she wanted to know what motivates the owners to keep their houses going. I would like to take this opportunity to thank her for all her wonderful support over the years and wish her every success with her book.

Justin Green
Ballyvolane House, Castlelyons, County Cork
www.ballyvolanehouse.ie
September 2012

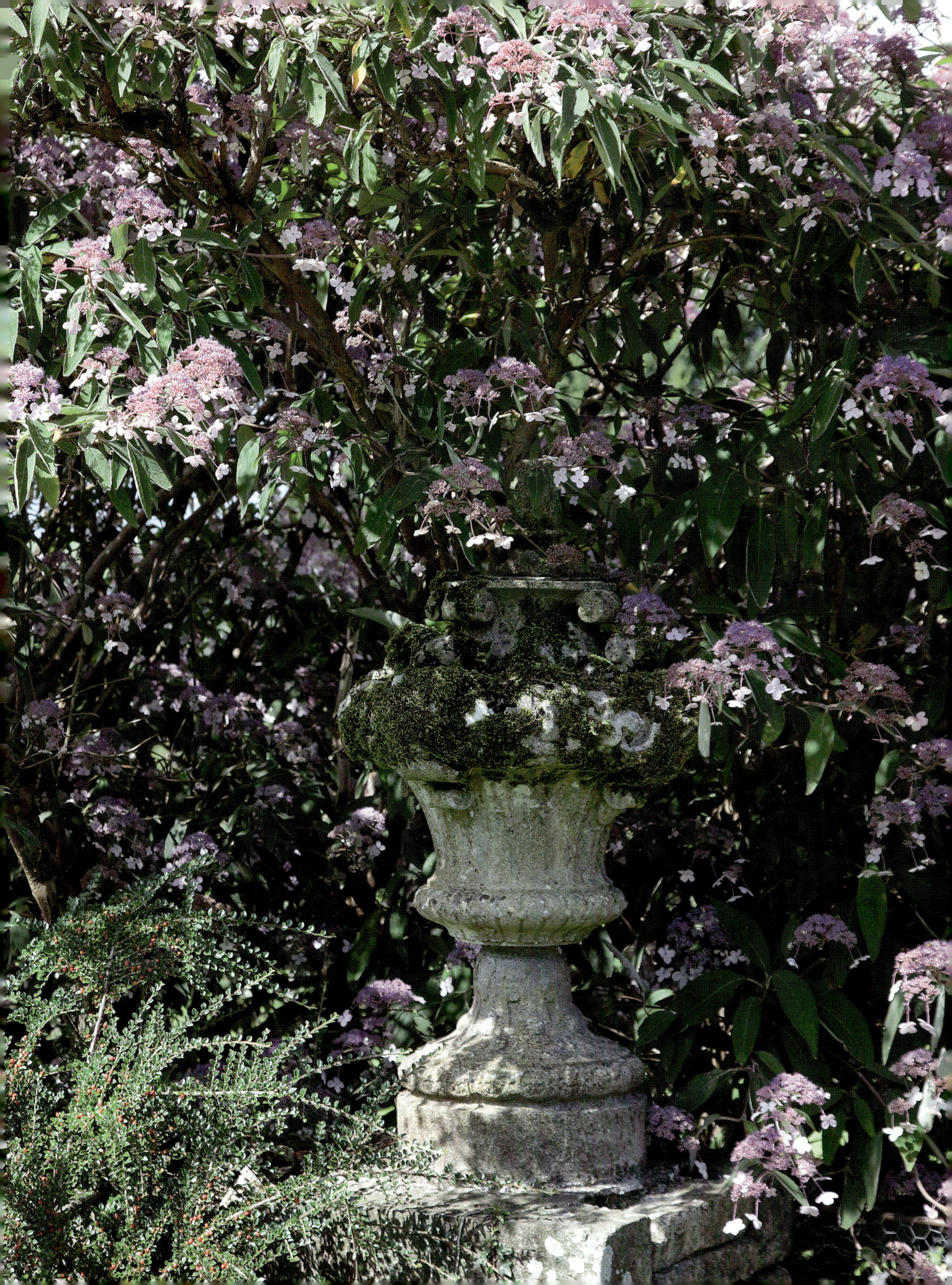

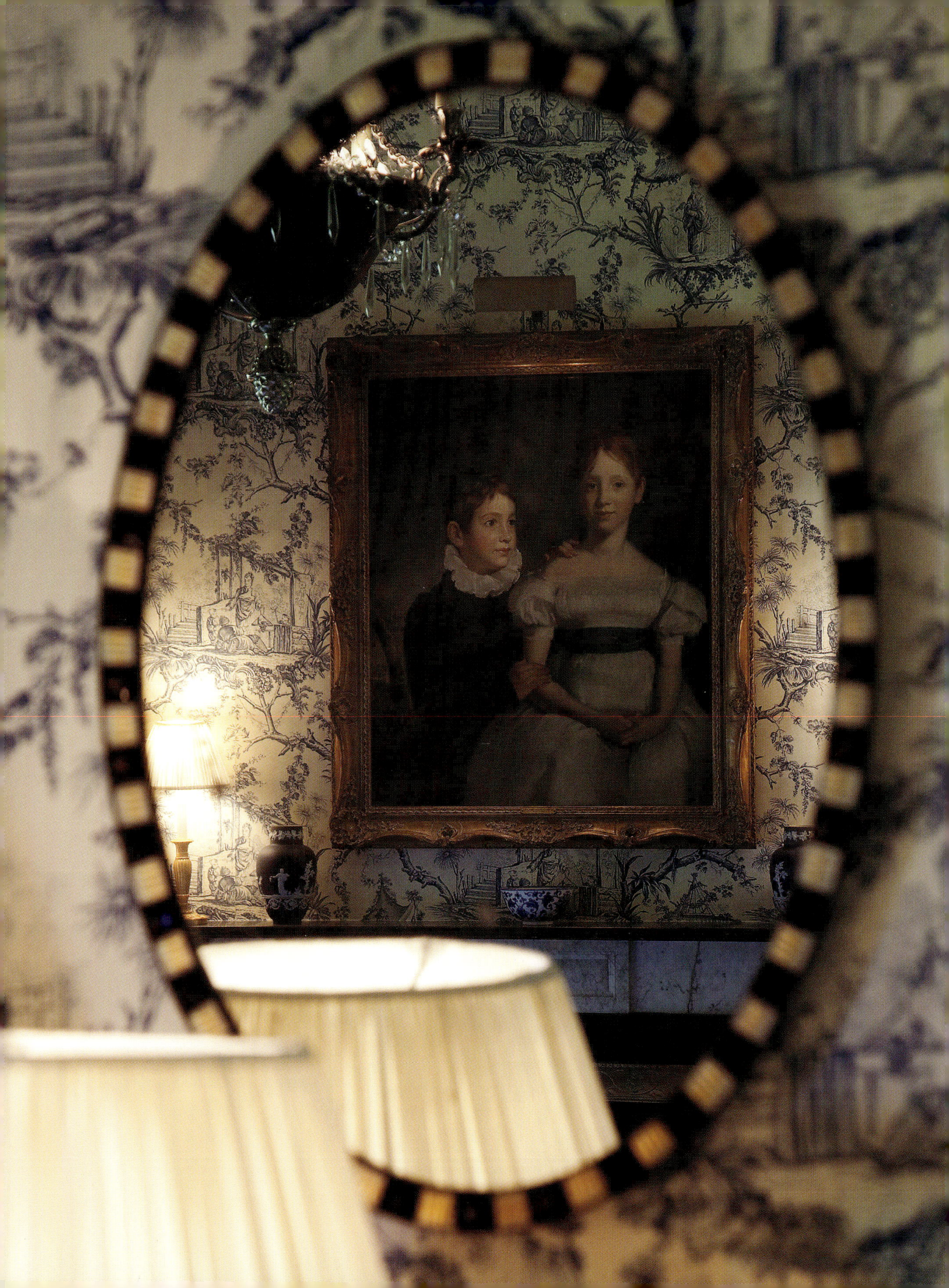

Abbeyknockmoy

County Galway

Tuam is swimming in history: its fifth-century foundation is dated from a settlement by St Iarlath (or Jarleth) and as the town and its hinterland became one of the principal seats of the O Conor kingship it seemed likely for a while to become the capital of Connacht. But the coming of the Normans to Ireland gradually diluted Tuam's prominence, concluding finally with the rout in 1316 of King Felim O Conor, his ally the King of Ui Mhaine and 8,000 of their followers. There had been a glorious few centuries of supremacy and plenty, an epoch celebrated in the still-resonant evocation of James Clarence Mangan's 'Vision of Connaught in the Thirteenth Century':

> But it was the time,
> It was in the reign
> Of Cathal More of the wine-red hand.

The verses learned at school echo as I try to find my way to the last resting place of Cathal Mor, Cathal Crobhdearg O Conor. Historian William Henry of Galway has told me that this is at Abbeyknockmoy, near Tuam. The countryside is lush, the air laden with the aromas of a west of Ireland summer, and my journey has taken me on a marvellous tour of Craughwell, Loughrea, Monivea and Athenry. It has introduced me to Mount Bellew Bridge and to the roadside gardens at Ballyclunin Bridge and finally to Noreen Fahy in her garden centre who directs me to Abbeyknockmoy.

I stop at O'Donoghue's pub and shop (and petrol station, undertakers, agricultural machinery, wool buyers, hardware and seeds) and Sean O'Donoghue supplies coffee and sandwiches and a quick guide (he's a busy man) to the abbey, which is practically across the road. How could this magical place be left unmarked and unknown? Yet, succumbing to its serenity and timelessness as I walk in the daisied meadow near the river Abbert and stand by the ditch to feel the breath of the cows on my hand, I feel it should be kept hidden.

The shattered spread of the abbey of Knockmoy was built by Cathal Mor in 1189 to celebrate a victory over the invading Anglo-Normans. This Cistercian abbey of Collis Victoriae reputedly took its familiar name from the nearby hill, Cnoc mBuaidhe, or the Hill of Victory. Cathal was expelled from the abbey in 1200 during his ruthless campaign to secure his kingship, but once restored to his titles and holdings in 1202 he maintained his rule over Connacht until his death in 1224. He was buried here, and also lying here is his kinsman Roderick O Conor, the youngest son of the last High King of Ireland.

After its dissolution in 1542 the abbey's story flows with the tide of landed families in the area, the last of whom were the Blakes of Ballyclunin, until in 1908 the local tenants acquired the lands surrounding the

The Cistercian abbey of Knockmoy is the burial place of King Cathal Mór O Conor, who founded it in 1189. (image courtesy of the National Monuments Service, Department of Arts, Heritage and the Gaeltacht)

abbey, which by now was in ruins. A leaning stand at the inner entrance reveals the presence of the Office of Public Works (OPW), whose attention was given to the abbey by virtue of its other great claim to national importance: in the chancel, here is one of the last surviving medieval frescoes in Ireland. Dating from the fifteenth century it carries the inscription 'Pray for the souls of Malachie O Nollan and Consire O Eddichan who caused me to be made'. Originally the paintings covered the entire northern wall of the chancel but now the only remaining pictures are those of a seriously arrow-pierced St Sebastian, with three living kings confronting three crowned skeletons. Under the kings the script reminds those lucky enough to get this close that 'we have been as you are, you shall be as we are'.

Now Eithne O'Donoghue of Abbey sends me some reading material which makes it perfectly clear that Cathal Mor was not to be trifled with. An obituary in the thirteenth-century Annals of Connaught, for example, describes him as 'the king who was fiercest and harshest towards his enemies that ever lived; the king who most blinded, killed and mutilated rebellious and disaffected subjects.'

The record goes on to describe Cathal as 'the king who most comforted clerks and poor men with food and fire on the floor of his own habitation; the king whom of all the kings in Ireland God made the most perfect in every good quality . . . the king who best established peace and tranquillity of all the kings of Ireland'.

Peace and tranquillity were what James Clarence Mangan remembered, while abroad in Germany, when he wrote his 'Vision of Connaught'. The final nightmare verse imagines the change 'From light to darkness, from joy to woe!' which followed the last days of reign of Cathal Mór of the Wine-Red Hand, buried now in Knockmoy Abbey near Mountbellew Bridge in County Galway. ♣

AT HOME IN IRELAND

Adelaide Memorial Church

County Carlow

It's no Taj Mahal, but the Church of Christ the Redeemer in Myshall, County Carlow, is just as much a testament to love as that famous Indian monument. The Irish church has its own atmosphere of distinction, grace and tranquillity, standing in its yew-lined churchyard above the village.

It seems too big for its location, perhaps even too elegant. Beyond it, sheep graze a reedy field, and the village houses and shops, freshly painted and glowing on this summer afternoon, are in proportion only to one another and not to this high-roofed grey monument on the hill. It comes as no great surprise therefore to learn that, designed by the architect G.C. Ashlin, it was intended to replicate the style of Salisbury Cathedral.

Yet it is all of a piece, for the love which it commemorates began and ended here. John and Adelaide Duguid and their two daughters were a devoted family living in England. When the elder daughter married the rector of Myshall, Constance, affectionately known as Conny, visited the couple at Myshall, Glebe. There she met Mr Brady of Myshall House, to whom she became engaged, but shortly before the wedding day she had an accident while hunting and died in Myshall a few days later.

Even as I stand in the shaded avenue I am told of a suspicion that the 'accident' had been arranged – not perhaps with a view to murder, but maybe to disfigurement or disablement, or discomfort so tedious as to discourage the lovers. Conny is recalled now in a statue of Sicilian marble commissioned by her mother and father: 'Remembering the admiration with which she used to view similar monuments in Italy this statue of Innocence fully representing her is placed here in memory of "Conny" Constance Louise Eugenie Duguid by her sorrowing parents, 1888.' The statue stood in the grounds of the old church of Christ the Redeemer at Myshall until, fifteen years after Conny, her mother Adelaide died. Having expressed the wish to be buried beside her daughter, her body was brought to Myshall. Here the old church was deteriorating, and Mr John Duguid decided to build a new church on the same site in memory of his daughter and of his wife. Now these three Duguids are here, John having died a year before the building was consecrated in 1913, and his ashes are interred in the wall of the mortuary chapel. Their portraits hang in the vestry, where Constance smiles from an oval gold-leaf frame, her hair high and ringleted.

Today I have the company of Jack Corrigan who, as he walks through the churchyard, is surrounded by relatives. Even the rest room near the chancel is dedicated in memory of Ethel and John W. Corrigan of Cappagh, and all around us are the headstones of the Corrigans of Lisgarvan and nearby townlands.

Despite its mass of local granite and contoured limestone from Stradbally, the internal proportions

The Church of Christ the Redeemer at Myshall was consecrated in 1913. The portrait is of Constance Louise Duguid, whose father had the church built to commemorate her death and that of his wife Adelaide. (images Dylan Vaughan)

of the church allow all the attractive detail to shine through. The windows are stained-glass depictions of celebratory themes, from the *Te Deum* sequence in the chancel to the Benedicte or Praise windows of the nave. Appropriately enough there are plenty of women – Ruth and Hannah, Mary and Elizabeth and, in the mortuary chapel, the women waiting at the Easter tomb. In marble, mosaic, timber and ironwork, personal and biblical connections are vividly expressed, and at the point where the nave and chancel meet, the four evangelists surround the intertwined initials of John and Adelaide Duguid.

The marble floor of the chancel copies that of St Mark's Basilica in Venice; the wrought-iron grille around the Duguid tombs is copied from a screen at St Giles in Edinburgh. In the baptistry the marble font, with an enamel inlay in blue and silver, stands on a floral mosaic floor. The windows are separated by six groups of five narrow pillars upholding the virtues of humility, faith, charity, hope and fortitude and the baptismal inscription: 'Walk humbly, steadfast in faith, robed in charity, joyful through hope and strong in the Lord.'

Jack Corrigan's father was the last person to be christened in the old church here; his friend Joe Deacon was the first to be christened in the new one. Now, with help from the Heritage Council and the generous involvement of the local community, the thirty or so families from the Union of Myshall, Fenagh, Aghade and Ardoyne are in the last phase of a three-year restoration programme supervised by engineer Colm Hassett of Naas. Like so many small parish buildings, this church is layered now with the associations of generations. It has flourished with the goodwill of a village which takes pride in this lovely monument.

AT HOME IN IRELAND

Airfield House

Dundrum, Dublin

All three elements of Airfield House work in conjunction according to the bequest of Naomi and Letitia Overend, independent ladies of means who left their estate to be run as a charitable trust with the emphasis on education. The public are invited to inspect the gardens, to take the Airfield Walk through the fields which wander up to the fringes of the Dublin Mountains, to shop at the Mulberry Market (organic wines, cheeses, fruit and vegetables, along with varieties of the unusual – and usual – plants and shrubs grown in the garden), to enjoy the vintage vehicles in the car museum, to eat and drink in the popular tearooms opened in the house itself and to attend any or all of a series of programmes run under the Trust's educational remit.

Naomi and Letitia were the daughters of Trevor and Lily Overend; he was a successful solicitor who, like many of his colleagues in Dublin, preferred to live on the rural outskirts of the city and moved to Airfield in 1894. The house had been built in the 1820s in what was then undisturbed countryside; the two girls were brought up in Edwardian comfort but were also – even in those days when no woman went out of doors without a hat – encouraged to be self-sufficient and adventurous. They travelled widely, studied mechanics as part of their interest in cars, developed the farm by acquiring more land and establishing their Dromartin herd of Jersey cattle, and maintained the beautiful gardens familiar to them since childhood.

Now Airfield House retains all its architectural elegance, even if it is no longer possible to imagine (apart from old photographs) what it was like in its heyday. Archivist Deirdre Heaphy takes time off from sifting through a collection of over 150,000 documents to explain how the trust works under its chief executive Brian Dornan. Expensive restoration was required for the interior, so the charge to visitors is one way of helping with the costs of running the whole place. Rental income, for lectures and recitals and meetings, is another, but with a full-time staff of nine people Airfield has to market itself as productively as possible.

The complex has a gentle, traditional atmosphere. Different areas are clearly distinguished; the Laurel Walk borders the front field, where Connemara ponies vie for petting at the railing and, typical of the sometimes ambitious planting of leisured landowners, its interest is multiplied a little further on in the Yew Walk. Trees and shrubs manage to hide the fact that this farm in what is almost the heart of Dublin is increasingly surrounded by suburban infrastructure. Yet the actual Airfield Walk can take a couple of hours (picnic baskets are available), with views of the Dublin Mountains and the Wicklow Hills expanding from the farm fields. The lawns carry fine trees, including a Giant Redwood, and the

The gardens at Airfield House and (below) daughters of the owners, the Misses Naomi and Letitia Overend at Airfield in the late 1930s. (images courtesy of Airfield Trust)

woodland plot known as Tot's Garden has the Persian ironwood with its flaming autumn colour as well as bay laurels underplanted with hellebores and golden woodruff.

The many different borders offer delight after delight but, of them all, perhaps the walled garden is the one which must not be missed: when the Trust was established in 1993 Arthur Shackleton advised on the garden restoration, and this section was redesigned in formal style in 1996. No fewer than thirty varieties of old climbing and rambling roses were used here, from Alberic Barbier to Lady Hillingdon and Henri Martin. The Queen of Denmark twines with Rose de Rescht, Rose Mundi rivals Ferdinand Pritchard, the soft pinks of Fantin Latour chime with the densely cupped purple flowers of Tuscany Superb, while the amber Buff Beauty and the tall arching Bobby Joe roof the iron frame. Ducks and hens patrol the orchard, where greengages, medlars (who has these any more?), cherries, pears and damsons grow in the happy company of a collection of old Irish apples, saved here to give us the pleasure of inspecting fruit called Blood of the Boyne or Pig's Nose Pippin. The other great joy is the kitchen garden with the Victorian greenhouse and its stained-glass doorway, and the tropical abundance of its contents. Airfield seems unforced, but it is not a location for a hasty garden tour. Its magic is almost casual, which is the great achievement of its staff and a great tribute to its donors.

Airfield House will be closed for major refurbishments until spring 2013; Kathy Purcell is now Director of the Airfield Trust.

The Airfield Trust, House and Gardens,
Upper Kilmacud Road, Dundrum, Dublin 14.
Tel: 01 298 4301

Annesbrook

County Meath

Everything edible on Kate Sweetman's dinner table this evening has come from the garden behind her house at Annesbrook, County Meath. Everything, that is, except the fresh wild salmon which comes from Drogheda, and the wine which is another story altogether. And perhaps the bread which, if not exactly made from flour milled from her own wheat was at least baked in her own kitchen and tastes every bit of it.

A farmhouse made grander through the generations, this seventeenth-century residence grew by the eighteenth to accommodate a family with fourteen children; the back of the house is layered with passages leading to bedrooms big and small, some overlooking the courtyard with its climbing roses and vines and its big old meat safe in the centre, some looking out on the plains of Royal Meath, ribbed with woods and golden in the sunlight.

Downstairs the kitchen wing is hidden behind the hall's arches; on each side the large dining-room and larger sitting-room are lit by floor-to-ceiling windows set in front under relieving arches. In the evening light the glass mellows with the greens and golds of a summer sunset. Fields stretch beyond the lawns, deep

BELOW: *Mellow in the evening light: the sitting-room at Annesbrook.*

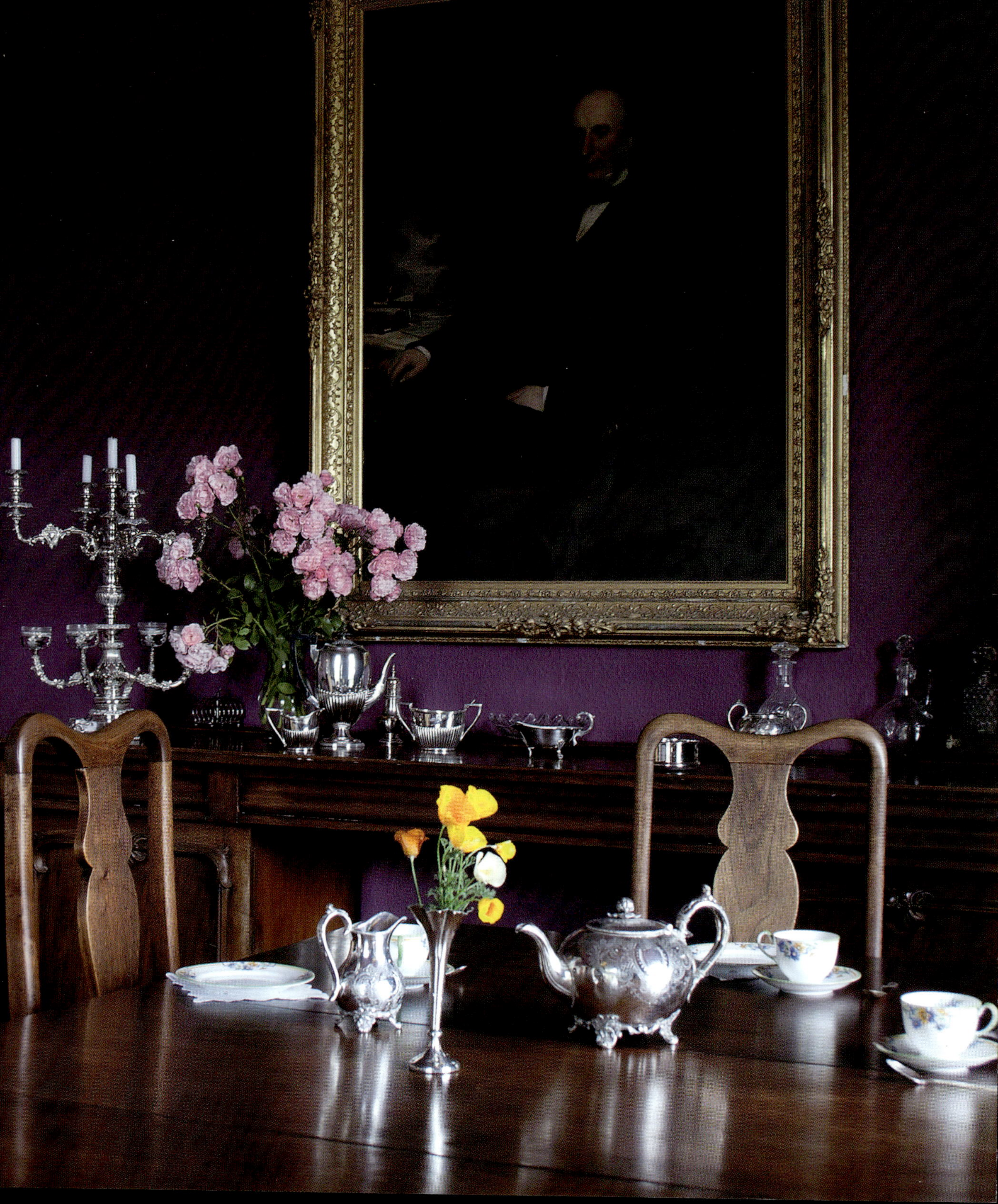

LEFT: *Contemporary and familiar: a bedroom at Annesbrook.*
RIGHT: *Waiting for the Prince Regent; detail of the portico.*
OPPOSITE: *The dining-room.*

hedges fence the meadows and troughs of woodland mark these historic acres. Duleek was famous for its monasteries and after the Battle of Clontarf the bodies of Brian Boru and his son lay here in state in 1014. Duleek still holds two tenth-century crosses and remnants of its fifth-century church and there are other pre-Norman relics, as well as medieval tombs and towers in the ruins of St Mary's Abbey.

In the village itself and in the surrounding area a series of wayside crosses commemorate Genet (or Jennet) Dowdall and her husband William Bathe. One of these is just outside the entrance to Annesbrook and, with the little lodge inside the gate, ties the demesne to a timeless landscape, somewhere history has been happening all the time and where, when the Jacobites fled from Donore Hill above the Boyne in 1690 and regrouped at Duleek, they were just one more army at just one more battle.

That was in July too, I think, as I sit washed by evening sunlight, surrounded by the paintings of Kate's daughter Sadhbh Sweetman, her niece Katie Sweetman and their friend Sarah Durcan. With other modern artists their work enlivens a graceful room, making it contemporary as well as familiar and filling it with the kind of youthful, searching vitality essential to the survival of beloved old houses. While Kate admits that she herself only paints the walls, she describes her life here since 1975 and her decision to open a bed and breakfast business as 'brilliant'. Even the labour (with which she has some help) of getting part of the enormous walled garden back into working order has been enjoyable. Its bounties are everywhere – a vast multicoloured bowl of sweet peas scents the sitting-room – and they begin at the grand front-door portico where Californian poppies riot through the gravel. The walled garden, the

LEFT: *The plains of Royal Meath viewed from Annesbrook's front door.* RIGHT: *Bedroom comfort.* (images courtesy of Shane McElveen)

orchard and the old well tower are all embraced by the massed chestnuts, beeches and sycamores which shelter Annesbrook while accommodating the local squirrels, which seem particularly attracted to Kate's strawberries.

'This was never a grand house', she says, 'but it had its pretensions.' Thus the huge portico and the marvellous banqueting hall which were built by Henry Smith (he of the fourteen children) and decorated in 1821 in expectation of a visit from the Prince Regent, then a guest of Lady Conyngham at Slane. But the future George IV never saw its Gothic arches and traceries and beautifully moulded ceiling, preferring to dine outside in the clement August weather.

I take Kate's grant application for the restoration of this room to read in bed, although it is eclipsed immediately by the treasure trove of her bookshelves, where I find the 1949 edition of Maurice Healy's enchanting book *Stay Me With Flagons*. I fall asleep steeped in its advice about wine and thinking of the query overheard from the kitchen about what was to be done with these gooseberries. Perhaps they'll appear for breakfast, I hope, as I drift off under my patchwork quilt and, with porridge, warm scones, loganberry jam, eggs, bacon and excellent coffee, they do.

The management of Annesbrook House is now shared between Kate and her son Shane McElveen. The banqueting hall was refurbished with the help of an award from the Irish Georgian Society and the house is a venue for corporate and private events and meetings, with bed and breakfast accommodation provided only for special occasions or to large groups.

Annesbrook, Duleek, County Meath
Tel: 041 982 3293
www.annesbrook.com

Ardgillan Castle

County Dublin

There is probably a 'best time' for visiting Ardgillan Castle in north County Dublin, but a sunny morning in March seems just as good a time as any other. The avenue is long and trimmed with hedge-high daffodils which later spread out into golden lakes beneath the trees. From the gently undulating parkland a curve shielded by trees suddenly presents a vista: greensward, woodland, grey battlements in the distance and beyond them the vast and unexpected ocean.

The house sits on a little esplanade of steps and terraces. Its administrator, Michael McElligott, explains that this was once called Prospect House and that, at least, is not to be wondered at. From the drawing-room, where the gilding and stencilling can be noticed at leisure, the initial impact is a retrospective envy that once the people who lived here could gaze across the parkland to the sea, the clustering houses on the far coastline and beyond them again to the dark blue shadows of the Mountains of Mourne.

In its day Ardgillan could hardly have been called a pretentious house. The stucco is delicately moulded and, although the carved Italianate wainscotting of the dining-room (brilliantly copied on a sideboard by FÁS trainees) is impressive, still it has an atmosphere of gentility rather than aristocracy. Perhaps the families here had no need to declare themselves; they lived comfortably and elegantly and had the good sense to leave well alone. The current phase of restoration by Fingal County Council will show that the servants too lived with a basic comfort, although they had to enter the house through underground passages.

As fluently ready to expound on the pine floorboards and their parquet edgings as on the chandeliers of Bohemian glass, Michael McElligott is especially erudite on the fortunes of the families at Ardgillan. The demesne was ruled by the O Casey clan, which later gave way to the Earls of Tyrconnell, but Cromwell and his successors had their own ideas of land ownership and parcelled the country out as rewards or restitutions. By 1737 Ardgillan belonged to the Reverend Robert Taylor, Dean of Clonfert. Robert's grandfather, Thomas Taylor, was a surveyor who assisted Dr William Petty in the compilation of the Down Survey from 1654 to 1656, which produced the first scientific cartography of Ireland. Its original barony maps are held by the French National Library in Paris, but copies are on exhibition at Ardgillan. The maps are coloured and full of detail; one enchanting decoration is the drawing dated 1654 of a dolphin to mark the coast near Dingle. Incidentally, the exhibition rooms are shared at the moment with a display of drawings for the coach-builders John Hutton & Sons of Dublin, makers of the Irish State Coach. Lovers of Georgette Heyer's Regency novels will enjoy the

Originally named Prospect House, the 194-acre demesne of Ardgillan was acquired by the local authority in 1982. (image courtesy of Fingal County Council)

phaetons, barouches, landaus and curricles painted by Rudolph Ackerman, along with swatches of carriage wallpapers and upholstery.

Robert Taylor's country house carries his mark in the inner hall, where a tablet over the fireplace is dated 1738 and inscribed with a verse from the 'Odes of Horace', celebrating – rather oddly in a house built by a clergyman – the laws and power of the pre-Christian emperor Augustus. Contradictions add to the attractions of Ardgillan, which was fairly ruthlessly embellished between 1807 and 1852; according to Mark Bence-Jones, 'Over each of the wings was thrown, literally speaking, a Gothic cloak of battlements and pointed arches.' It had been inherited by the Revd Henry Edward Taylor, fifth son of the First Earl of Bective and husband of Marianne St Leger of Doneraile. Their son Thomas was MP for Dublin and served as a minister in Disraeli's cabinet. The family continued here until 1962, when the property was sold to the German industrialist Heinrich Potts, from whom it was bought by Dublin County Council – now re-born in this area as Fingal – in 1982.

There are 194 acres at Ardgillan, managed by Senior Park Superintendent Michael Lynch. This visit in March cannot indicate the summertime fullness and bounty of the gardens maintained by Dominica McEvitt. There is the national collection of potentillas and kitchen and herb gardens with patterned planting giving prominence to the alcove wall used for tender fruit trees such as peaches and nectarines. And in the rose garden the pillars and loops of climbers such as Mme Grégoire Staechelin, Mme Alfred Carrière, Zéphirine Drouhin and Climbing Compassion will be the highlight of your visit to Ardgillan. ♣

Ardgillan Castle,
Balbriggan, County Dublin
Tel: 01 8492212

Ardtara Country House Hotel

County Derry

Linen is described in Ulster as 'the aristocrat of textiles', so it is appropriate that I should be making my first acquaintance with the province's famous industry as an aristocrat of the tourist trade. This is Ardtara Country House, near the village of Upperlands in County Derry, and in the dining-room the tables are laid with immaculate white damask cloths and napkins as if to proclaim the supremacy of this region over all other linen-producing areas. I am dining in what was once the billiard room, under a ceiling formed by a glass pyramid complete with rotating fan; the panelled walls and carved timber fireplace are set off by a deep frieze painted by John Alden with engaging hunting exploits in the style of 1930's illustrations.

BELOW: *The sitting-room. The nobility of linen and the aristocracy of golf unite at Ardtara.*

ABOVE: *The entrance front of Ardtara.* OPPOSITE: *The hall: visitors are drawn by Ardtara's combination of serenity, comfort and cuisine.* (images courtesy of Ireland's Blue Book)

Ardtara was built as a family home by Harry Jackson Clark in 1896 and is now maintained as a country hotel by Dr Alastair Hanna and his wife, the Revd Nancy Hanna. The gardens and grounds were restored as the proper setting so lawns and trees and flower beds surround it, shielding it from the road which runs past to the village of Upperlands. I am distracted from my dinner by my company in the shape of a book – *Linen on the Green* – which was written by the historian Wallace Clarke and tells the story not just of the manufacturing company William Clarke & Sons Ltd but of Upperlands and, because linen was such a core industry in the north, almost of Ulster itself.

It is the tale of an Irish mill village established in 1730, of sealmasters, lappers, blanchers, of bleaching greens and beetling mills, and of the changes in the nature and significance of the linen trade after 1914. The Clarke company diversified into non-woven fabrics; its modern factory is set back from the road a short distance from Ardtara House. At the other side of the road traces of the system of weirs and streams harnessed to provide early power can still be seen, and it is no surprise to find that this generous book is dedicated to the Clady River which, the author says, 'has clothed and fed us all at Upperlands for 240 years'.

As I digest all this I notice that the group of hearty but courteous men I met earlier in the drawing-room have now come in to dine. Despite concentrating almost equally on my roast smoked and fresh salmon with celeriac remoulade and on my introduction to the linen industry, I realise through overheard snatches of conversation that they are golfers. The stories and the laughter filter through my enjoyment

AT HOME IN IRELAND

of a fillet of local beef done lusciously as I specified and accompanied by fondant potato, buttered greens and truffle cream, and it becomes clear that they are headed for a Seniors (or could it be Veterans?) championship at Royal Portrush. But it's not until I've got to the lemon crème brûlée with raspberries and a lemon sorbet, presented like a work of art on a triangle of sugar-dusted crystal, that I grasp the fact that I am dining with Ben Crenshaw.

His group are regulars among the golfers favouring Ardtara, drawn by its unique combination of serenity, comfort and cuisine and by its closeness to Royal Portrush, which everyone says is 'just up the road'. However, it seems that if golf isn't your thing you won't be ostracised at Ardtara because so many fishermen come to scour the river Bann for salmon and trout with coarse as well as game fishing available.

Ardtara has kept its sense of style. There's a lot of old wood, some elegant mantelpieces, plentiful bookcases, armchairs and sofas, well-placed lamps, paintings and photographs, books and magazines. It's not a large house – only eight bedrooms – but this makes staying here a more authentic experience. The entrance hall is attractively finished; a playful plaster frieze in the staircase hall is an additional pleasure and the period touches are effective (my deep, hipped bath is terrific), but modern convenience is an unobtrusive priority in a house maintaining the late Victorian atmosphere of gracious living.

In the morning the white damask has been replaced by green on the tables. I breakfast on local sausages and potato bread and watch the golfers pack their cars and drive off to Royal Portrush. Aristocracy is catching, I think: the house, the linen and now the great golfers of the world.

Ardtara Country House,
Upperlands, County Derry
Tel: 028 7964 4490

Ashley Park House

County Tipperary

Country houses live in their communities in ways town dwellers do not suspect. When Sean Mounsey begins to tell the story of Ashley Park House he unfolds not simply a series of family events but a succession of legends, of local rumours which have the status of consensus, aspects of rural history undisclosed in any casual response to his charming eighteenth-century home near Nenagh.

Nenagh itself is a town with all the charm of a place which has moved with the times but without leaving the best of the past behind. One of its most notable attributes is Peter Ward's thronged shop at Country Choice, which supplies restaurants all over Ireland and also plays a part in the hospitality offered at Ashley Park House. Here Sean Mounsey and his daughter Margaret are assisted by staff who maintain a personalised but efficient tradition of welcome for the travelling guest. Although when my dog Bobbie and I find ourselves at Ashley Park the desire to travel any further at all vanishes utterly, and here's why: my big brass bed; the electric blanket; the high-styled bedside lamps; the walls of dusky pink enhanced by white woodwork and deeply valanced floral curtains; the fireplace with its turf basket and lidded bucket of coal – both of which I take for decoration until I am shown where the matches are; the light from the bay windows reflected in the gilded overmantel; it is the cool green light of the lake beyond the garden.

And the invitation to Bobbie to share my room: she is half-afraid to believe her luck and hesitates before following us up the stairs but then, although I place her basket by the bathroom door, she takes to the carpeted comforts as if she had been born here.

The morning is heralded by the cries of peacocks. A white fan-tailed pigeon is grooming herself on the window ledge and the dew sparkles like frost on the lawn, the light breaking in waves of silver and gold on the lake. A house was built here on the shores of Lough Ourna in 1700 by John Head; his son John built the present house in the mid-century, but the Heads were newcomers to a site known as Rathone, where a series of neolithic ring forts were gradually absorbed into a landed estate – more recently covering 2,000 acres – and recorded in 1660 as belonging to Peter Foxwell. When young John Head died bankrupt, the house eventually came to a new owner living in South Africa, who sold it in 1983. By then the grounds and gardens had become overgrown and in many ways the house wasn't much better. Looking now at the lovely rooms, the drawing-room opening into a little rotunda before developing itself as the delightful Chinese room, the sheer quality of the bedroom décor, which remains both cosy and serene, it is hard to believe that when the Mounseys took over 'the floors were so rotten you couldn't get in the door!'

The transformation came about because Sean

Mounsey and his late wife Nora had a feeling for the house and for the value of old things: the door handles, the shutters, even the bulbous light switches were all rescued from what were often ruined rooms. That sensitivity to the place is matched by the choice of solid country furniture, by the decorative style employed by Margaret Mounsey and her colleague Anne Tuohy, and by the warm, well-equipped bathrooms.

From the outside the house has a French air, with its external shutters and its embracing green-painted verandah. Yet it is all of a piece with Sean Mounsey, a devout and quiet-spoken man whose distinguished face is half-hidden by the flat cap he wears indoors and out. Formerly a small farmer and clerical officer with the county council, he relives the night of the auction. 'I had to go after it,' he explains. 'My late wife had come up this way, her family had farmed some of this land. So there were four of them, three children and the wife, all persuading me! Even though the verandah was all strewn around the place, and there wasn't much feeling for the house around here – I had to go after it!' Two of the adult children went to work in America to get the money needed for

Ashley Park House is all of a piece from inner hall to drawing-room.

ASHLEY PARK HOUSE   17

the ten-year-long restoration. Sean Mounsey speaks of a family yearning, of 'a woeful wish for land', which goes back generations. Now his 75 acres include three fairy forts, about which he is almost as reverent as about church. And the trees – 'Some of them are 300 years old,' he says, 'they would talk to you. We hate to have a storm here, we hate to see the trees fall.'

It is night, and we have eaten at immaculate Dromineer after Bobbie's swim in Lough Derg. We have met the horses in the avenue paddocks and wandered, listening, through the groves of beeches and oaks. All that remains as dusk fills the room with its tender light is sleep, and as I switch off the lamps I hear, from the rug near the bathroom door, a deep contented sigh. ♠

Ashley Park House,
Sean and Margaret Mounsey,
Nenagh, County Tipperary
Tel: 067 38223
E-mail: margaret@ashleypark.com

ABOVE LEFT AND RIGHT: *Details from the drawing-room and bedroom at Ashley Park and (below) one of the house peacocks guards the front door.* (images courtesy of Margaret Mounsey)

Ballaghmore Castle

County Laois

The pride of Grace Pym's life is her castle at Ballaghmore, near Borris-in-Ossory in County Laois, little more than a ruin when she found it in 1990. Set in 30 acres of Ireland's monastic midlands, it is so prominent that its battlements provide a viewing point for 80 miles of surrounding countryside. The castle dates from 1480 on a site straddling the Slighe Dala, one of the four main routes to Tara and the ancient gateway to Munster. It was built for the Mac Giolla Phadraig Lords of Upper Ossory; Barnaby Mac Giolla Phadraig was held as a hostage by Henry VIII and reared with the future Edward VI; on his death, the teenage Barnaby returned to become the 1st Earl of Ossory. Lured by the riches of north Munster, rival clans challenged the Fitzpatrick dominance; later invaders included Cromwell's troops and eventually Ballaghmore was left in the hands of the Ely family, a name now being promoted in the new tourism designation of the Ely O'Carroll territories.

The castle was a bit of a ruin that Cromwell knocked about a bit, but Grace Pym has restored and furnished it with such a sense of its earliest history that its atmosphere, like its architecture, is more medieval than Cromwellian. With its storeys floored and its windows glazed, the castle is more reconstructed than modernised, and this treatment, despite the ingenuity in the bedrooms and bathrooms, maintains the sense of antiquity breathed out by the 10-foot-thick stone walls, the vaulted ceilings and the musket embrasures. After a restoration in 1836 the castle had become derelict again when its rescue was masterminded by Grace, working with Martin Carroll, Joe Sullivan, ironmaster Pat Fogarty and cabinet-maker Mark Bulfin. With this team of wonder-workers it was given an imaginative charge: massive, decorated outside only by a rampant síle-na-gig, brooding over the great plain stretching on every side, it is a keep in nature as well as name.

The adjoining sixteenth-century manor house is where Grace has made her home. She has given herself a conservatory of Victorian Gothic character by retrieving the windows and doors from a demolished church in Castletown. No one who knows Grace could have been at all surprised at this. Trained as a sculptor, gilder and specialist in antique frames, with a gallery in Galway, she was also widely respected in Dublin and London for the success of her art gallery in Duke Street. Looking at a portrait of Grace now, I notice how the painter has caught that raised, assessing eyebrow, that interrogative look with which she encounters both pictures and people.

At Ballaghmore that sensitivity to, and eye for, old and beautiful things has created a house both practical and lovely. In ways it is a kind of nursery-rhyme house, with cupboards and niches and little passages all to be discovered, just as the arches of roses between this house and the neighbouring two-storey cottage and the baskets hanging from the conservatory ceiling are themselves a kind of coded link to Grace's life as a child and to her favourite Aunt Dinah. It was the castle which initially looked to Grace to be totally beyond redemption. Once she grasped that the scaffolding alone would cost an honest man's yearly wage, she decided that if it were to be tackled at all it would be from the ground up, which is exactly how it was done, so that each phase of the restoration work could rest on the foundations laid down by the previous one. The panelling disguising the thoroughly efficient plumbing was made from discarded Georgian shutters, a half-tester bed stands under a roof of raw stone, more panelling encases the garderobe.

ABOVE: *The castle keep at Ballaghmore overlooks the more recent manor house.* OPPOSITE: *Sleep in medieval style within the castle walls and (below) the manor house conservatory.* (images courtesy of Grace Pym and Grant Hutchinson)

She takes me to the battlements to see not just the woods and fields and streams spread out below but also the many roofs which keep the castle dry and warm (assisted by central heating). Enjoying the sweet nostalgic drift of turf smoke from the manor chimneys, I'm happy to be outside on this June evening knowing that under the sloping ceilings of my bedroom the country-cottage furniture includes a bed with a wonderfully receptive mattress and an embroidered counterpane. As the sky fades in tints of rose and gold the buttercup-laden fields seem to breathe out their perfumes and the ponies come slowly to greet us at the fence. Essences of woodbine, elderflower and clover mingle with the warm must from the horses. A stream rustles beneath the castle where once there was a moat. It is night, in the summer, in the monastic midlands, and from the manor house the lamps gleam among the roses.

The castle and cottage at Ballaghmore are available for private rental. ♣

Ballaghmore Castle,
Borris-in-Ossory, County Laois
Tel: 0505 21453
www.elyocarroll.com

BALLAGHMORE CASTLE

Ballaghtobin

Callan, County Kilkenny

The Gabbetts of Ballaghtobin talk about their creeper-clad home as 'the modern house'. In a way they are right, but there's nothing about Ballaghtobin which seems, or is, disconcertingly contemporary. It is the very model of an Irish country house, arranged so as to provide graceful accommodation while still serving the needs of a big, centuries-old farm.

Its 500 acres, to which Mickey Gabbett returned in 1977, are filled now with tillage, blackcurrants and Christmas trees, all managed and harvested by two men and some massive machinery. And that still leaves time for Mickey's passion for vintage cars, which move at a pace which seems to suit the character of Ballaghtobin. Both Catherine and Mickey Gabbett are powerhouses in themselves, yet again there is that vintage quality, as if, with minor exceptions such as the occasional change in the cast of characters, Ballaghtobin has remained undisturbed and untroubled for centuries.

The truth is that this is a re-made house, the result of rebuilding which imposed a Georgian symmetry on the earlier outlines while incorporating strong indications of the house, or houses, on this site since the Tobins arrived in the mid-seventeenth century. They were dispossessed in favour of the Baker family, from which, via the Knox connection, the estate passed to Mickey's father Robin, aged all of twelve. There are traces of all these people and their lives on this Kilkenny land, from the dovecote and the seventeenth-century kennels for the favourite wolfhounds to the remains of a little chapel and graveyard across the lawn. (All this history is given in more detail in some fascinating documents prepared by Miss Sophie Gabbett when a twelve-year-old schoolgirl.)

Maybe it's the wolfhound connection (although the biggest dog on the lawn right now is a lurcher) which makes Catherine suggest that I might like to bring my own bitch Bobbie up to my room for the night. I'm travelling with her on a trail of houses willing to accept the canine pets of their guests and after supper in Callan I take her for a protracted twilight stroll along the avenue. It is high summer, and the trees stand clear of the mellow fields; well-tended, they show off their fullness, their perfection of contour, the spread of branches and flow of foliage declaring, as trees can when given the opportunity, their imperturbable immensity. This is what a visit to the country can do: perception changes, the ordinary day fades and otherwise unnoticed or undervalued parts of life are allowed to seep into our consciousness.

Soothed by this precautionary walk I find the lamplit charm of my bedroom so soporific that I'm asleep before I can do justice to the books, the bedside tables with their mineral water, clock radio, torch and tissues, or even to the commodious bathroom with its

Ballaghtobin. An Irish country house arranged to provide graceful accommodation while meeting the needs of a big modern farm.

quantity of towels, its bathrobes, packed vanity case, slippers and unguents and oils. We're in the older part of the house, where the ceilings are low, the windows have cushioned window seats, the armchairs flank the parkland and farmland views.

The size of the house, the looming departure of their children, a major downturn in farm economics and – 'really, I think it was the hole in the roof!' – combined to persuade Catherine to follow the example of her sister in Northern Ireland and open Ballaghtobin to guests. 'I enjoy it more than I thought I might, even though I only started this because I wanted to. But we meet lovely people – the great thing about this is that you meet people at their best, they become their better selves. It's a little like being in love: you want to deserve it.'

BALLAGHTOBIN

ABOVE: *'The hospitality you offer to good friends': the dining-room at Ballaghtobin.* RIGHT: *The sitting-room.* (images courtesy of James Fennell)

Such lucky people find at Ballaghtobin the kind of hospitality which, as Catherine says, is the hospitality you offer to good friends, beginning with welcoming drinks in the drawing-room. It's style with generosity, I think next day as Mickey and I take all the dogs to walk the land. It's a languorous morning, and the blue-grey expanses of oats undulate as the mist lifts from the fields. Agri-business is personalised as Mickey explains the policies of blackcurrants and the Noble Fir, how farming can be developed on a European scale among landowners in Ireland, Poland and other eastern countries, and the real importance of the Gordon Bennett international rally. But I am distracted by the dogs racing along the headlands, by the occasional startled cock-pheasant, by the squirrels and, for one ecstatic second, by a hare. ♣

Ballaghtobin,
Callan, County Kilkenny
Tel: 056 772 5227
www.ballaghtobin.com

Ballinacurra House

Midleton, County Cork

Whatever else may be growing in and around Midleton, houses are in full bloom. Acres of pastureland are succumbing to the insatiable appetite for residential development. Yet in the face of such sprawl the land itself seems in good heart. All along the coastal districts the fields glow with a golden autumn harvest, a bright promise of good faith between farmer and field. If farmers in Ireland are abandoning the land, it's not the land's fault.

Allan Navratil knows where to put the blame. Farming all his life, he has followed every move in the economic policies which had dictated rather than directed so much of what has happened to agriculture in Ireland and across Europe. Sitting in the sunny kitchen of this old manor house near Midleton, seeing birds swoop and flutter along the box-hedged garden, hearing the raucous call of the herons and egrets roosting in the harbour inlet below the walls, is to feel at once both involved in and immune from the controversies of the recent past. But it is here that Allan Navratil explains how a future can be recovered from the shocking closures of the past twelve months.

This, it has to be admitted, is not what I came for. I came for a house on a site occupied since the late twelfth century. Or even earlier, depending on the mound reached by a spiral path cut through laurels above the river; this could be a burial mound pre-dating the Normans or might instead be a relic of the Normans themselves. Just beyond the garden wall the ruins of a thirteenth-century church remain, and the early eighteenth-century house itself, mellow in its simplicity among lawns and shrubberies, passed in its many years of history through several families before reaching Henry Garde's daughter Clothilde, whose husband Andrew Rowland sold it to Alfred Navratil in 1939.

The Irish sugar industry was the brainchild of two opposing politicians, William Cosgrave and Eamon de Valera. The start-up expertise came mainly in the person of Alfred Navratil, who arrived from what is now the Czech Republic in 1926. He was the chief engineer for the Carlow factory and later manager of the Mallow plant. Settling in Ireland with his Czech wife, Navratil anticipated a shortage of imported beet seed due to the looming war; because his warnings went unheeded, he decided to grow his own. For this he would need a farm, and so he bought this house with about 100 acres near Midleton in 1939.

Allan Navratil explains all this with such affection for the process and the people involved that it is impossible not to respond to the idea of a great native industry, home-grown and thriving, and yet suddenly slipping away into history. And it didn't stop with sugar, for along came General Michael Costello – 'a tremenduous visionary, well aware of the need of Irish farmers for a market'. Costello developed Erin

The farmyard gate at Ballinacurra. (image courtesy of the *Irish Examiner*)

Foods, hugely important to tillage farmers all over Ireland. 'Because of his vision we had something to grow,' says Navratil. 'There was one period where I was growing fifteen crops, employing a lot of people, involved as a director in East Cork Foods.' With privatisation in 1991 came Greencore, and the change to a business run according to shareholders' best interests. Navratil, like others whose voices so often seem to be deliberately ignored, is concerned for the social impact of political decisions which led to the closure of the sugar factories and the obliteration of the beet industry in Ireland.

With his colleagues in the Irish Biofuels Initiative, Navratil proposes other uses for the beet crop. The production of ethanol as a fuel is one such alternative and in these days of diminishing oil supplies an increasingly urgent one. Provided the factories are left standing, Navratil and his colleagues say that the Carlow and Mallow plants are better than oil wells because, with the feedstock supplied by Irish farmers and the fuel produced by Irish workers, they constitute an infinitely renewable source of energy. These biofuel chemists, scientists, engineers and farmers have taken their intensely argued and well-documented case to those who have the power and, one imagines, the intelligence to consider it. But here, strolling along the gravel paths above the harbour inlet, the question has to be: is anybody listening? ♠

The Carlow and Mallow sugar factories were dismantled. Allan Navratil still farms near Midleton and points out that two recent independent professional studies unequivocally promote the economics of sugar industry reinstatement as soon as possible.

Ballinkeele Country House

County Wexford

There are not many country house hotels where, once dinner is over, the covers removed and the port passed round, the entire kitchen staff decamp to the opera. Without, let it be said, any noticeable effect on the standard of breakfast served the following morning. Yet this is the custom of the country in which Ballinkeele House is set, in the village of Ballymurn, only a few miles from Wexford town and its three weekends of international opera festival.

The departing guests are making reservations for next year as I wait for Margaret Maher to give me the history of the house and of the family which

BELOW: *The entrance hall at Ballinkeele.*

built it in 1840 on the site of an earlier, eighteenth-century residence. Before 1825 the house had been home to Edward Hay, noted in these parts for his *History of the Insurrection of the County of Wexford AD 1798*. Since then – as the well-kept stable block might indicate – it had become famous for its racing stables, producing both Frigate, the first mare to win the Aintree Grand National which she did in 1889, and, among other valuable horses, two winners of the Irish Derby: Kentish Fire in 1890 and Bowline in 1893.

Margaret's husband John Maher farms the 360 acres of largely arable land and a herd of twenty suckler cows, yet he fits without apparent effort into the early-morning routine of cooking to meet the needs of those guests who, after a long night at the opera (and, make no mistake, one production this year lasted for four hours) are fit for another day exploring the county before returning for dinner. This is served at 6pm; even seconds late at curtain up and you don't get in until the next act.

Although Margaret trained as a nurse in her native Edinburgh, she went to work at the small hotel at Craigieburn made famous by her mother Margaret Hislop. Coming to Ireland after her marriage she settled down to what could be called normal country life. But 'settle' is not a word easily applied to Margaret; when I join her in the kitchen after dinner she no sooner finishes her own meal than she begins to bake the bread for the next morning's breakfast.

When the fragrant corrugated loaves lie on the counter-top she goes off to the opera party. I go to my room in the wing, reached downstairs by a long flagged passage leading off the main hall, which itself is inside the entrance hall. Both these halls are very attractive, the outer rather stately, the inner warmed by an enormous wood-burning stove. The curtaining may be rich, the wallpapers old and fine, the pictures many and interesting (including some of Margaret's

OPPOSITE: *Room to relax after the opera.* LEFT: *The dining-room, full of the atmosphere of a beloved family residence and (right) detail of the ceiling cornice.* (images courtesy of The Hidden Ireland)

own studies; yes, she does sit down sometimes), the furniture having that combination of finesse and function which distinguishes so much Victorian craftsmanship, yet there is still the atmosphere of a beloved family residence.

'I wanted the guests to feel that they were coming to a home. If you destroy that, there's nothing to make it special for people. Also we were very anxious to keep the house feeling right for ourselves and the children, to protect its tradition as a family home, which has been unbroken ever since John's people came here.'

My room is carpeted, white-painted, with shutters at the window and print curtains matching the quilted coverlet on the generously pillowed bed; lamps are positioned just where they are needed for easy reading. Once in bed I drift into dreamless slumber, waking in the morning to see the pheasants twittering at one another through the long stubble fields outside my window.

Margaret has no regrets about the decision taken nine years ago to open up for guests. She was more or less doing something of the kind anyway, as the snipe bog and the autumnal fields brought groups of friends on shooting parties. She loves cooking and it shows, but the house also has a freshness which reveals the care lavished on it.

Belonging to The Hidden Ireland organisation keeps the Mahers in touch with other people who, like themselves, are determined to keep their old homes together, properly maintained and full of a modern approximation to the kind of life for which these houses were built in the first place. ♣

I regret to say that John Maher died in October 2011; he and Margaret had already agreed to be included in this publication and his family subsequently decided to let that decision stand.

Ballinkeele Country House,
Ballymurn, Enniscorthy,
County Wexford
Tel: 053 9138105

Ballyboy House

Clogheen, County Tipperary

I arrive at Ballyboy House near the village of Clogheen in sunny humour, given that the temperature is soaring, the sky cloudless, the grass of a piercing green brilliance, the mountains shadowed only by their own heathery masses. At the end of this journey is the promise of a garden and lunch and friendly conversation – a taste of what is on offer to those who appreciate Breeda Moran's home in Ballyboy. As we walk across the paddock, now a lawn smooth enough for tennis, she reminds me again of the pleasures she finds in keeping everything going here, in the constant stream of visitors and in the unending vista of the Knockmealdown Mountains on one side, the Galtees on the other and all the abundant greenery of the valley.

'People come just to relax,' she says. 'Just being here is enough. They find their way about, we tell them everything that's going on, they make their choices.'

Beyond the garden a gap in the old wall gives access to the ruins of Ballyboy Castle, demolished for strategic reasons in 1597. Shortly after this the Everards built Ballyboy Manor, a late arrival in the history of this family, one of whom is reputed to have fought beside William the Conqueror at Hastings in 1066. Martin Everard accompanied Prince John to Ireland in 1187, and Laurence Everard of Tipperary fought at Agincourt in 1415. Nothing of this belligerent career is evident now, where Breeda's husband John maintains the family's 150-acre dairy farm, with his mother's butter barrel in a place of honour in the roomy kitchen.

Encouraged by Brid Burke of Teagasc, Breeda took the opportunity of a general farm redevelopment to open for guests in 1991 and has 'never looked back since'. This is not a grand house nor even a particularly big one, but the main reception rooms are large and they and the attractive hall are of considerable character, the long windows are replacements but match the style of the house and even on this brilliant day in June there is a snapping fire in the sitting-room, scenting the house as it always does because it always did.

The manor house was inherited by Sir Richard Everard, in 1624, but became a Georgian farmhouse in the eighteenth century. Breeda has not tried to obliterate that typical personality combining grace with function; the house and its farm buildings sit naturally into a landscape to which they have belonged for so many centuries. Off one of the bedrooms a large bathroom has been created out of a loft which was once where the farm labourers slept over the kitchen. The bathroom for another bedroom is what was known as the feather room, because it was here that the pillows and quilts were stuffed.

A chalice commemorating the marriage of Sir

OPPOSITE: *Ballyboy House. The farmhouse sits beneath the foothills of the Knockmealdown Mountains.* (image courtesy of the *Irish Examiner*) BELOW: *The dining-room at Ballyboy.* (courtesy of Brendan Davis)

Richard Everard and Catherine Tobin of Fethard is still used in the diocese. The couple left Ballyboy for their new castle of Clogheen, dated 1641 and known as Burncourt: the name enshrines the decision of Lady Catherine to burn it down in 1649 rather than let it fall to Cromwell's men. Ballyboy itself went through the hands of several families after the departure of the Everards, until a Fennessy–Moran marriage brought the Moran family to Ballyboy and the Morans have been here ever since. The valley area includes Cahir Castle and the Rock of Cashel, but first of all there are two and a half unsequestered miles of trout fishing on the Tar available to guests, literally at the bottom of the garden. The Suir is within easy driving distance, so is the Blackwater.

Every salmon caught in one of these waters is worth £600 to the local community, a fact which the government prefers to ignore, placating the commercial interests with permissions for ruinous drift-nets. A massive fish kill on the Suir was reported the day after my visit to Ballyboy. Found guilty of contaminating the public water supply of the town of Nenagh (admittedly with some help from the county council's own deficiencies), Proctor & Gamble were fined the risible sum of £1,500, although Nenagh Urban District Council had to provide an emergency alternative source at a cost of £330,000. This is a joke, and the joke is on us, on the fish and on the tourism and its most dedicated promoters, like Breeda Moran of Clogheen. ♠

Drift-net fishing was banned in Ireland in 2007.

Ballyboy House,
Clogheen, County Tipperary
Tel: 052 7465297

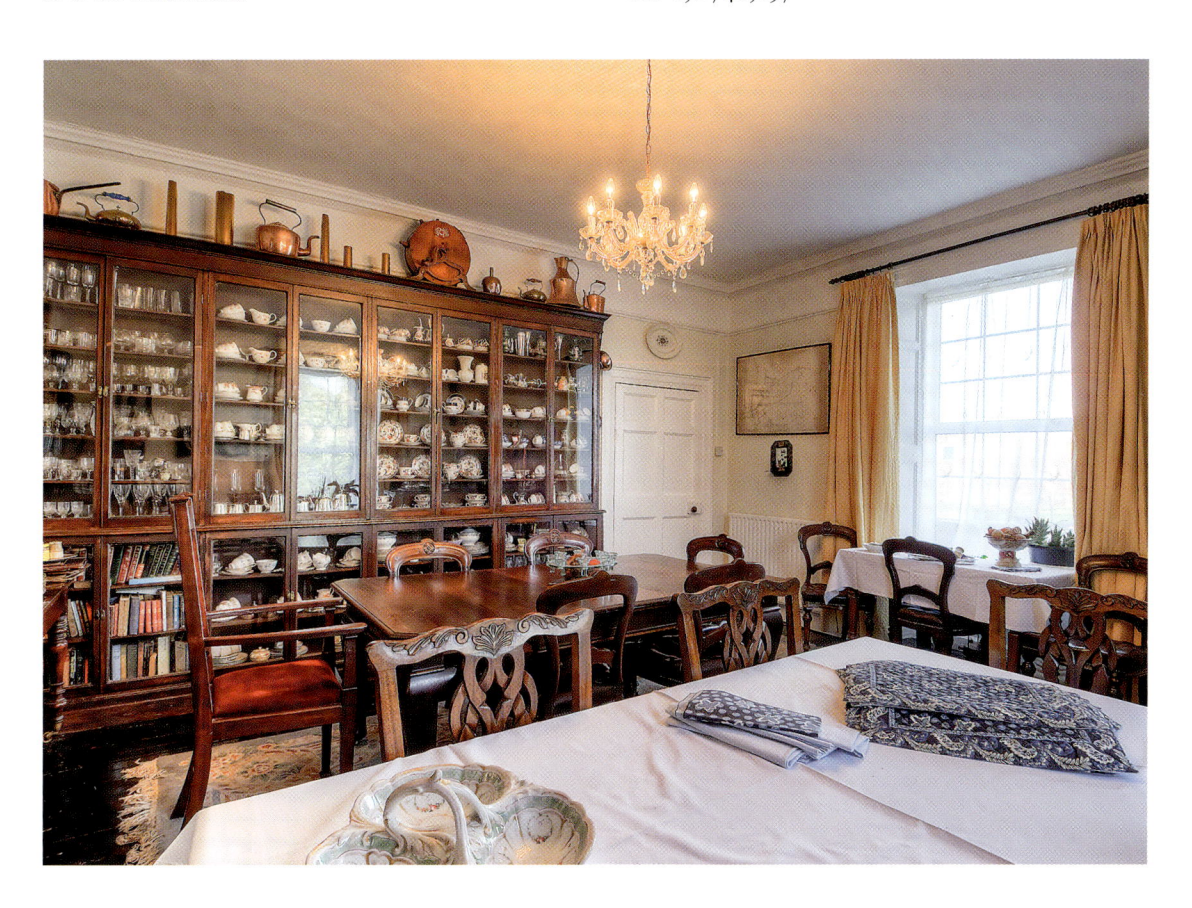

Ballyduff House

Thomastown, County Kilkenny

'Life here is a juggling act,' says Brede Thomas as she supervises the boxing of a pony which is to be driven off to Pony Camp in Kilkenny. Maybe it is, but Brede spent twelve years in America as manager of a chain of smart restaurants, so she's the one who does the juggling at Ballyduff House, not her guests. The River Nore is below the dining-room; some of the guests have been fishing and they are tying up the boat and shouldering their baskets and shaking out their waders before climbing back up to shower, change and enjoy sherry in the library. There is no formality to this; the atmosphere is casual, but traditional, given that we are in a country house attached to a castle and that hospitality has been practised and perfected here for centuries.

This Georgian property was inherited by Marguerite Solly-Flood, and then by her daughter and son-in-law Major and Mrs D.J.O. Thomas. Brede, who comes from a farming background herself, married their son Peter Thomas but was widowed very early in her marriage while her two children were little more than infants. For several years she shared the house with her late parents-in-law, absorbing all the history of the place, of the 240 acres of farmland, of the river and its townlands and of the busy village of Thomastown.

On my arrival with my dog Bobbie I am greeted by the very competent Rachel, for Brede is taken up with the pony club event and later will be providing supper for the men making silage. Soothed by the pink-patterned walls and tulip-print curtaining of my bedroom, by books and magazines and flowers on the dresser and tall windows letting in acres of soft evening light, I decide to absent myself from the silage supper. I lure Bobbie away from the splashing delights of the river and into a roomy loosebox and then, finding that the entire population of Thomastown is on the streets to celebrate the arrival of the Special Olympics team from Alaska, I head off to Pakies in Knocktopher.

Ballyduff's 700-year-old keep has been roofed and repaired and transformed into generous self-catering accommodation, much loved by the fishing folk from France and Belgium who come here year after year. Brede has learned that 'even in a castle people like their carpets', and she provides stylish bedrooms with their en-suite bathrooms, a well-equipped kitchen and the freezer, which is essential to holiday satisfaction, as this is where the catch is frozen before being carried back to the Continent.

Although there are lawns and shrubberies around the house, and the façade is softened with wisteria and climbing roses, it is a place with enchanting hidden plots like the walled acreage somewhere under an arched hedge behind the stables. Herbaceous borders riot with colour and scent, fruit ripens on canes and

Above: *Brede Thomas in the hall at Ballyduff House and (left) contentment in the library.*

trees, herbs and vegetables together fill more beds and in the paddock beyond some glossy horses muse and munch contentedly.

'I love having people around and, although it's only possible to manage a place like this by being out there and getting it done, people adapt to the atmosphere here, they become part of the place and they seem to enjoy the fact that it's a farm and things are going on,' says Brede. I think of this later in the evening as I settle down in the library, surrounded by the books from many generations of the same family, cocooned in lamplight and sofas with a cool glass of

BALLYDUFF HOUSE   33

Friendly and traditional is the keynote at Ballyduff. (images courtesy of Ballyduff House and Marie Dunne)

white wine to hand. At breakfast I hear Brede sing the praises of housekeeper Mary Butler and remember that the night before I had gone to walk the dog and passed the men putting the silage under cover in the barn. We skirted the headlands of newly-mown fields, shielded from the blaze of the setting sun by the woods which emboss all this part of Kilkenny. As we made our way home again we found the men gone, the silage covered, the yards empty and quiet, the day's work done. With Bobbie fed and watered and bedded down, all I had to do was reach the library, my choice of books, my glass of wine, and sweet content. ♣

Ballyduff House,
Thomastown, County Kilkenny
Tel: 056 775 8488
Email: ballydhouse@eircom.net

Ballyfin Country House Hotel

Mountrath, County Laois

'Yes,' says Brother Maurice Murphy, 'yes, my life has fallen in pleasant lines.' We are looking, as we looked exactly ten years ago, across the ornamental lake at Ballyfin, where the woodland is reddening and the rooks cluster like a cloud over the trees. I wonder aloud if he had ever thought he would see such a day. Not so much the autumn sunshine, or the serenity of these 600 midland acres, or even the glinting thirteen-bay array of windows in the great house behind us. No – the wonder to us both is that so much is happening. Brother Maurice agrees with me. He had never thought to have seen this day. The last time we met it was to consider the possible future of Ballyfin House, then badly in need of expensive repairs. It had been bought by the Patrician Order in

BELOW: *Seen in its lakeside setting, Ballyfin reflects the motto of its Coote family builders: 'cost what it may'.*

Opposite: *The grisaille paintings in the Van Der Hagen room came originally from Mount Congreve in County Waterford.* Below: *The library.* Right: *The Marquise de Massigny de la Pierre room celebrates the French son-in-law of Sir Charles and Lady Caroline Coote.*

1928 and opened as a school – attended by the young Maurice Murphy – in 1932. Since then, the Brothers had kept the interior of the house intact and as close as possible to its original style. The Irish Georgian Society helped with this, as did the Irish Heritage Council, but in 1997 it was becoming very obvious that Ballyfin needed more than the Patricians could bring to its future prospects.

Now, however, it looks as if the Patricians, by selling it to the business consortium which is transforming it into as splendid a hotel as it was once a splendid house, have saved it again. And in a way Brother Maurice himself is part of that rescue operation, having known the house through three lives: as a school boarder, as a teacher, and acting as a kind of curator until its sale three years ago. He knew where things had once stood and where they had been stored. He had, and still has, tales to tell of the water-tanks, the painted panels in the saloon, the turf-lined walls of the bedroom passages. He can point out where the damaged roundels above the portico have been copied and replaced, identifying the old from the new at an enviable glance. A lyre motif garlanded by the extended tails of exotic birds patterning a cornice is explained, as is the moulding of a door-frame. In an upstairs bedroom men are kneeling to insert, leaf by gilded leaf, the decoration of a window-frame, and Brother Maurice appraises this minutely finished work with a kind of reminiscent tick – yes, it's as it used to be.

This wondrous house was built to echo the family motto, *coute que coute* – cost what it may. In itself the motto is a kind of pun on the Cootes, who bought Ballyfin in 1814 from William Wellesley Pole, 1st Lord Maryborough and 3rd Lord Mornington and brother of the better-known Duke of Wellington. Pole's relatively plain house had been built in 1778; Sir Charles Coote, married to Catherine Whaley, commissioned the local architect Dominic Madden to rebuild the house and then engaged Sir Richard Morrison and his son William Vitruvius to adapt Madden's plans.

Costing about £20,000 at the time, the completed house is undeniably and triumphantly more Morrison than Madden. Architectural historian Edward McParland has described both the influences on and the spatial significance of the stunning enfilade the Morrisons created through the house, achieving a drama of top-lit spaces, of pillared screens, painted niches, domes and lanterns from one end of the building to the other. The coved ceiling of the saloon is acclaimed as one of the greatest technical achievements of Irish decorative plasterwork. The library wing, ending in the Turner conservatory (faithfully preserved from dereliction by the late Brother Joseph) has a curved bow, pillared on the outside and almost as grand as the thirteen-bay entrance front with its portico supported by Ionic columns.

Mark Bence-Jones describes Ballyfin as 'the grandest and most lavishly appointed early nineteenth-century Classical house in Ireland' and this is what

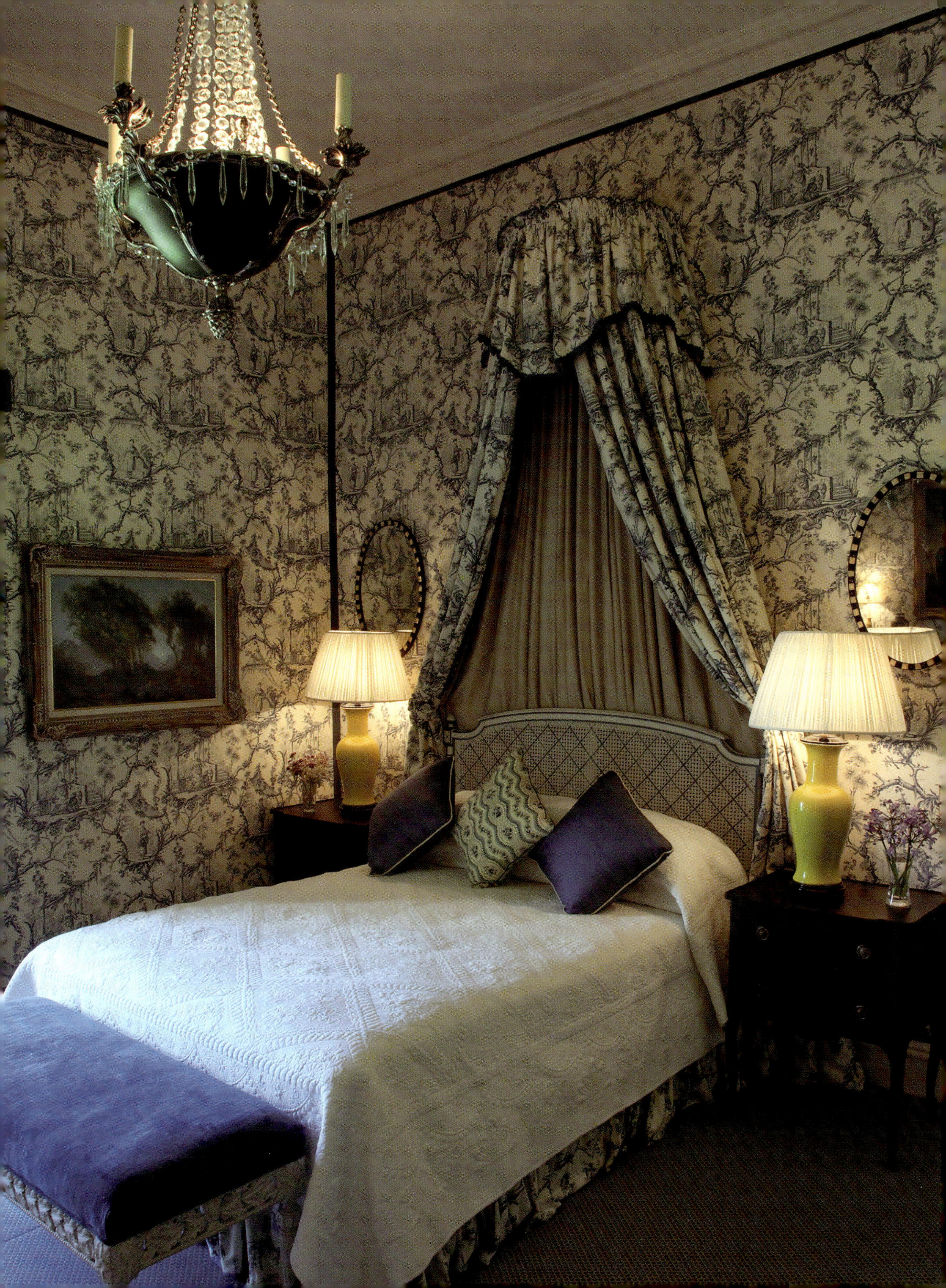

ABOVE: *The portrait by Thomas Carlton in the entrance hall is that of Sir Audley Mervyn, who was connected by marriage to the former owners of Ballyfin House.* (images by James Fennell for Ballyfin House and Demesne)

its new proprietors want to offer their guests: a stay in the traditional style of the greatest of great houses. The marble and mahogany, maple and bog-oak, satinwood, rosewood and cherry, marquetry and rediscovered inlay are all attaining a new shine. Several thousand books are ready for the glazed library shelves, the fireplaces in every reception room will be in working order, the repaired conservatory will hint at the groves, the walled gardens, the grotto and follies and the 40 new acres of oak planting in the parkland. Although the long-term plans include the whole range of estate buildings, from cow-house to gardener's bothy, this will not be an enormous expanse of hotel. Instead its forty-five bedrooms and suites will be generous, the furnishings as authentic as possible in one of the grandest adventures in restoration Ireland has ever known. All its participants, in one way or another, listen to Brother Maurice Murphy, who can say now, as we watch the fall of sunlight on the distant hills, that the work of the Patrician Brothers at Ballyfin has been completed. And, given the chance, 'I'd do it all again.' ♣

The Patrician Brothers and their school have moved to new premises near Ballyfin. The consortium led by its chairman Fred Krehbiel of Chicago (and Kerry) has completed its restoration of the house, which now includes a fine collection of classical and modern art. It opened as a private country house hotel in 2010.

Ballyfin Country House Hotel,
Mountrath, County Laois
Tel: 057 875 5866
www.ballyfin.com

Ballymacmoy House

Kilavullen, County Cork

Ballymacmoy House is in a kind of active limbo, being gradually brought back to the light of what will be uncommon day, if its owner Frederic Hennessy has anything to say about it. 'My ideal is that it will be a guesthouse, something as perfect as Ballyvolane House in Castlelyons,' he tells me as we stand in the frozen mud outside his front door. And I believe him. Even as we thread our way through spaces left by absent doors, beneath ceilings revealing their underwear of lathe and twining cobweb, along a little enfilade of rooms where the gaping floorboards seem aghast at his promise of en-suite bathrooms and restored cornices – even with all this, I believe him.

Frederic Hennessy has a visionary optimism which is quite infectious. His belief is founded on the evidence of work in progress: windows in, roof securely on, floors reboarded, walls replastered, the adjacent coach house already restored as an attractive apartment, storehouse and workroom. With 3½ miles of riverbank with four fishing beats, Ballymacmoy makes its argument by rising above the scaffolding and over the dilapidated orchard and walled garden, its character and location surpassing even the detritus of builders' rubble. It is a process which began a very long time ago. My guide is the eighth generation of the French Hennessys, the Cognac line which began here at Killavullen on a precipice above the Blackwater.

As Frederic explains it, 'My ancestor Richard Hennessy at that time was living on this estate although not in this house; he lived about three miles away from here before he left Ireland in 1740. The cousinships lapsed through the generations but this house of Ballymacmoy, which was built in 1818 on the foundations of an earlier house, came back to us in 1932 when my great-grandfather bought it from the last Hennessy living here.'

Frederic was born in Paris, shares wine-growing hectares in Cognac with his family and has worked extensively further abroad but most recently in London. His older brother Maurice is chairman of Hennessy Cognac for Ireland, and it was he who passed Ballymacmoy on to Frederic. 'It was a present, but I'm not sure I would have been fighting to get it,' says Frederic now, although he acknowledges that 'this is where we come from, Killavullen.'

The Richard Hennessy who was born at Ballymacmoy in 1720 married Ellen Barrett, a cousin of statesman and orator Edmund Burke. For a time Hennessy and Burke shared a place in the same hedge school under the walls of Monanimy Castle. Its grey keep is visible from here, gleaming through the winter trees on its crag above the river. An earlier marriage was that of Ellen Nagle of Monanimy to Sylvanus, son of Edmund Spenser of Kilcolman. In all these births, marriages and deaths the Blackwater remains the stream of inspiration and solidarity for

ABOVE: *Now restored and open to guests, Ballymacmoy House rises above the river Blackwater in north Cork.* OPPOSITE TOP: *The curved dining-room and (bottom) old and newer in the entrance front of the house, which dates from 1818.* (images by Gabriel de la Bassetiere, courtesy of Frederic Hennessy)

the Catholics of this valley, just as France remains their place of refuge. No wonder Burke spoke with such passion about the fate of the queen of France during the Revolution: 'I thought ten thousand swords must have leaped from their scabbards, to avenge even a look that threatened her with insult.'

Sir Richard Nagle of Carrigacunna Castle further along the stream was Attorney-General for King James II and followed him into exile; a year before Richard Hennessy's departure for France, John Nagle of Monanimy was killed at the Battle of Knockanuss, near Kanturk.

The working avenue for Ballymacmoy opens from the main road through Killavullen. More challenging is the formal avenue, its long curving lines making a ghostly shadow on the fields which cover it between the town and the river. Between the house and the sheer edge of the rock a terrace was laid out, overlooked by Wyatt windows on both floors. Eventual guests will enjoy the view from these windows, which now show the river in full winter spate and beyond it fields of striped stubble and hedges thick with haws.

Working with architects Murray O Laoire, Frederic has been identifying the character of the house with its cornices, its delicate plasterwork, its arches and beamed ceiling. So far as possible he has employed only local people on the restoration of Ballymacmoy and has tried to make sure that all his materials come from Irish sources. Settling in to his 23 acres of Irish countryside he makes no great architectural claims, gesturing only to the fields and to the ramparts of the Ballyhoura hills on one side, the Nagle Mountains on the other, brown and golden in the frosty air.

The restoration of Ballymacmoy was completed in 2011 and the house is now open for guests.

Ballymacmoy House,
Kilavullen, County Cork
Email: info@ballymacmoy.com
www.ballymacmoy.com

AT HOME IN IRELAND

BALLYMACMOY HOUSE

Ballymote House

Downpatrick, County Down

All around me are vast fields empty of everything except cattle and cross-country fences. When the wind dies down, I can hear in the quiet the roll of the incoming tide on one of Ireland's loveliest beaches. The creeper-cloaked house in front of me is silent and vacant; even the stable yard behind yields only an amiable lurcher and a wheelbarrow piled with the morning's muck. But it isn't morning, it's getting deeper and deeper into the evening, with the shades of night pulling themselves down ruthlessly. My overnight booking seems to have gone astray and it's time to search for alternative accommodation, but turning up unannounced at nine in the evening isn't the best introduction to any proprietor.

However, Nicola Manningham-Buller is a specialist in the art of rescue. She has had to be, given that her children are pony and polo mad and her own riding career has had its moments of danger. She immediately unleashes a series of forensic telephone calls, produces a much-needed cup of tea, offers accommodation, sends one child to a neighbour for fresh eggs (those already in the house have been requisitioned for Dash, a nursing bitch whose five-strong litter cuddles together in their box near the Aga) and the other into the garden for courgettes and chives and parsley and lettuces, while she herself raids the cellar for a bottle of white wine.

Few misunderstandings in my career have turned out quite so well as this, I think, as I eat in the friendly kitchen, the atmosphere alive with the children's talk of friends and ponies and competitions and teams. And I thank my lucky stars again – those stars which led me through Downpatrick's streets to the Killough Road – as I finally retire to a calm bedroom and fade into sleep on the feeling that what could have been an upsetting experience in Northern Ireland has been transformed into a miracle of welcome and wellbeing.

Nicola is a child of these parts, who met her husband James while working in London, where they lived for a while. When Ballymote, already well known to Nicola, became available, it was here they decided to settle. Taking guests was an extension of the plan, born from Nicola's family habit of having lots of people around more or less all the time.

She loves this house of 1730, with the trees and lawns stretching from the avenue to the door and its immaculate farmyards hiding the garden layout behind. She's a finder and a keeper, everything gets reused, even the silk curtains in my bedroom were found in Paris and date from 1890. In the dining-room the gilded pelmets were recovered from a house that was being refitted and, although almost in bits from exposure when retrieved they have found a new life here. The floor in the sitting-room had been concreted over, the window-frames had rotted and the shutters had been nailed back: all this has

ABOVE: *A serenely confident personality is expressed at Ballymote House.*

been repaired, relaid and reinstalled, while the new kitchen and utility rooms were given old sills and a huge recovered flagstone floor, with the help of a local builder who managed all the Georgian timberwork on windows and architraves.

Family photographs (usually with a strong equine involvement), prints, fine mirrors and mantelpieces sit so easily here as to be taken almost for granted. Yet as I sit down to a breakfast in which, because of my own curiosity, soda, brown and potato breads are major constituents, I'm aware that I am eating 'properly' in the dining-room, given that last night's meal was in the kitchen. I must see and use the house according to its real personality. As expressed by Nicola and her family, that personality is confident and serenely hospitable in the very best traditions of the neighbourhood.

And what a neighbourhood, I think, as I drive later into Killough, a tree-lined town at the edge of the sea. Downpatrick is behind, Rowellane and Mount Stewart are ahead, with the Royal County Down Golf Club within easy reach. The long beaches here stretch almost to the foot of the Mourne

ABOVE: *A corner of the hall and (right) the kitchen: a haven of welcome and wellbeing.* (images courtesy of Alan Lewis)

Mountains, which lurk like a sheltering mass behind the fields of grain. The trees all tilt away from the sea, where yachts like confetti decorate the coves at Kilclief and introduce the gradual, lingering unveiling of Strangford Lough.

Ballymote House remains open for guests.

Ballymote House,
84 Killough Road, Downpatrick, County Down
Tel: 04844615500
E-mail: BandB@ballymotehouse.com
www.ballymotehouse.com

Ballynatray House

County Waterford

Ballynatray is a house with a past. Unlike many such houses, it is also a place with a future, an estate famously engaging the hearts and minds of its proprietors and subject to episodes of what can only be called re-creation. Time after time through 1,500 years, it has seduced proprietors and visitors alike. This time, in the care of Henry Gwyn Jones, it is welcoming the public from the end of May to the first of August not just to its ancient abbey but to the parkland, shrubberies and organic kitchen garden. Also several of the properties on the estate are available as self-catering rentals, including the dramatic studio space above the boathouse and the little riverside house called the love nest.

Ballynatray carries romance within its title like spores within its woodlands. It seems as if geography and imagination feed one another still, as they have done for a thousand years. The deer-park folds back up into the hills above the Glendine River, which meets the Blackwater just where the twin gatehouses give acess to the estate. Walking the land, as estate manager Neil Porteous explains what has been done and

BELOW: *Ballynatray. The boathouse on the river.*

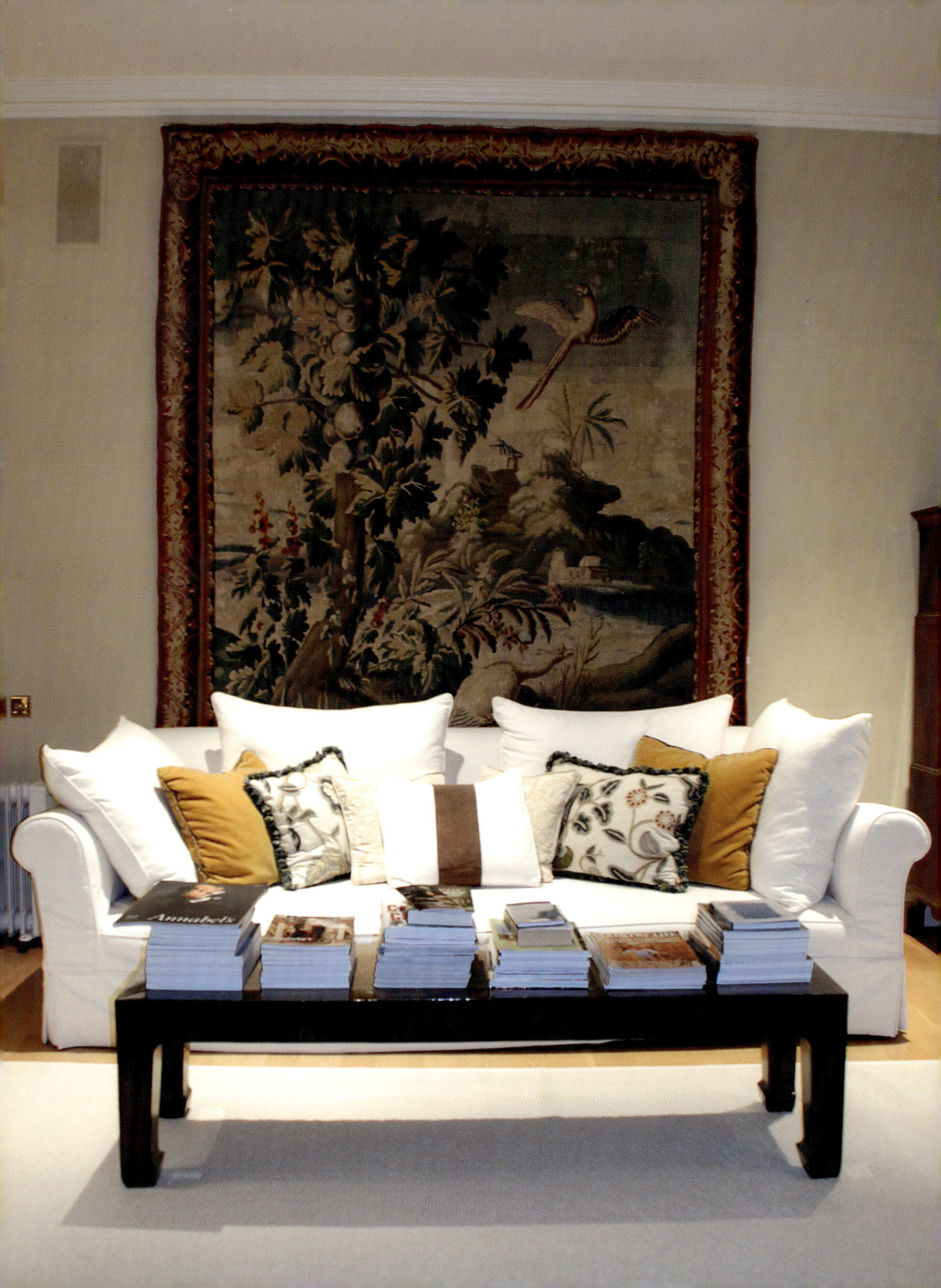
Annabels

what is to be done, I am reminded of Adam Nicolson's story of Arcadia, that vision of an idealised house and landscape fashioned as a retreat from the world.

Up the hill behind the house, through old gates patrolled by hens, lie the eight sloping acres which were once the walled garden. Porteous decodes its sandstone, its brickwork, its outcrops of decayed structures from boiler house to bothy, its flued walls, service sheds and what's left of the melon pit, fuelled by tanners' bark, a by-product of the leather industry. Tenanted now only by the hives from which Pat Deasy produces his Deise honey, this incline is the planned location for a Palladian pavilion and orangery designed by Robert Adam Architects. Closer to the house a greenhouse in the kitchen garden warms the apricots and nectarines and a hen pheasant nests among the sprouting broccoli. From the stable yard, which is now the business hub of the enterprise, the changes made by his immediate predecessors, Serge and Henriette Boissevain, have been adapted by Henry Gwyn Jones.

Ballynatray House sits on a ledge above a wide curve of the Blackwater as the river winds towards the sea at Youghal. When Grice Smyth built this house in 1795, probably with Cork architect Alexander Deane, the site had been fortified for centuries as a defence against incursions from the sea. It was from this front door that his daughter Penelope eloped in 1836 with Charles Frederick Borbone, prince of Capua, a Gretna Green marriage which scandalised Europe. Between the lawns and the tide the seventh-century abbey of Molana, now a picturesque ruin, was founded by St Molanfhaide of Lismore. It passed from Sir Walter Raleigh to Richard Boyle, 1st Earl of Cork, through whom the connection to Elizabeth Boyle, wife of Edmund Spenser, is made. One of its most famous residents was Thomas Harriott, friend of the geographer Richard Hakluyt. It was as Raleigh's scientific adviser that Harriott journeyed to America and later wrote his *Briefe and True Report of the New Found Land of Virginia*. But there were earlier writers at Molana. Rubin (or Reuben) Mac Connadh, known as the Scribe of Munster', died in 725, but was famous in his time as one of the compilers of the influential eighth-century treatise *Collectio canonum*

ABOVE: *The garden front overlooks the Blackwater, seducing both proprietors and visitors through the centuries.* OPPOSITE: *In the sitting-room at Ballynatray.* (images courtesy of Richard Salaman)

Hibernensis, a guide to church laws and disciplines which was respected all over Europe. Cloaked in ivy, with the purple stars of vinca nestled in the windowed crevices, the abbey's choir, cloister court, nave, chancel and pulpit recess are reached by the causeway built by Grice Smyth in 1806. A memorial put up by the Smyths in the early nineteenth century announces the tomb of Raymond le Gros, Stongbow's henchman who died while the invading Normans were making their way upriver into Munster.

After six years Henry Gwyn Jones isn't sure that, if he had known what he was taking on at Ballynatray, he would have stayed with the project, but thinks that to begin such an adventure one has to have some naïvete along with a sense of purpose. He believes also that the enjoyment of 'a jewel like this' should be shared, and as to the Arcadian vision he acknowledges that his approach to Ballynatray is 'a bit romantic, but you have to live your dreams when you can'.

Neil Porteous is now the National Trust's Head Gardener at Mount Stewart, County Down.
There are driven shoots on the Ballynatray estate in winter.

Ballynatray House,
Youghal, County Cork
Tel: 024 97460
www.ballynatray.com

BALLYNATRAY HOUSE

Ballyteigue House

Bruree, County Limerick

There are no sweeter words known to the wayworn traveller on arrival than that there's no need to dress for dinner – except the next question which falls from Margaret Johnson's lips: 'What would you like to drink?' If I were not already so pleased to be at Ballyteigue House, Margaret's welcoming enquiries would have repaid all the trials of a rain-sodden journey on a bleak Friday afternoon, with weekend traffic building inexorably into tail-backs and the process of passing each pantechnicon feeling like nothing so much as driving under the sea. This turn off the main road from Cork to Limerick leads immediately away from speed and noise and frenzy; all of a sudden there is a view, the lowering clouds clearing to let the sun varnish the distant Ballyhouras.

In the drawing-room there is a fire blazing in one of the house's several imposing fireplaces; the modern windows have been double glazed and shut out everything except the view. The walls are laden with dashing hunting prints, with portraits of horses and hounds, with photographs of meets and point-to-points, with men and women on horses, holding horses and about, from the look of things, about to fall off horses. On the landing outside my bedroom a mature fox is stilled in his docile stance, as immobilised as Lot's wife. This is hunting territory and, although neither Margaret nor her husband Richard follow the hounds, they met at the riding school centred here at Ballyteigue.

Widowed when her first husband, Thomas Wrixon, died six years after their marriage, Margaret had two children when she married widower Richard Johnson, a veterinary surgeon who had seven. This combined immediate family of nine formed an amiable group of step-siblings, and it was only when they all began to move on that Margaret and Richard decided to reopen the house to visitors, as Margaret had done during her widowhood. 'We got very good breaks,' says Margaret. 'We got very good publicity and people's reactions were reassuring, making us more positive in our approach. We also find that, because the major tourism areas such as Killarney and west Cork are so crowded, people love to find a quiet place like this from which all those places are accessible.'

Richard remembers when country houses like Ballyteigue were the poor relations of the tourism industry; that has changed now, largely because small towns and villages have taken affairs into their own energetic hands, prompted by rural development schemes and Leader programmes. From this house, good river fishing is only a couple of miles away; there are the measured walks in the Ballyhoura hills, a wealth of archaeological discovery, the attractive village of Bruree at the other side of the main road with Adare, Limerick itself, Kilmallock and Croom among the many interesting places within easy reach. There is golf. And there is hunting or more sedate riding expeditions.

Ballyteigue House is one of those typical countryside properties, Georgian in character and simple in design. Complete with their old fireplaces and sunny with generous windows, these are plain rooms which take on style and comfort from the owners: the result is cosy, familiar and welcoming. Richard explains that the house was originally a hunting lodge for the Conyers family, its last resident of that name being Dorothy Conyers, a novelist – and

Top and Above Right: *The entrance hall at Ballyteigue House.*
Above left: *A typical country house property, Georgian in character and simple in design.*

BALLYTEIGUE HOUSE 49

ABOVE: *The restored coachyard and (right) a living-room in one of the self-catering apartments.* (images courtesy of Shamrock Cottages)

actress – who wrote popular fiction with (amazingly!) a hunting background and whose exploits entertained the neighbourhood. The family name is maintained in Castletown Conyers at Ballyagran, County Limerick, and Rockhill itself is an historic townland named after Captain Rock of Whiteboys fame. Its prominent church and parochial house were once the home of the Land League priest Fr Sheehy, an acknowledged influence on Eamon de Valera, who served him as an altar boy during much of his childhood and schooldays here.

Ballyteigue is a reminder of the need to take that turn off the motorway, to take what Robert Frost called the road 'less travelled by'. I think of this as I eventually retire to my room, clutching the book recommended by Richard Johnson: *The Ryan Family and the Scarteen Hounds*. This fabled hunting family and their unique two-tone hounds accompany me into bed, where I gratefully remember the third most welcome phrase in the Irish guesthouse lexicon: 'Your electric blanket has been switched on.'

Ballyteigue House,
Bruree, County Limerick
Tel: 063 90575

50   AT HOME IN IRELAND

Ballyvolane House

Castlelyons, County Cork

The Greens of Ballyvolane House are discussing their plans for the future and for a wild moment I think of the Mad Hatter's tea party: 'Let's all move up one place!' The imagery from *Alice in Wonderland* is not so inappropriate, for there has always been an element of fantasy at this house deep in the countryside of east Cork. Merrie and Jeremy Green are the most rooted and realistic of people, yet somehow together they have created a magical atmosphere. It has something to do with attainable luxury, a promise they have kept with stunning style through the years since they first

BELOW: *Woodland and pasture surround Ballyvolane House.* (images courtesy of the Green family and The Hidden Ireland)

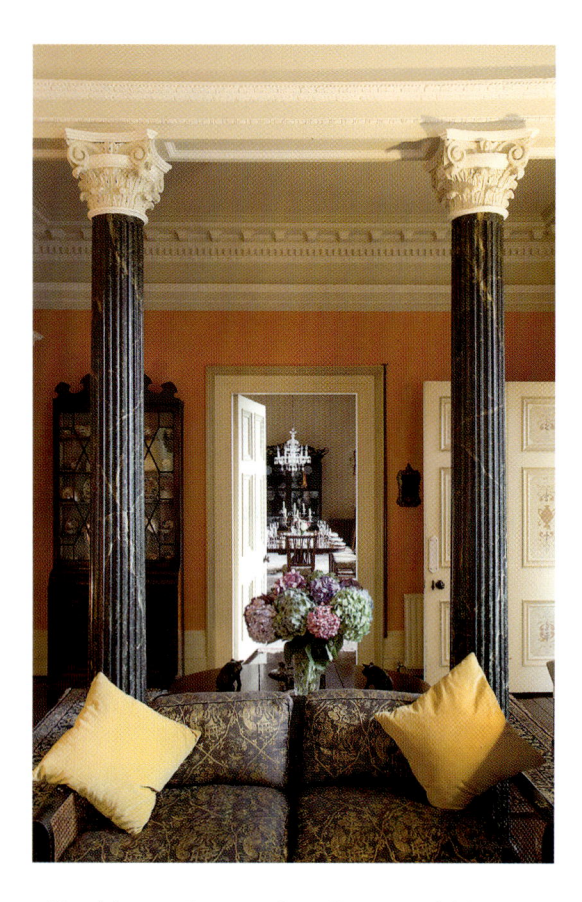

offered hospitality to a friend's party of fishermen.

As Justin Green and his wife Jenny move in, there are four generations of Greens living at Ballyvolane, while Merrie's own parents live in the refurbished coachman's house further along the farm avenue, where Merrie and Jeremy lived when they first married. This marvellous roundabout began with farming, and remembering his family's arrival at Ballyvolane in 1953, after his father's career as the proprietor of rubber plantations in Malaya, Jeremy says that he thinks the estate was bought for him. He was dispatched to agricultural college within a year and he quickly settled into the kind of mixed farming he believes should never have been abandoned in Ireland.

'Irish farmers were advised to become more specific and we had to specialise, so I chose dairy farming; in fact I still run a few cattle on the fields here.' Special or not, it wasn't enough, so Jeremy, who had married Merrie Benson in 1965 and had taken over the big house at Ballyvolane after his father's death in 1971, agreed to spend a little more time and trouble on the idea of farmhouse hospitality. It's true: elegant Ballyvolane is not the kind of house one thinks of as a farmhouse, yet that, essentially, was what it was. Its front door opens out on a landscape of hilly pastures, with small trout lakes in the hollows. The lowing of cattle can be heard from the kitchen garden and, even if Jeremy has eased up on daily farming activities, he still manages the small but labour-intensive group of amiable donkeys who wander up to the railings.

ABOVE LEFT: *The pillared hall at Ballyvolane House and (right) Jeremy Green in the kitchen garden.* OPPOSITE: *A bathroom with a view.*

'We weren't serious at all when we began,' recalls Jeremy. 'I used to spend a lot of the winter shooting, which I love, and Merrie's passion was fishing – she actually became the ghillie for Peter Dempster on his Blackwater salmon fishery.' Yet, as they got more

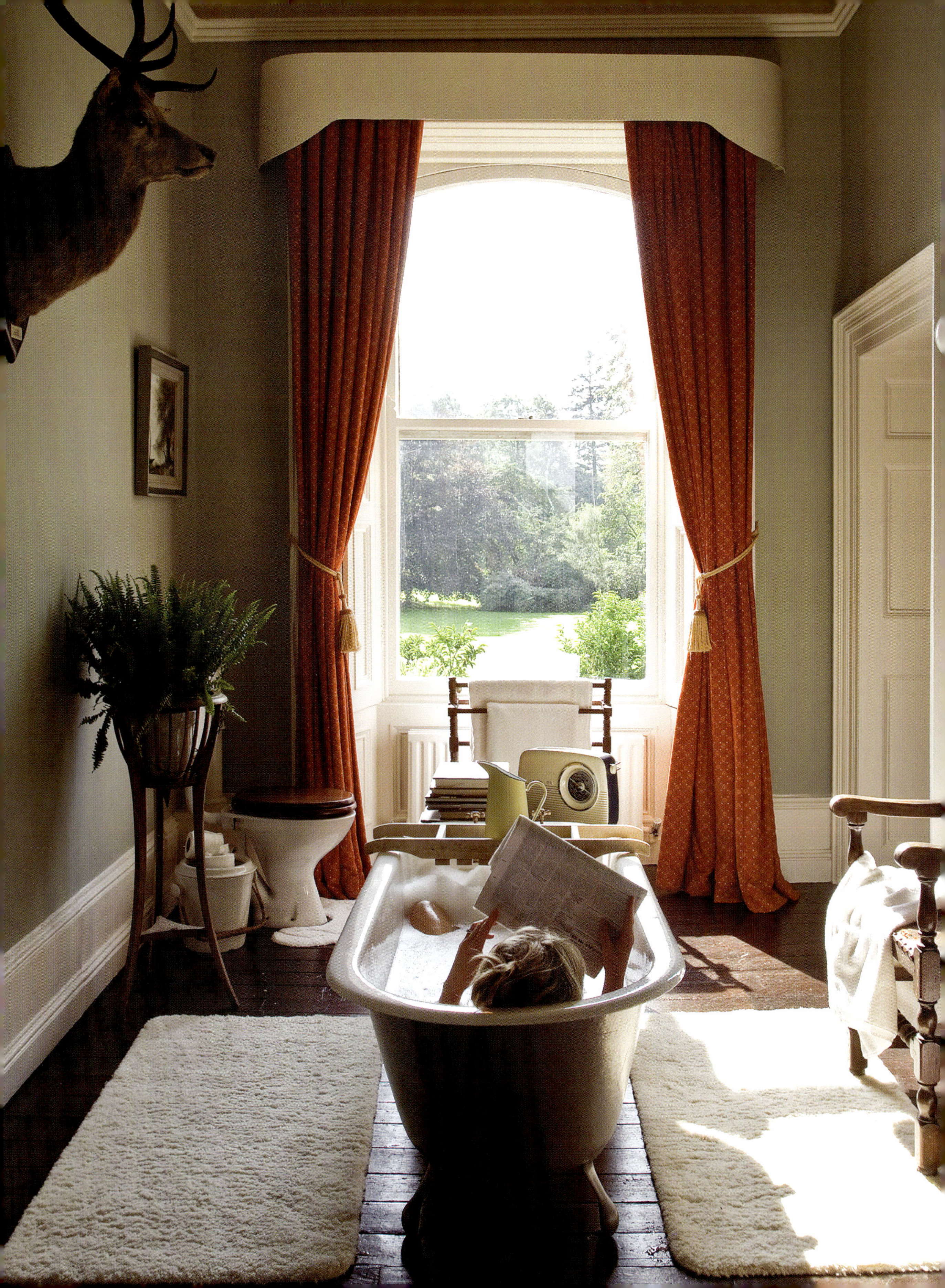

RIGHT: *Justin Green at the front door of the house.*

committed to the tradition of Irish hospitality, they became founder members of The Hidden Ireland, the marketing organisation which has ensured the future of so many of Ireland's fine country houses. Jeremy explains that John Coakley was the catalyst, along with Johnnie Madden of Hilton Park, Nick Wilkinson of Nenagh and six or seven others.

The Hidden Ireland imposes standards of accommodation and amenities. These are all heritage houses too, with a story to tell, a character which can be found nowhere else, and a family in residence to give a living, breathing sense of activity and welcome. Italianate Ballyvolane, improved in the nineteenth century from the original of 1728, is now regarded as the epitome of The Hidden Ireland at its best, so it is fitting that Jeremy has been awarded the title of first honorary president of the organisation.

Like many others who know and love this house and its keepers, I am a little dismayed that Merrie and Jeremy are taking their hands from the reins and passing the house to a new generation. Yet this must happen if properties such as Ballyvolane are to have that future which their membership of The Hidden Ireland organisation seemed to promise. This responsibility has been accepted by Justin and Jenny, back in Cork after their years abroad, most recently with Babington House in Somerset.

These junior Greens understand pampering. They have worked in the most sophisticated ambience with a celebrity clientele and feel that management of Ballyvolane House is not so much a change of direction as a change of emphasis, with client wellbeing still the central objective. In a cosmopolitan hotel, this might be achieved through a leisure centre, gym, swimming-pool and all the amenities of a particular kind of luxury. In a country house it comes in a different wrapping – quiet, space, timelessness, traditional country pursuits, books and conversation, superb food and, as the day ends and the curtains close against the terraced lawns, a lamp-lit drink by a fire of logs. ♣

Justin and Jenny Green have introduced a unique wedding service to Ballyvolane House, where Jeremy continues in charge of the gardens and livestock. Justin Green is now marketing manager for The Hidden Ireland organisation. Merrie Green died in 2004.

Ballyvolane House and Blackwater Salmon Fishery,
Castlelyons, County Cork
Tel: 025 36349
E-mail: ballyvol@iol.ie

Bantry House

Bantry, County Cork

Climbing the one hundred steps behind Bantry House shows, from the top, how the house itself is set into a natural shelf in a vast cliff. The steps cleave through a series of small terraces, with shrubbery rampant on either side; they culminate in a screen of trees. But to look down is to see the widest of these terraces holding the house, its central block flanked by set-back wings. At ground level, box-edged parterres frame the pergola, cloaked with voluminous wisteria which, in the rainy dusk of this evening, hangs in fragrant grape-blue clusters, scattering little raindrops on the gravel as if to keep time with the fountain it encircles. On the opposite shore the Caha Mountains surge into sunset promontories which sheltered the remains of the scattered French armada of 1797 while the local defences were rallied by Richard White of Blackrock, now known as Bantry House.

It is from that momentous Christmas of 1797 that the mansion's years of grandeur began. While personally discomfited by the troops he had invited to defend Bantry, who were promptly and properly billeted at his own house, Richard White was rewarded with an earldom. His eldest son, Richard Viscount Berehaven, travelled extensively, became a sophisticated collector and finally supervised the extension and modernisation of the house and grounds to reflect the influences of the famous gardens of Italy and France. The years have blurred some of the effects he achieved, but the grand design has remained intact. The two stable blocks with their arches and cupolas (one now a museum devoted to the French armada) still stand on either side of the great stairway to the sky. The small sculptures by Alexander Sokolov which now decorate the garden balustrade are another reminder that the generations who live in this house affect it in different ways.

Opened to the public in 1946 by Clodagh Shelswell-White, mother of the present owner Egerton, a guest wing has been created for overnight visitors. The comfortable bedrooms and bathrooms are reached through a private entrance; the view from my deep-silled and cushioned window opens on the pergola, the perfume from the blossoms like a glow in the room. The guest wing, however, is not the house, and the house is an experience in itself, rich with the furniture, the hangings, the mirrors and paintings which have been added to by descendants of equal discrimination. The coloured mosaic floor panels – *Cave Canem* – in the main hall came from Pompeii in 1828. The Aubusson tapestries in the Rose room have insets designed by Boucher (whose favourite model was La Grande Morphée, the exile from Ireland and mistress, for a time, of Louis XV of France) which were reputedly made for the wedding of Marie Antoinette and Louis XVI. There are the Savonnerie carpet, or the firedogs from the Petit

AT HOME IN IRELAND

OPPOSITE TOP: *Seen from the 120-step stairway, Bantry House stands above the bay, with the Caha Mountains in the distance.* BELOW: *A corner of the parterre.* ABOVE: *The library remains a central venue for concerts, especially during the West Cork Chamber Music festival.* (images courtesy of Sophie Shelswell-White)

Trianon at Versailles, or the Gobelin tapestry in the aptly named Gobelin room, the windows flanked by floor-to-ceiling mirrors.

In the library with its rosewood shelving the Blüthner grand piano is tuned to concert pitch. The continental theme is not exclusive: there is a fireplace from Bandon, a mantelpiece from Kinsale, chairs made beautifully and locally of local wood. There is wainscoting of Spanish leather, a chandelier decorated with Meissen flowers, the formal dining-room has sideboards which curve in ornate sections the length of the walls, and picture-frames so gilded as to properly belong in a cathedral. At every turn there is evidence of a defining vision for the house, even in the way in which the upstairs landings relate their curves to the Gothic arches of the ceilings.

Brigitte Shelswell-White's part in the domestic industry of this house is many-sided and includes the care of four children, three cats, two dogs and the garden, where the original design is to be reinstated as part of the Great Gardens of Ireland Restoration programme. She looks forward to this new demand as part of the family commitment to handing on the house in good working order to the next generation. That commitment is one of the reasons why the Shelswell-Whites have given University College Cork the Bantry House Archive, an immense collection of documents, letters and diaries, a history of a family, a house, a town, a country. 'You can't be greedy,' Brigitte says. 'The house is part of a continuum. When you step back from it, as you must, you see that it goes on; the archive is a record of its survival.'

Bantry House is now managed by Sophie Shelswell-White, who has refurbished the guest accommodation; the Garden Restoration programme was successfully completed and the house continues as a central venue for the annual West Cork Chamber Music Festival.

Bantry House,
Bantry, County Cork
Tel: 027 50047

Barberstown Castle

Straffan, County Kildare

The thing about Barberstown Castle is that it's not so much which room you want as which century. If your choice is an ancient Gaelic aura in which to pick up your knife (or dagger) and fork, that can be arranged. An Elizabethan atmosphere in which to lay your head? No trouble. Victorian or Edwardian? Yes, that's on offer too. And modern with a look of heritage to soften the contemporary comforts? Here it is, just through one of the several doors that lead the visitor through a house which spans aeons of Irish life while remaining sophisticated, efficient and welcoming.

Admittedly, its location in one of Ireland's most interesting, and possibly most affluent, villages is a help when it comes to establishing Barberstown as a quality hotel. Straffan is at the hub of the horse-breeding and training industry; most traffic jams through the village are caused by convoys of boxes and horse lorries, but at least the tail-backs give a chance to enjoy the vicinity, including a church with a lych gate. The delightful space called The Tea Room at Barberstown is murmuring with people dawdling over their afternoon tea, lulled by the open fire, the quality of the food, from light lunches to sandwiches, and by the combined aroma of burning logs and fresh flowers.

Being shown around by such an enthusiastic guide as proprietor Ken Healy means that I lose the run of the place entirely, so that eventually the different corridors, floor-levels and apparently unending roof trusses extending from the great stone keep into a banqueting hall all merge into a fascinating scoot through the centuries. Conference clients have the meeting-rooms and every IT connection in the new wing.

Anthony Reddy Associates are the architects for the tearoom area, which introduces the main hotel entrance, but diners go in a little further down the garden front. There the door opens into another hall, the main staircase mounting between gilt-framed portraits and paintings, heavily draped windows and splendid overmantels, plush-covered sofas and armchairs and, in the dining-room, layers of white linen, glass and glistening cutlery. Ken Healy is working in a hospitality environment which has changed completely in the last ten years – 'it's a different world,' he says of the way in which patterns in dining out have been altered by drink–driving regulations or differences in rural living. Adaptability is all and, with a background in the family business at the Black Lion Inn, Healy is prepared to invest both money and creativity in his commitment to Barberstown.

This is particularly obvious in the way in which the stables and courtyard have been transformed, architects John Duffy Associates achieving a sense of authenticity with oak roof beams, carvings and

Pick your century at Barberstown Castle. (images courtesy of Ireland's Blue Book)

reproduction tapestries highlighting a matching sense of occasion. Originally a FitzGerald property (a phrase which seems to re-echo through Irish architectural history), Barberstown was built as a castle by Nicholas Barby towards the end of the thirteenth century. It has to be said that the livestock – from moose, elk, deer, buffalo, wildebeest and ram, not to mention a sad little Irish hare – which decorate the inner walls of the keep suggest that Nicholas Barby had a blood-lust that transcended geography. The battered walls include two towers and several crenulated musket loops; one of the towers was used as a kind of mausoleum in order to evade the terms of a lease which would run out at the time of the tenant's burial. This usage did not deter later generations, so that the central section of the long building was further developed between 1550 and 1600.

Literary-minded visitors will enjoy the fact that Bartholomew Van Homreigh owned the property for a while. His daughter Esther was the ardent 'Vanessa', admired by Dean Swift, although a ferocious row shortly before her death caused her to leave her considerable estate to the philosopher George Berkeley, who used it to fund his mission to America. Another proprietor was Hugh Barton, who built the Georgian/Victorian section at Barberstown before building Straffan House, while the list of later owners culminated in Eric Clapton, who sold it to Kenneth Healy in the late 1980s.

Ken Healy has found a way of suiting his rooms to their centuries. Despite the suggestion of segmentation, the whole house has an appealing unity and sits in its lawns, its stands of trees and its hedges of roses as secure and hospitable now as it has ever been. ♣

Barberstown Castle,
Straffan, County Kildare
Tel: 01 6288157
info@barberstowncastle.ie
www.barberstowncastle.ie

BARBERSTOWN CASTLE

Barnabrow Country House

Cloyne, County Cork

At Barnabrow Country House the beds are not just made. They are constructed. My own is like a galleon in full sail, its muslin curtains sweeping from the ceiling, its pillows and cushions billowing behind my head. Just as the beds are big business in Barnabrow, so is the whole enterprise which has transformed this attractive old farmhouse near Cloyne. Transformation is the right word; another is imaginative, if that word could be given weight and substance to include the essence of determination, skill and vision which all come together here on this little hilly farm above the gleaming plain that stretches to the sea between Garryvoe and Ballycotton.

This old house was built from about 1639 as a central, three-storey block with flanking single-storey wings. It was the home of Timothy Lane in 1814, later of J.R. Wilkinson and more recently of Leuitenant-Commander Whitehouse, and its history is summed up in its modest exterior and homely function. The rear of the house is of plain stone, matching the fabric of the former coach houses, stables and labourers' cottages.

When I first met proprietor Geraldine Kidd she was awaiting the arrival from Liscarrol Donkey Sanctuary of Rosie and Sadie. This pair now drowse in the shade of the fine oak in their paddock; elsewhere in the 30-acre holding more trees are being planted, lime and beeches with hedge species of thorn, rose and woodbine. Environmental friendliness is carried in Geraldine's genes and traces of it appear throughout the house and promote the organic sources of the food served in the restaurant behind it.

A guest television room with books, sofas; a fine fireplace with flaming logs enlivening the marble opens from the inner hall and leads into another sitting-room. The floors are of teak and throughout the house the sash windows move smoothly up and down. Some of the bedrooms in the house have papered walls, and there is a cottage-type room of particular charm, the small windows and raftered ceiling reducing the light yet creating an atmosphere of rustic comfort; others have a finish of painted rough plaster. Some of the colours are deep, some soft; in some rooms the walls are plain white, all enhanced by the addition of cushions, by a rich-hued throw, an embroidered bedspread, by lamps and rugs and pictures.

'Every single thing I ever had, or hoarded, or that my father hoarded, is used here,' says Geraldine, who also mentions O'Regan's Antiques on Lavitt's Quay. When I can finally be prised off some bed or other, she adds that those marvellous thick white bedspreads used for every bedroom with all the linen and the densely piled towels come from Forgotten Cottons in

OPPOSITE: *Barnabrow: a bathroom in the main house.*

BARNABROW COUNTRY HOUSE

ABOVE: *The blue bedroom in one of the restored out-offices at Barnabrow.* (images courtesy of Geraldine Kidd)

the Savoy Arcade. When I remark on the impeccable housekeeping Geraldine gives all the credit to Anne Cusack, a perfectionist caring for everything from floors to flowers. It is this mixture of the exotic and the local, the strange and the familiar, which makes the house so diverting. But that's not enough for comfort, I muse, as I lie back at last against my Himalya of pillows under a canopy of spangled muslin. Wildflowers and rhododendrons decorate an elegant table. There are no curtains but plain shades close off the deep-set windows. Before I sleep I lift these again for the sake of the morning light and that long vista of fields: plough, meadow, grain, grass, hedgerows deep as laneways and beyond them all the silver glisten of the sea.

Having enjoyed dinner here so much, the choices at breakfast have to be restrained. But after really fresh orange juice, a sprinkling of muesli over raspberries and blackcurrants (or apricots and apples and prunes) with yogurt, I agree to a taste of O'Flynn's spicy sausage and potato cake. Plus coffee. And then the house breads and fresh butter and homemade marmalade. Oh dear …

'There was no major master plan when we came,' says Geraldine. 'It just evolved. The problems with the house were the usual ones: roof, dry rot, rising damp, rotten joists and a tree growing up through the hall. Local workmen did all the work, including the lining and panelling of the doors and windows. So, although there wasn't any overall scheme, it has remained coherent.' Barnabrow House, for all its individuality, is coherent and consistent as a country house of intrinsic character which has taken on a new colour and excitement without losing any of its integrity.

Barnabrow Country House,
Cloyne, County Cork
Tel: 021 4652534

Beaufort House

Killarney, County Kerry

After the merciless shearing of greenery, with hedgerows and trees butchered at the behest of Kerry County Council, it is a relief to find that the bridge over the river Laune leads to a long bowered avenue, the grassy verges starred with primroses. The trees stand in shoals of bluebells, the fields themselves are studded with sheep and the avenue winds at one side by the meadows, at the other by the stream (terrific trout, I'm told) which curls off from the river, with the river itself a foaming brown flood just a few yards away.

BELOW: *The simple formality of the sitting-room at Beaufort House.*

ABOVE: *Surrounded by woods, the house occupies the former site of a short castle and later of a hunting lodge.* OPPOSITE: *The sitting-room of one of the self-catering courtyard cottages at Beaufort House.* (images courtesy of the Cameron family)

Here, with Mangerton and the Reeks and the Derrynasaggart Mountains all rearing above the valley in which Beaufort House is set, a small industry has been created. The family spare room is piled with fabrics in the shape of curtains, bedspreads, table-linen, cushions, all Rachel Cameron's handiwork, a way, she says with some wonderment, of passing the winter. These raw materials are the stuff of a new venture at the house, the Courtyard Cottages converted from the fine stone outbuildings which form a cobbled square at the back of the house.

They don't hang about, Rachel and Donald Cameron. 'All we've done is try to put back what was there originally as sympathetically as possible and within our means,' explains Rachel, recalling that when she and Donald decided to leave their lives in London the old house was beginning to get fragile and a family decision had to be made about its future. Just as I get sympathetic about their choice to retire, in Rachel's case from a career as a clock restorer with the Phillips Auction House and Donald's later transfer from dealing in architectural antiques, Rachel says that she was going to stop work anyway as they didn't want to bring up their children in London.

Not only that: although people said they were mad to be taking on a financial commitment which would last for the rest of their lives, they both felt the undertaking to be more of an opportunity than a risk. 'This is such a glorious place – you'd make any sacrifice for it!'

The house is undoubtedly glorious in an intimate, scaled-down style. The layout has the simple formality of the best Georgian domestic architecture and Rachel's décor allows the space and the light to show up the elegance both of the furniture and of the proportions of the building itself. 'We're not going to look fake. We want to achieve the atmosphere by peeling away the Victorian clutter, but we're also trying to ensure that the house looks what it is, a family home in a certain tradition.'

Donald grew up at Beaufort House, which his parents had purchased in the mid-1960s when Donald's father, Norman Cameron, decided to retire from his sheep farm in the Falkland Islands. The first building on the site was what is known as a short castle, low-storeyed but built on high ground. By 1654 this had been demolished by Cromwellian forces; the method was that only one wall would be knocked down, making the castle indefensible without wasting any more ammunition on it. A century later the Mullens family of Ventry built a hunting-lodge around the ruins – the Camerons think the thick-walled hall is the central castle area – and when eventually promoted to De Molyns they occupied it in the person of Frederick William De Molyns, MP for Kerry, a friend of The Liberator Daniel O'Connell until they quarrelled in 1837. In the meantime the house had undergone several transformations, the most significant being its nineteenth-century reduction from three storeys to two, the building out of the bays under the projecting eaves and the planting of many, many trees.

But now we sit in the library, the log fire putting the dogs into a snoring trance, the fir-green library lamps matching the dark walls, books thronging the shelving with its columned trim of limed oak. 'We're very committed to this now,' says Donald. ' We want it to work and now we find that many of the people who come here hardly leave it at all. It's casual and relaxed and that's the way we want it to be.' Rachel adds, 'We're here because we want to be. You only have an opportunity to do something like this once in a lifetime, so you have to embrace it heartily. It's all or nothing.'

The Camerons now provide self-catering accommodation at Beaufort House cottages.

Beaufort House
near Killarney County Kerry
Tel: 064 6644764

BEAUFORT HOUSE

Belvedere House

Mullingar, County Westmeath

Brigid Geoghan of Belvedere explains: 'This was not a practical family house.' That's just as well, for its notorious owner was not a practical family man, and the surprise here is that so pleasing a property should also have been the preferred home of so vengeful a husband as Robert Rochfort, 1st Earl of Belvedere.

Belvedere House, gardens and park are in the careful management of Westmeath County Council. Bordering the shores of Lough Ennel, near Mullingar, the estate now covers 160 acres; immediately, as one steps from the visitor centre into the park, it is as if one were stepping into not just another landscape but another world, for Belvedere was created as a retreat and the illusion of isolation combined with splendour is profound. It was built close to 1740 for Robert Rochfort of Gaulston and is accepted as the work of Richard Castle or Cassels, author of Russborough and other Irish mansions. Gaulston, about six miles away, was the family seat and it was there that Robert took his second wife, the sixteen-year-old Mary Molesworth, when they married in 1736. As Belvedere progressed it became more villa than sporting box; its restoration by architect David Slattery has emphasised attributes obliterated in the past century, especially by replacing the original Diocletian windows at either end of the second storey, which had been removed during the nineteenth century.

The Victorian Italianate terracing on the garden front with its arched balustrades and adjacent rockery serves now as an attractive graduation towards the lawned shore. While the overall estate was laid out by a professional landscape designer in the 1740s, the marvellous garden dates from the 1850s and was the work of one of Belvedere's later owners, Charles Brinsley Marley. As an example of the ornamental demesne, Belvedere includes a mock-Gothic arch of 1760 and an octagonal gazebo of the same date. The English antiquarian Thomas Wright was responsible for these and perhaps also for the Jealous Wall. This three-storey, 180-feet-long façade is a sham ruin which had a real purpose, that of blocking the view of another house, Tudenham, possibly also by Cassels and, although now a ruin itself, built for Rochfort's brother George.

Jealous is a gentle word when used to describe the pathological revenges of Rochfort, Lord Belvedere. Something alerted him to the possibility of a liaison between his young wife Mary and another brother, Arthur. From hint to fact was a quick step: he accused Arthur of adultery, then known as criminal conversation, and over several years pressed the charges with such energy that Arthur was convicted, fined £20,000 and died in a debtors' prison. Mary was confined to Gaulston, with servants her only company and her presence signalled by the bell she was forced to carry. After twelve years, during which

ABOVE: *Wintry Belvedere House suggests the bleak tragedy of Lady Mary Molesworth, wife of its notorious owner Robert Rochford, Earl of Belvedere.* BELOW: *One of the restored windows at Belvedere overlooks Lough Ennel.* (images courtesy of Westmeath County Council)

at times she was allowed at least to see her children, she escaped to the house of her father, Viscount Molesworth, where she made a terrible mistake. Thinking she would be divorced by her husband and thus become free of him, and even though later on her deathbed she declared her innocence, she admitted adultery. As a result her father sent her back to her husband and for the next eighteen years of her life she was completely imprisoned at Gaulston, deprived of all contact and left to rot in such poverty that her only clothes were those she possessed when her misery began. It ended at her husband's death in 1774, when she was released by her son George, the second Earl.

When George died the estate passed to his sister Jane, Lady Lanesborough, and through her to Charles Brinsley Marley and then to the mountaineer Colonel Charles K. Howard-Bury. He died in 1963 and left Belvedere to his companion Rex Beaumont, who sold the property to the county council six years before his own death in 1988. In a way, those last decades of the house as a home come almost full circle, for Howard-Bury and Beaumont enjoyed it both as a retreat and as a centre of entertainment. That was how the first Lord Belvedere used it while his wife was a captive at Gaulston.

Almost humorous in their detail and ebullience, Belvedere's ground-floor ceilings by Bartholomew Cramillion are reputedly among the finest rococo examples in Europe. Seeing these through Brigid Geoghan's eyes is to see them intimately. As education officer, her knowledge of local history is enriched with a personal affection for the house which banishes the tragedy of that lady whose name is forever associated with it, although she never lived here. ♣

With its grounds now including a Narnia trail, Belvedere has a busy schedule of public events.

Belvedere House,
Mullingar, County Westmeath
Tel: 044 9349060
www.belvedere-house.ie

BELVEDERE HOUSE   67

Blackwater Castle

Castletownroche, County Cork

Blackwater Castle has such a cosmopolitan air to it these days that it is difficult to remember that once it was the scene of sieges, attacks, romantic assignations (they probably still go on) and brutal miscarriages of what was the brutal justice of the times. But now, at least three names and many centuries later, it shines with wellbeing above the wooded ravine cut by the sweep of the Awbeg, a tributary of the river Blackwater. Having survived the reprisals following the Desmond rebellion, the castle was later besieged on Cromwell's behalf by Lord Broghill, son of the 1st Earl of Cork. It was defended by Lady Roche in the absence of her Royalist husband Maurice. This was Ellen Power of Curraghmore in County Waterford, and she paid for her defence with her life.

After the Restoration the castle went to a Colonel John Widenham, and Castle Widenham was rebuilt during the early eighteenth century from the ruins left after the siege. The great keep was still standing, however, just as it is today. Although Blackwater Castle has passed through several other hands in the meantime, its welcoming atmosphere is largely due to the efforts not just of a family but of a family trust, represented in Castletownroche by Patrick Nordstrom, well known among the fraternity for his book *Motor Cycle Tours in the South of Ireland,* written with Bartho Buckley.

It was Patrick's parents Ninna and the late Dr Rabbe Nordstrom of Finland who fell in love with the castle while visiting Ireland. When they bought it the plan was to use it as a residential headquarters for Dr Nordstroem's medical research company with a cultural programme supported by a trust fund. His untimely death meant a major readjustment for everyone; Patrick came to settle in north Cork and the fund was redirected to the restoration of the castle and its future use for cultural and recreational enterprises. As a multi-instrument musician Patrick, by then also a successful businessman, must have found this something of a challenge. Now, he says, 'I'm just happy if I do something substantial. In our family life we've been the kind of people who when offered a choice between an easy, secure life or a challenge, we have always gone for the challenge.'

The main entrance to the castle faces on to a sweep from which the yards and gardens expand as far as the woods which shadow the long avenue. Here Patrick has planted more than 500 German oaks in a process of renewal which includes the reclaimed coachyard, where the well-kept farm buildings open onto little patios with individual terraces of shrubs and flowers, the divisions marked by decorative willow fencing.

Much of the harvest from the walled garden is brought to the local farmers' market, but some is taken for the castle itself where a large modern catering kitchen can be used for functions such as receptions, banquets and weddings (already a successful enterprise).

ABOVE: *Originally Castle Widenham after a former owner, Blackwater Castle is dominated by its great tower-house.* BELOW: *A sitting-room in the early nineteenth-century building.* (images courtesy of Patrick Nordstroem)

When the house was castellated in the 1800s the internal enhancement was carried out with a light hand, so that it retains many features such as the lovely spiral staircase at one end of the hall, a quirky counterbalance to the more formal stairs at the other. A more personalised character distinguishes each of the bedroom and bathroom suites, reached from corridors where the décor includes paintings by family and friends. Alive to contemporary art, the Nordstroms persuade modern shapes, colours and textures to marry happily with the old prints and paintings of a past dominated by Scandinavian shipping lines.

While the restoration of the tower house itself is a major commitment, Patrick is also evaluating the remains of a twelfth-century round tower and chapel on the precipitous terrace. 'This is a place with good vibrations,' says Patrick, surveying the work of local wood-turner Mick Gibbons and of his father, the stonemason Mick senior, who has carried out all the courtyard and tower restorations in tune with architect Frank Scherer.

'A trust is not a game, or something to be played around with for tax purposes. It means a lot to us that we make a contribution to the next generation. And taking over the responsibility for a place that has been standing for 800 years isn't an easy decision. It is our concern that we live up to that responsibility.'

Blackwater Castle now includes an Outdoor Activity Centre in the grounds, with a campsite for attending groups.

Blackwater Castle,
Castletownroche, County Cork
Tel: 022 26333
www.blackwatercastle.com

Blanchville House

Dunbell, Maddoxtown, County Kilkenny

At one point in our conversation Monica Phelan describes Blanchville House as 'double-barrelled'. The modern avenue curves up to a more imposing front door than a farmhouse usually wears, yet this is undeniably a farm, with winter wheat flourishing outside one window and Charolais cattle basking outside another.

There is a sense of easy fusion, so that those enjoying Monica Phelan's version of a bed-and-breakfast service can also taste the real life of the country. It is beautiful country, the roads suddenly, surprisingly running along a riverside with a railway line bringing what traffic might be passing to a dozy halt under arches of greenery. This is high summer, the cornfields almost rust-coloured in their readiness for harvest and the heat slowing everything to a gentle untroubled pace.

One can relish country pastimes at Blanchville but this is also a place for just simply switching off, especially as afternoon tea arrives, with crustless sandwiches and a raspberry roulade oozing fruit and cream; a china teapot, napkins and all the appurtenances of gracious living in a book-crowded sitting-room overlooking the next bit of the Blanchville story: the bell tower. The Norman family of de Blancheville settled in the townlands between Gowran and Kilkenny. Here at Maddoxtown the site of their original castle was Bhearann an Bhluinseolaigh, and they stayed here and hereabouts until the Nicholas de Blancheville of 1690 supported the Jacobite cause and, with that defeat, his castle was razed to the ground.

All this landscape for centuries had been known as Blanchevillestown, and the house built here in 1800 was the demesne house, Blanchville. By the mid-eighteenth century the estate was in the hands of the Kearneys, an old Irish family to which David Kearney, the Archbishop of Cashel who died in 1624, belonged. Later men of note were James Kearney, solicitor and MP for Thomastown, County Kilkenny, and his son and heir James Charles, a former Dragoon. Although solitary and reclusive, James was not untouched by the events of his time, and engaged the architect David Robertson to design a coach house and stable block in a programme for famine relief. He also converted the rear wing of the house into a magnificent ballroom in which, music being his abiding passion, he installed an organ made in 1823 by Walkers of London. Here he invited the leading musicians of the country to perform to an audience of one: James Kearney himself.

He also loved the sound of bells and Robertson designed the bell tower on the lawn. The bells have gone to the Augustinians in Limerick, while the Austrian clock established on the tower's façade has been returned to Vienna. But the structure stands like a tower upon a tower, its arched and empty windows paired by granite mullions. When James died in 1847 he left the estate to his sister; she installed a caretaker,

Above: *The architect David Robertson was commissioned to design the coach-house and stable block at Blanchville House as part of a relief scheme during the Great Famine.* Below: *James Charles Kearney also asked Robertson to design the belltower on Blanchfield's lawn.* (images courtesy of the Phelan family)

The Hidden Ireland group without disrupting family life. She likes to close for the winter to make sure she doesn't get stale but says that the ten years she's been taking guests either in the house or in the self-catering cottages adapted from the coach-houses have been a great experience. 'People can be wonderful,' she says; their response is worth the extra effort she makes for their sake. She's making another now, for me, as I prepare my way on to Carlow. 'Take the Dublin road,' she says, looking across the fields to the Blackstairs Mountains, but I can see no sign of a road anywhere nor any sound of one either. Then her daughter Niamh comes in from the kitchen with news of a toffee sponge just out of the oven and somehow the Dublin road disappears even further into the distance.

Mr Cantley, who stayed until 1916, and from then on this was known as Cantley's Tower.

'Everyone said we should build a bungalow.' Monica remembers buying the house where the land adjoined her husband's home farm. Blanchville is built with the front and back sections linked but quite separate, so Monica can carry on her business as part of

Blanchville House now also offers art therapy courses and spa treatments.

Blanchville House,
Maddoxtown County Kilkenny
Tel: 05677 27197

BLANCHVILLE HOUSE

Boherwilliam

Modeligo, County Waterford

Designer Ciara Gormley had told me precisely the right and best way to get back to Cork from Modeligo in County Waterford. But I took the road into the Drumm hills and to the long avenue of beeches ending at the church of St Patrick. It's the avenue which attracts every return journey: the trees growing out of the mossed stone walls, the old stile near the church hinting at a mass path from long ago, the beauty and surprise of such an arrangement of church, stile and avenue in such a place; those of us who know of it cannot resist its gentle magnetism. Stopping briefly here was a reminder of the choices people make, in this case the choice of Ciara Gormley and her husband Rob Lynch in deciding to make their home in a Victorian property in the heart of the country.

'At the time we had been living in a terrace house in Dublin and when we saw this place it couldn't have looked worse.' But Ciara isn't an arts history graduate and Rob isn't an archaeologist for nothing: 'It had a nice feel to it, though. And it was surrounded by a garden – well, by land really, eight acres of it.' Explaining that their arrival here was not a plan but something that just happened, Ciara talks about her discovery of this district through art classes in the area. Then she and her family found O'Brien's Bar for sale in Lismore and a consortium of herself, Rob, her brother, sister and father bought it and introduced Barca, a tapas bar. At the end of two years the degree of commitment required from all involved was taking its toll, so the bar was sold to Justin Green (and reopened as O'Brien Chop House) and Ciara and Rob set about tackling the house they had bought in the meantime.

Ciara is a meantime kind of person: there's always something else to be doing. From university she moved directly into film work, designing sets, doing all the research and ensuring the accuracy of architectural detail. 'It's a great business, but it's freelance and can involve very long hours, long weeks, absences, and then times when there's no work at all.' Those were meantimes, and in them Ciara went to night school or to additional professional courses. One of these has influenced her choice for the future: her main commitment now, having studied the subject at the Dublin Institute of Technology, is garden design.

As we walk through her house, with its high, wide windows looking south to Colligan Wood and further on again to the dusky slopes of the Comeraghs, her talent for this kind of work is very obvious, even on a blustery day when what was green looks grey and the scarlets and pinks of surviving roses seem to be fading in the wind. But here the cobble-edged paths are tidy, the lawn reached by stone steps from the front of the house stretching into the dull golds of stubble fields and the shadows of wooded ditches. The borders are

ABOVE: *Ciara Gormley and her son Conor in the family kitchen at Modeligo and (right) a view of the refurbished parochial house* (images courtesy of the *Irish Examiner*)

still vibrant with shrubs, the orchard rich with its apples, pears, plums, cherries and quinces.

The date of the house is uncertain, although 1820 is carved on a stone on the property. It was the parochial house – an arched window in the dining-room is a reminder of a former oratory – and most of it is single-storey, a kind of Regency villa, 'awkward' says Ciara with a smile which suggests the pleasure of getting it right. Everything was brought back to the rubble walls, which were then covered with a lime plaster. An outhouse was joined to the main building to make an additional bedroom and bathroom, and all this part with the long hall running horizontally through the house and including the kitchen was floored with Portuguese limestone, giving the layout a calming perspective.

The kitchen with its coved ceiling was fitted, the demolished outbuildings re-erected on their original footprint, the old embellished cast-iron fireplaces with their tiled borders and hearths were dipped and polished, while the old floorboards were sanded and varnished. Rob and Ciara took some advice, got their specifications from a quantity surveyor, found the people and sources they wanted to work with, and got on with what Ciara now says was 'really a refurbishment'. The feeling is that perhaps Ciara has decided to shelve interior design for a while and is going to concentrate on gardens. But there's a meantime: she's also continuing with her painting classes. ♣

E-mail: ciaragormley10@gmail.com

Cahernane House

Killarney, County Kerry

This is all Ted Newenham's fault, I remind myself as I square up to the burly stag at the other side of the fenced avenue leading to Cahernane House Hotel in Killarney. If it weren't for Ted Newenham and his passion for croquet, I wouldn't be in this stand-off situation with a creature whose size, habit and temperament are, to put it mildly, intimidating. I had only stopped to admire the croquet lawn and to identify the dog's-tooth violets sparkling on the close-mown grass. Yet here I stand, face to face with one of Ireland's most magnificent animals, the wild red deer. Behind him two smaller hinds stand tremulous but interested. Then in an instant the deer have sprinted up the rocky outcrops and into the oakwood which fringes the pastures, the stag halting for a brief, watchful moment before disappearing among the trees.

Now I turn reluctantly back from the fence; the native Irish red deer is something to be treasured, to be protected. I had known all that, yet seeing the animal brings absolute conviction: these are 'Stag at Eve' deer, heavily built with thick russet pelts and smelling breathing gusts of a wild world we so rarely encounter. How far away is this from croquet and its placid (and misleading!) suggestion of ladies and gentlemen strolling about on summer lawns? At Cahernane House it is as close as the fencing, although the deer are cautious beasts and delight the guests here only at early morning or towards dusk. I am in Killarney only because Cahernane House Hotel included among its 'facilities' a croquet lawn, which in these days of spas and leisure centres and gyms seems almost too old-fashioned to be genuine.

After the long, tree-shaded avenue the house appears, tall, narrow, obviously Victorian but with the strong imprint of an earlier age. Explained by Sales and Marketing Manager Marion O'Connor, this is a Herbert house, related to Muckross and, as in Muckross, this branch of the Herberts was to fall on evil or ill-managed times. Although these might have been anticipated by 1877, when Henry Herbert decided to improve his family status by demolishing the existing Queen Anne house, he persisted in ruinous spending on the new Cahernane. All the same, the steeply pitched roof, the array of gables and dormer windows, the family crest, dragon arms and motto ('Every man according to his taste') carved over the door and the beautifully managed spaces still evoke the earlier building. Even the extension to one side is gabled; it is here that the modern suites are located, with cast-iron balconies and tall windows overlooking the woods and the neighbouring herd of Kerry cows. Torc and the Reeks ring the view, and here and there are glimpses of the lake.

Sometimes the new owners of old houses go mad for 'period' detail. Here the principle, guided

ABOVE: *A suite at Cahernane House, where nothing strikes a false note.* (image courtesy of Cahernane House Hotel)

by architect Kevin Murphy of Irish Country Homes and managed by Weir Interiors of Cork, has been to keep calm. Original decoration was used as the design footprint, so that the fine latticed oak staircase and oaken floors, the fretted hall ceiling supported by corbels carved with family initials and the panelled window-frames set a pattern of authenticity and restraint. Proprietor Jimmy Browne, whose daughter Sara is managing director of Cahernane, has made sure that there is no pretence here of being something the house is not. Colours, as in the drawing-room, for example, are taken from the veining of the marble fireplaces with their insets of Dutch tiles. Nothing is declamatory and nothing strikes a false note.

Even the modern conservatory, walled in white, furnished with white-cushioned rattan and rippling with a fountain of Italian stone, matches the high-pointed gables both of the old house and the new wing, which it links together before stepping down to the cellar bar. Here the low vaulting of the ceilings is relieved by flooring of gleaming Liscannor slate and by the introduction, in the bar counter and around the fireplace, of the pink and grey Muckross marble found on the demesne. A bar menu is served on Wedgewood porcelain, the hand-made breads arrive wrapped in damask napkins. From menu to wine list to the magnificent antlered stag's head in the hall (oh dear!), to the panelled bedroom corridor with its little domestic mural of a long-ago duck, even to the dog's-tooth violets on the croquet lawn, Cahernane House is a very special place, as genuine in its way as the red deer are in theirs.

Cahernane House Hotel,
Killarney, County Kerry
Tel: 064 6631895
www.cahernane.com

Cairbre House

Abbeyside, Dungarvan, County Waterford

Brian Wickham attributes the success of Cairbre House to his grandmother-in-law, if such a designation is easily understood. Margaret Norris was the grandmother of his late wife Geraldine and, although Brian and Geraldine spent most of their married life away from Dungarvan, they responded to a sense of tradition as well as inheritance in their decision to relocate to Geraldine's native town and to the house in which she was reared.

It stands at an angle to the causeway at Abbeyside, on the edge of the Colligan river estuary, with the foothills of the Comeraghs mounting gently behind it. This impression of distance from the busy town of Dungarvan was precisely why Cairbre House was established in 1819 as a fever hospital. At that time its small peninsula was virtually an island, reached on foot only at low tide. A garden wall is broken on the riverside by the 'sea gate', from which patients who had succumbed to the frequent outbreaks of cholera were taken away by boat to what was known as the cholera graveyard.

The district belonged to the Irish Devonshire estates centred at Lismore Castle, and in a 40-year-long spurt of improvements in their Munster properties the 5th and 6th Dukes of Devonshire built the single-arch bridge which brought the hospital closer to the town. It was from the Devonshire estate that Margaret Norris and her husband James bought the old hospital in 1913 for £211. It had long outlived its original purpose by then, although in the interim it had served as an asylum during the Great Famine. When Margaret Norris and her husband renovated it as a small private hotel she renamed it 'Cairbre' in memory of her native west Cork. Margaret had been educated in poultry-keeping at Reading University and worked as a poultry instructor in County Waterford while rearing five children and running the hotel all at the same time. James Norris devoted himself to the gardens and orchard, keeping chickens and pigs on the small acreage which would always be the first in the county to produce the new potatoes.

As Brian Wickham explains her family background, her independence and her campaign of investment and management, I wonder if Margaret Norris had not been ahead of her time. 'Was she what!' he responds, remembering that at her death at the age of ninety-six she was still bright, broadminded and wise: 'She and the house were at the core of the family.' It's not hard to see why the house should have remained important: there is nothing of the hospital about it, nothing at all of its feverish and famine-stricken past. Instead it is like a large cottage, its ceilings boarded, most of its rooms relatively small, its stairs and landings interrupted by little cupboards, by steps leading to a narrow passage or to a panelled bathroom. Its country furniture looks as if it was

ABOVE: *Cairbre is a house very much of its time and its place: a bedroom at Cairbre House and (below) the new conservatory.* (images courtesy of Brian Wickham)

made for these rooms, as it probably was. And to this have been added the rugs, the fleecy towels, the fresh bed linen, the over-bed reading lamps, the disguised television sets and the electric blankets.

Son of Commandant Thomas Wickham, who was killed on the Golan Heights while serving with the United Nations during the Six-Day War, Brian took early retirement from the Irish army to move back to Dungarvan with Geraldine in 1994. They had not planned on taking over at Cairbre House, but when Geraldine's mother Maire Keegan retired they thought it all through again. They spent the next few years repairing, restoring, re-panelling, uncovering old fireplaces and, with John Kelly of Kilbrittain, refitting or replacing old sash windows and their shutters and sourcing crown glass for the panes. 'It's still very much a house of its time and its place,' says Brian, 'our whole object was to keep as much as possible, to hold on to its atmosphere. It's unique, it's not a clone – you won't find any artificial fires or artificial flowers in the house.'

After the shock of Geraldine's sudden death in 2001, Brian and his family decided to keep Cairbre House in business, difficult though the first few years might have been. 'She was just a magical person,' Brian says now, 'she was packed with energy – and it all just came to a stop. But we had worked as a team and the house was part of me by then. I loved it as she had done.' It's not hard to see why.

Continuing work at Cairbre House includes a new conservatory and renovations throughout the house.

Cairbre House,
Abbeyside, Dungarvan, County Waterford
Tel: 058 42338
www.cairbrehouse.com

Carrig House

Caragh Lake, Killorglin, County Kerry

A bat, a sickle moon, a splash, and all else is silence and stillness at nightfall at Caragh Lake. As the evening wanes, the colours darken and the hills become mountains, the stream beside the road becomes a river, the uplands slanting away are washed with fading, golding light. The bog road (there is even a bog village here) drops to a fertile valley dense with trees. Mangerton looms black in the far distance and Carrantuohill is higher than the cloud over the MacGillicuddy Reeks. Just when I think I'll sell my soul to see the lake, glimpsed here and there through the greenery, the gateway to Carrig House beckons. Beyond it lie the mountains, the moon, the bat, the splashing trout and, at last, the house. From the

OPPOSITE: *Comfort and elegance are the priority at Carrig House.* ABOVE: *A bedroom window looks out on Caragh Lake.* (images courtesy of Frank and Mary Slattery)

windows lamplight spreads its gleam over the lawn and garden paths, candles flicker in the bow windows of the dining-room. From the sitting-room with its bookshelves and armchairs comes the inviting and familiar tang of turf blazing in the wide hearth. I have to make my way back from the lakeshore before dark if I don't want them to send out search parties.

In fact, this dusky enchantment is not isolated. The oak woods growing almost from the waterline disguise the amount of building going on here, the few remaining Victorian houses still cloaked in trees, the newer, often incongruous modern dwellings pitched so that only a rooftop here, or a window there, breaks the ancient calm of the landscape. How long this can last is uncertain; everywhere there are site notices or signs for a plot for sale, with collies panting like auctioneers at each signpost.

It was to this house that Senator Arthur Vincent came when he remarried after the death of Maud Bourn, his first wife, daughter of the American Bowers Bourn who had given the Vincents a wedding present of Muckross House in Killarney. Carrig House had already had a succession of owners since it was built in the 1850s; after Arthur Vincent it was sold to Sir Aubrey Metcalfe, a cousin of The MacGillicuddy and one of the last ministers of the British administration in India. Then came Lord Brocket, who owned several other notable houses including Carton and Cashel Palace. With this embarrassment of homes to choose from, he only visited Carrig a few times a year, until it was sold first in 1983 and then in 1996 to Frank and Mary Slattery. They and their children left their bar and restaurant in Tralee to realise a dream they had kept alive for twelve years.

Now William Morris wallpaper, elegant curtaining, glittering glassware and cutlery on white napery with simple garden flowers everywhere present a style which is both fresh and sophisticated. The renowned kitchen is also open to non-residents and, when I drag myself back from the lakeside, I sit down to seafood pudding on carrageen moss with a saffron vinaigrette followed by sweet potato soup, seared scallops with spicy couscous and green tomato salsa. I won't even mention the desserts. But I must mention the music of Áine Nic Gabhainn, on harp and then piano. Her melodies lie on the night air like a romantic charm.

All of the six bedrooms – more are being added this winter – are different but look out on four acres of garden and on the lake with its rampart of mountains. In the morning light this is breathtaking. I drink it in with my orange juice at breakfast and, when planning my drive home, Frank and Mary guide me to their favourite places in the hills. For them, the business they run at Carrig House is a labour of love and this knowledgeable advice, like the bowls of brilliant apples from the old orchard, is another indication of the care they take to get it right.

As I circumnavigate Glencar, I leave for another day what remains, in Glenbeigh, of Winn's Folly, the mansion designed in 1867 by Edward William Godwin for the Hon. Rowland Winn. Winn was an eccentric of one kind, Godwin, who eloped with Ellen Terry, of another, and Winn's son, the 5th Lord Headley, added to local legend by adopting the Muslim faith with such ardour that he became president of the British Muslim Society. I turn instead for Blackstone Bridge, staying in second gear, intimidated by the fringe of massive sheep along the roadside. A blue boat lies on the shore, Lickeen Wood emerges from the oak thickets, Cloon Lough and Lough Acoose fill the hollows with their steel-grey waters, while horned free-range cattle calmly block the little bridges. The streams plunge into a maze of tributaries all rushing to their home in Caragh Lake.

Carrig House,
Caragh Lake, Killorglin County Kerry
Tel: 066 9769100
www.carrighouse.com

Cashel Palace Hotel

Cashel, County Tipperary

Every good garden has its own particular feature: in Susan and Patrick Murphy's garden the feature is the Rock of Cashel, reached by the path known as the Bishop's Walk and part of the 28 acres they took on when they bought this famous house.

Although the monument itself is owned by the Irish state, the rock and the rocky fields immediately around it belong to the Palace; the Murphys are content to let the land adjacent to the garden be used

BELOW: *Sleep in the shadow of the Rock of Cashel at Cashel Palace Hotel.*

ABOVE: *A long tradition of hospitality is expressed in the hotel sitting-room.* OPPOSITE: *One of the bathrooms features window shutters and internal arches.* (images courtesy of Ireland's Blue Book)

for grazing, which in any case has an amenity value of its own. To stand in the garden of the Cashel Palace Hotel with the house on one hand and the rock with its tiara of turrets and chapels on the other is to experience a shock of continuity. The garden front of the house is built in shimmering limestone, and its almost liquid quality seems only to harden into the great limestone pile beyond the trees. Mercifully, neither of the Murphys seems in any way interested in enhancing this magical interchange between building and rock; it simply exists in a quiet relationship which has lasted for so many centuries that, as Susan Murphy remarks, the owners of the Palace cannot ever have been more than custodians.

The pity is that those in control of Cashel as a

AT HOME IN IRELAND

town don't use the same caution. Visible from this garden, a raw new housing development is growing on a neighbouring hill, rupturing the town's fragile atmosphere of heritage and ruining the pastoral landscape around the ancient ruins of Hore Abbey in the valley. The Palace gardens are private, their immaculate lawns bounded on one side by sections of the old town walls and surrounded by trees of vast height and impressive age. On the lawn nearest the house are the wide-spreading branches of two ancient mulberries planted, it is believed, in 1702 to commemorate the coronation of Queen Anne of England. In the thriving herb garden two of the hotel's chefs are carefully selecting both culinary and decorative leaves for the evening's menu. This is an enticing document, but my interest was more thoroughly stirred by the breakfast menu, after which one might feel inclined not only to climb the Rock of Cashel but to carry it away single-handed.

When Susan and Pat came to the Palace in 1998 they found it structurally in very good condition, if looking a little tired. It had been built as the residence of the bishops of the Church of Ireland in 1732, when Bishop Theophilus Bolton, famed scholar and keeper of the marvellous library now housed in the Bolton Library across the road, commissioned the design for the house from architect Sir Edward Lovett Pearce. The entrance front has something of the style of a French château in its rosy brick façade but, although the notable string courses and coigns, the Palladian doorway and Venetian windows at each wing suggest different influences, there is an immense structural harmony uniting the whole. Quietly graceful, with a wide driveway off the main street, the Palace looks what it is, a place, as described in Loveday's Tour of 1732, 'of notable hospitality'. The hotel is a tribute to Susan's collaboration with consultant Daphne Daunt, with whom all the interiors have been not just refreshed but re-thought, with the intention, beautifully achieved, of indicating how the house is to be used and enjoyed by its guests.

The sense of relaxation and of luxury is not ostentatious, but speaks of the sophisticated deliberation with which a venerable building can earn its living without losing its dignity. This combination of style and restraint, coupled with the quality of its kitchen, has won the Cashel Palace the distinction, already, of the Les Routiers award as the Best Hotel in Ireland for 2001. On the street side the old coach house now offers a series of delightful rooms, so that the tree-shaded mews is almost as popular as the house itself. And the railings of the Palace terrace are still entwined with the hops from which one Richard Guinis, agent for the Bishop of Cashel in the 1740s and father of Arthur, brewed his first beer. Guests lingering under the willows as dusk falls will find all the scented pleasures of an old garden promising the bounties of many years of its new history.

Cashel Palace Hotel,
Cashel, County Tipperary
Tel: 062 62707

Castle Durrow

Durrow, County Laois

The exuberant personality of Shelley Stokes infuses everything that happens at Castle Durrow, and makes it perfectly understandable that the magnificently tiered chandelier suspended over the stairwell is the product of a flatpack self-assembly kit. Flatpacks are not what one might expect at Castle Durrow, despite Shelley's insistence that this is a contemporary country house hotel. She and her husband Peter have not altered it in any physical way, but their sense of style is another decorative layer on an already marked, if somewhat anonymous, history.

There is no record of an architect for one of the grandest houses in the county. Its European hints finally resolve themselves into something of a Dutch influence, reasonable enough given its date of 1712–16, and following the grand plan of the fashionable architecture of its time. The builder Benjamin Crawley used a fine blue-shaded limestone for the core of the house with its high-pitched roof and dormer attic windows.

'It was Georgianised later on,' explains Shelley, whose Dutch nationality may explain the instant affinity she felt for Castle Durrow. She came to Ireland for a long weekend in 1992, met Peter – famous for his Cooper's Restaurant in Dublin – and the weekend stretched to cover marriage, four children and the move to Durrow. Castle Durrow has taken off, its wedding business especially building on the opportunities provided by the setting, the amenities of the hotel, the restaurant run by David Rousse and the unique combination of ancestral atmosphere allied to efficiency and a pervading homely warmth.

It was built for Colonel William Flower, MP, later 1st Lord Castle Durrow. The Flowers went on to expand from barons to Viscounts Ashbrook and the house lived through a family history until it faltered with the Land Acts and finally, in 1922, with the withdrawal of the Flowers to their estates in Wales. The property remained empty for several years while its oak forests were sold off and the acres were divided by the Land Commission. In 1929 what remained around the house was bought for £1,800, and St Fintan's College was established there. Some woodland remains on the 30 acres which still surround the house and these, with the more formal gardens, the remnants of the fine lime tree avenue, the castellated gatehouse and the out-offices currently under restoration, unite with St Fintan's Church of Ireland church in a landscape which seems ageless.

Inside the house there are elements of moderate grandeur, particularly in the shallow stone flight of steps in the staircase hall illuminated by the stained-glass window and, now, by the Czech crystal facets of the Empire-style chandelier. 'The other chandeliers we bought all of a piece in Kilkenny, but these two big ones came in flatpacks – we had 1,800 separate

ABOVE: *A more ornamental character has been given to the converted library at Castle Durrow.* (images courtesy of Ireland's Blue Book)

strings of crystals laid out on the floor while we were trying to put them together!'

The management of light is a characteristic feature of Shelley's tenure of the house; the bookless library (the built-in covered bookcases are used for ornaments while the books are in the sitting-room) with its panelling and elaborate ceiling has been converted as an example of chinoiserie, once the fashionable décor of gentry drawing-rooms. Its hand-painted silk carries traceries of birds and branches, while the cornices and plasterwork here and in the other ground-floor rooms have been beautifully regilded by Dick Bradish. Shelley explains that she didn't want an 'old' feel in the house and so she wasn't going for authenticity at all costs. The carpets were dyed in France to reproduce the Aubusson quality and style; the tapestries are excellent modern versions of the traditional. Some of the old lead from the roof, which, like the floorboards, had to be completely replaced, was used to restore the sash weights in all the windows, with the curtains in the library a lovely example of the *changeant* fabric she uses to such effect, even under glass for her coffee tables.

Some of the effects are immediate, some more gradual. Both Peter, who works as overall manager and supervisor of all the continuing exterior restoration and development, and Shelley who keeps both hotel and wedding business balanced and thriving, are in love with this house, and it shows. 'In a way,' Shelley remembers, 'we feel the house was waiting for us. The sun was shining on the day we first saw it and ever since then there have been little coincidences which make us feel that the house is happy we bought it!'

Shelley Stokes now also manages Bramley's, the furniture shop and restaurant at Abbeyleix.

Castle Durrow,
Durrow, County Laois
Tel: 057 8736555
www.castledurrow.com

Castle Oliver

Ardpatrick, County Limerick

Leaving after my first visit to Castle Oliver, I thought I'd never return. Grim, gloomy and neglected, I thought then, despite the atmospherics of the place, its striking location and the quality of its strong Scottish Baronial style carried out in red sandstone. But now I revisit Castle Oliver on a bright spring day. The resident terrier Harley accompanies my own Bobbie along the cleared avenues and under the cut-back scrub; they race in circles across the terraced lawns, which seem somehow to vault over the hidden road and merge with the sloping fields that climb to the Ballyhoura hills. Decoy ducks on the ornamental pond cut out between the drawing-room (when I was last here there was no drawing-room, not to mention a pond) and the formal garden lure Bobbie into a diving swim; Harley stays on shore, but as Bobbie shakes her coat free of the water the two of them take off again, the haze of moisture around them both glinting and dazzling in the sun.

Nicholas Browne joins me on the lawn and remembers that, when he began house-hunting in Ireland, the price for houses like this seemed cheap by UK standards. 'I thought I wanted a castle, something that had a touch of medieval grandeur, perhaps. Like vaulting, and battlements, a spiral stairs, things like that.'

At Castle Oliver medieval is on offer in spades. Vaulting lifts the hall ceiling and is repeated elegantly in the bedroom corridors. There are battlements at every opportunity. There are five flights of spiral stairs. There are, in fact, 110 rooms. So now Nicholas, having plied his trade of rebuilding and restoration around the world, is thinking of moving on. He has done his bit for Castle Oliver. The entrance hall is its own workshop, the ceiling down, the floorboards up, the corbels painted with armorial bearings neatly stacked and numbered, the great window replaced, although much of its painted glass depicting the life of St Patrick was destroyed by random stone-throwing while the house was empty. Still, the remaining iron struts hold their original shamrock detail, the oak shutters are back, the fireplace is framed by the outline of its enormous panelling and huge overmantel torchères. In the adjoining library the three-light window has been reinstalled, although here the ceiling, propped up by tree trunks when Nicholas arrived, is being repaired in conjunction with the flooring overhead. All sixty-five fireplaces can be used and, as I see for myself, the one in the sitting-room draws beautifully.

The sitting-room – or ballroom – like some of the reclaimed bedrooms and like the dining-room, also is a calm example of what such a room should be. There is no Victorian clutter, so the elements of the space are given their full emphasis, especially in the wide serene view of Glenisheen, that valley flowing between the Ballyhouras just beyond the garden. In a big room the fireplace is crucial and here the flames show up the remaining painted tiles, the ceiling lined with painted canvas panels picked out in gold and carried on through a gilded arched doorway to the ante-room with its coved ceiling.

That the high inner hall is here at all is a wonder, given that it was closed off and disintegrating the last time I saw it. Now the wide diamond-shaped skylight or lantern shines down on a chandelier of reclaimed, painted organ-pipes. The staircase of oak has been restored in immaculate style by Gerry Hamilton of Charleville and still incorporates the spindles turned by the builders of the house, Mary and Elizabeth Oliver-Gascoigne of Yorkshire. There are traces of these talented, philanthropic and immensely wealthy women everywhere, not least in the painted glass and tiles which still survive as examples of their own handiwork, not least either in the hand-made Minton tiles used in chimney-pieces and hearths.

Mary and Elizabeth had inherited a fortune, believed to be as much as £100 million in today's values. They commissioned Castle Oliver from architect G. Fowler Jones *circa* 1846–50 to relieve the distress of the Great Famine, and one consequence was that this neighbourhood was among the very few Irish rural districts to show an increase in its population during those famine years. Already a family estate, the earlier Castle Oliver had been the birthplace of Marie Gilbert, known to the world as Lola Montez, briefly but influentially mistress of Ludwig I of Bavaria, who was something of an expert in castles himself.

With Nicholas Browne I watch the scampering dogs and wonder about the future of this amazing, rewarding and unique place. He is, he says, a pragmatist, and Castle Oliver was taken on as a real-estate investment. But he is ready to tackle something different, ready to find a place in the sun. He is, one feels, entitled. If he once saw Castle Oliver as 'redeemable', he has indeed redeemed it, so that it too can take its place in the sun.

The major restoration project initiated by Nick Browne has now been completed by its latest proprietors, Declan and Emma Cormack. Following further extensive refurbishment, they run it successfully as a unique holiday venue.

Castle Oliver,
Ardpartrick, County Limerick
Tel: 063 91826
www.castleoliver.ie

There are 110 rooms and five flights of stairs at medieval Castle Oliver. (images courtesy of Emma Cormack)

CASTLE OLIVER

Clonalis House

Castlerea, County Roscommon

Pyers and Marguerite O Conor Nash get their name out of the way first: O Conor Don is simply a description, from the Irish *donn*, meaning brown. And while Pyers O Conor Nash of Clonalis House may have inherited the clan's ancestral home in County Roscommon, he can never be The O Conor Don, because he inherited through his mother and the female line is barred from this ancient Irish Catholic title.

The library at Clonalis, late on a summer's evening with logs smouldering gently in the vast grate, is exactly the place in which to have this kind of meandering, archival conversation. In a distant room hangs the harp of Turlough O Carolan, bard and

Opposite: *The library at Clonalis House, ideal for archival conversations.* Above and Right: *Clonalis was built for a native aristocracy.*

singer for the O Conors. The pillared hall leads to an oratory with its scroll of *Altare Privilegiatum*, a blessing for worshippers in the Penal days. Outside the front door, half-hidden by the woodbine which climbs to the bracketed eaves, stands the coronation stone of the O Conors, a slanted indentation indicating the fossilised imprint of the first high king of Ireland, a figure, in his time, to rival Alexander.

The library holds manuscripts, maps and genealogical tables; I note the cavities in the fireplace of Irish and Italian marble for the planks of raw turf on one side, timber on the other. A signature of the architect, explains Pyers; replicated in the dining-room, the design seems to indicate that this is not an Anglo-Irish house but one built to the style of a native aristocracy. Clonalis as it now stands was designed in 1875 as an Italianate mansion by F. Pepys Cockerell for Charles Owen O Conor Don, MP for Roscommon, but these acres at Castlereagh have been the seat of the most ancient royal family in Europe for more than a thousand years.

The current holder of the title is Desmond O Conor, resident in England. The name embraces almost the width of Ireland, the direct descent traced from Feredach the Just in AD 75 to Turlough Mor O Conor, first high king in 1156 and to his son Cathal Crodh Deargh. Buried at Abbeyknockmoy in County Galway in 1224, Cathal is now best remembered in the wistful lines by James Clarence Mangan celebrating the time of Cathal Mor of the Wine-Red Hand.

At Carnfree, near Tulsk, the coronation stone once stood on a hill among ring-barrows and pillar stones. The last king to be acclaimed there was Felim O Conor, killed in 1316 at the Battle of Athenry. Some centuries later, Donncadh Liaith (the grey) O Conor won back the lands lost through loyalty to James II and built the Hermitage, home of his son Charles at Bellangare. Charles died in 1791 but, as a noted farmer, antiquarian and genealogist, his influence lives on at Clonalis, where his personal archive survives, like the inauguration stone, under loving custody.

This inheritance fell to Pyers because a solitary uncle became a Jesuit priest. Although familiar with the house since childhood, Pyers was settled in Dublin with Marguerite (a native of Tullamore) and their young family and found himself facing a multiple inheritance tax and a very complex title. 'We

Dream of high kings and conquistadores at Clonalis House. (images courtesy of The Hidden Ireland)

didn't fully understand that at first. We came down to see if we could live here, and we almost went back again immediately, but someone reminded me that, if we didn't try to work something out, we would spend the rest of our lives wondering if we could have saved the place and all it stands for,' explains Pyers.

He left his job, uprooted his family and brought them to a house with no running water, one which hadn't been decorated for seventy years and was so cold, as Marguerite remembers it, 'that you could smell it!' A sympathetic government encouraged by the people of Roscommon allowed the sale of two-thirds of the estate, so Pyers and Marguerite could hold on to the house and its contents and the surrounding farmland, which gives it both its visual and historical context.

Clonalis bristles with Irish history which, for the benefit of a coach-load of awe-stricken listeners (including myself), Marguerite condenses from the time of the Milesians. Obviously the manuscript room is now the most important part of it, with its signatures of kings and princes, its story of the conquistador O Conor who governed Yucatan and founded Tucson, its legends of Conn of the Hundred Battles and of Daithi, the last pagan king of Ireland, brother of Niall of the Nine Hostages, the prince who captured Patrick and brought him to Ireland … Generations, as visiting poet Kathleen Raine wrote, 'who kept faith with the High King of an inner kingdom'. ♠

Clonalis now also offers self-catering accommodation and is open to the public during the summer season.

Clonalis House,
Castlerea, County Roscommon
Tel: 094 962 0014
www.clonalis.com

Coopershill House

Riverstown, County Sligo

'After about two months I knew I could do it,' says Lindy O'Hara of her first days in charge at Coopershill. 'Now I wouldn't dream of living anywhere else.' Although she first saw the house during the lovely summer of 1966, it was on a bleak December day twenty years later that she and her family realised that this damp and dreary landscape was to be their home. 'And then we reached Boyle and crossed over the Curlew Mountains and saw Lough Arrow – and the sun came out! That was the turning-point, I think – that and the fact that the huge O'Hara family in these parts meant that there was an instant and effortless social circle, which was a tremendous help with settling in.'

After a life lived largely abroad with her husband Brian O'Hara, Lindy admits that when they came back to Sligo they didn't know anything about running a house of this kind. The fact that Brian had held several diplomatic postings, which meant a lot of entertaining, was some help, as was the fact that neither of them was afraid of the really hard work involved when they took over both house and deer farm. Next door is another large family farm, where Brian's brother Tim concentrates on sheep and on vegetable processing.

Coopershill is a three-storey house, built in local ashlar, which has an almost luminous quality and sits in a glade of lawns and woodland. This façade, pierced by classically proportioned windows with a rusticated Venetian doorway occasionally patrolled by a very un-rusticated peacock (or two), presents a combination of elegance and solidity which seems typical of the life and enterprise within. Now in its sixth generation of the family, Coopershill began in 1755, when Arthur and Sarah Cooper decided to build a house to the design of Francis Bindon. The legend is that the Coopers set out two buckets of gold sovereigns and instructed the builder to keep going until the money was used up – although most of it was spent on first building a bridge (with the stones supported on sheepskins) across the river to reach the chosen site. Bindon himself was killed when his coach crashed during the twenty-year span of building; the change of builders is indicated in the stonework of the top storey, but the house looks totally all of a piece, serene and stalwart with an atmosphere of timelessness.

The family interchanges through the generations continued until the estate was inherited by Brian's father Frank. Back in Ireland, and back in agriculture after a career as a tea-planter, Frank and his wife Joan had adjusted to the demands of a young family and an old house and, once the children had left home, decided to offer holidays with tennis and ponies and dogs and all that parkland to paying guests during the summer months. An early member of

ABOVE: *Coopershill is surrounded by its deer park.* BELOW: *Alice.*

The Hidden Ireland organisation, Joan instilled that sense of stylish generosity maintained by Brian and Lindy since they took over in 1982 and for which Coopershill is renowned.

Here the atmosphere hinges on a strong sense of what is due both to the house – grand without grandeur – and to its guests. Old, time-worn, but never neglected, Coopershill is both fresh and refreshing. There are big beds, half-testers and canopied, but the upholstery is modern and beautifully suited to the rooms and their furniture. Although Lindy once did all the cooking herself, she now presides over a very competent kitchen staff; dinner is served in the formal dining-room, with linen and silverware in keeping with the gleaming mahogany. Coffee is taken in the drawing-room, where the homegrown logs

This is a house of contrasts, with its professional character combined with distinctive friendliness. (images courtesy of the O'Hara family)

keep the chill off the Irish summer evenings and the tables are laden with newspapers, magazines, books and garden flowers.

Coopershill is a house of contrasts. It has its professional character, its concentration on excellent cooking and dependable comfort, such as the turn-down service which prepares your bedroom for the night, and then it has its distinctive friendliness. The impressive hall, for example, with its recessed pediment doors and club fender has been familiarised by the hanging of hats on antlers and by the marshalling of boots, rods and other outdoor equipment. For all its history and its fame, Coopershill House is a place where such simple pleasures can be enjoyed to the full.

Following their retirement in 2007, Brian and Lindy have been succeeded at Coopershill House by their son Simon as manager and his partner Christina McAuley as head chef; Simon also assists his parents in the running of the deer farm. Tim and Jane O'Hara are now assisted by their son Mark on their adjacent farm.

Coopershill House,
Riverstown, County Sligo
Tel: 07191 65108
email: reservations@coopershill.com

COOPERSHILL HOUSE

Coursetown Country House

Athy, County Kildare

Jim Fox asked me to ring him back in half an hour because he was just sowing some peas. At least that's what I thought he had said and I wondered why sowing peas in a country garden should be such a major operation that he couldn't manage the mobile phone at the same time. But I had misheard; he was sowing sugar-beet, 19 acres of it this very day, and my call was interrupting the timeline established for a 34-acre schedule this week on his tillage farm near Athy.

But then it's hard not to interrupt Jim or his wife Iris at something; farming, welcoming guests, gardening with imagination and skill and operating as an advice, reference and production centre for information on wildlife, ornithology and local history are probably the major commitments of this couple, although it wouldn't surprise me a bit if there were several other aspects to their lives as well. Already I can think of another – the baking which Iris likes to do early in the morning so her visitors can enjoy bread and scones straight from the oven for breakfast.

Coursetown House sits with its side to the road, the long tillage fields stretching behind the farmyard or spread out like an enormous brown blanket at the other side of the roadway. Although he trained and worked for most of his life as an agricultural research scientist, Jim comes from a farming family near Dublin and retains all his youthful fascination with the mechanisation of farming which allows him to manage his acres of malting barley, sugar beet and winter wheat. I'm not a fan of these big wide ranges of open land but, as we drive along the headlands and he shows me the golden plover surging in dim swathes over the pleated soil, I understand that different kinds of farming can support different kinds of wildlife.

'We get the most interesting people – and they pay us for the privilege of meeting them!' Iris feels there was always an open house of a kind on the farm, not just family friends and neighbours, but all the callers looking for Jim to identify something, or to search for information in his reference books, or to look up his own writing in local and other journals. Now visitors are often on corporate business, but there are also tourists: people looking for somewhere a little different to the usual run of guesthouses.

Although modern in method, this is a working farm of almost traditional style in a bountiful countryside. But Iris puts her brand on things. My bed, for example, is a discovery, from the damask quilt and generous pillows to the pristine sheets and the satin-trimmed fleece blanket, while from the garden arise the drifting scents of thousands of narcissi pale as a mist in the evening light. Once morning comes and I see the spring blossom breaking on the trees, there's no keeping away from the garden, despite the yeasty smell of the bread still warm on the table.

Ornithology, farming and Irish apple trees unite on the old coach road, with Iris and Jim Fox at Coursetown Country House. (image courtesy of the Irish Examiner*)*

The lawn, herbaceous borders and glowing shrubs find room for some old apple trees: one a scarlet unblemished variety, Mère de Ménage, which Iris says was widely planted until about 1900; there's a Kerry Pippin among the Irish names – Jim had that tree at his home place. And here's what they call the Golden Noble, the Irish peach – 'you've never tasted anything like it!'

Jim and Iris came here in 1968 to a house situated on the old coach road from Dublin to Cork which had only changed hands once in 150 years. They concentrated first on getting the farm to rights, then turned to the house, where, as Jim remembers it, 'when Iris started to clean the kitchen the first thing she brought in was a spade!' In a way it looks as if the spade never left her hands, moving only from inside to outside. To encourage the garden, they planted a shelter belt of trees; 'As they say, you know you're growing old when the wood for the fire comes from the trees you planted yourself.' Inside, breakfast awaits with its offerings of pancakes, local cheeses, potato cakes, rashers from Abbeyleix and sausages from Mitchelstown. While huge lorries rumble by on the main road, inside all is peace, contentment and the promise of plenty. ♣

The Irish sugar-beet industry was eradicated since this piece was written. Jim now grows cereal crops at Coursetown.

Coursetown Country House,
Athy, County Kildare
Tel: 059 8631101

COURSETOWN COUNTRY HOUSE

Creagh House

Doneraile, County Cork

Michael O'Sullivan and Laura O'Mahony thought they'd like a cottage in west Cork, and that's why they are now the proprietors of a town house in north Cork. As Michael recalls: 'We saw a little hunting lodge in the west that we thought we'd like. We didn't get it, but it opened our minds to the possibilities of something a bit larger than we had intended. Then we saw another house in this locality but we had to let that one go too. And all the time we were actually passing this house without ever going in to take a look.'

Viewed while Creagh House was on the market, its enormous reception rooms were gaunt and cold, a ceiling was lowered here, a room partitioned there, the out-offices close to dereliction. The back garden was a field, the gates broken, outbuildings half-built or half-demolished, impossible to tell which. No problem, said Michael and Laura, along with both their families. The result, after two years' work, is a coherent reinstatement of a most distinguished house.

It stands at the end of a well-kept street, which begins with the secondary entrance to Doneraile Court and finishes with the former home of the writer and parish priest Canon Sheehan. The weathered limestone façade of Creagh House matches the town's immediacy of street to farmland. It also reflects the analytical approach of its owners, in that aspects of its character were given a real, although not predominating, importance in the renewal process. 'We had caught the bug by then,' says Michael, who has a touch of the 'no-problem' personality. 'Yes, we said, why not? We wanted a big house anyway, we had decided we would take guests, and the house has a good feel to it, although if we had known just what was involved we might have held off …'

What was involved in bringing that good feel to the surface was not just the restitution of timber floors and doors and shutters and ceilings, but running length after eight-foot length of plaster in order to renew the ceiling stucco. Lionel Powell came to explain how to cut the moulding, but after two days they were on their own. With most of the interior work done, three guest bedrooms are ready, one with bedsteads which could only be called episcopal and which came from Fleurys in Cahir. The bathroom panelling, alcove presses and radiator covers are a quiet tribute to the skills of Billy O'Sullivan, master carpenter. With thirty large and twenty small windows to restore, more than 200 panes of glass had to be inserted, with the help of glazier Mick O'Sullivan of Doneraile.

At the back of the house, the courtyard effect will be emphasised when the fine, double-fronted coach

OPPOSITE: *Sunlight on a corner of the drawing-room at Creagh House.*

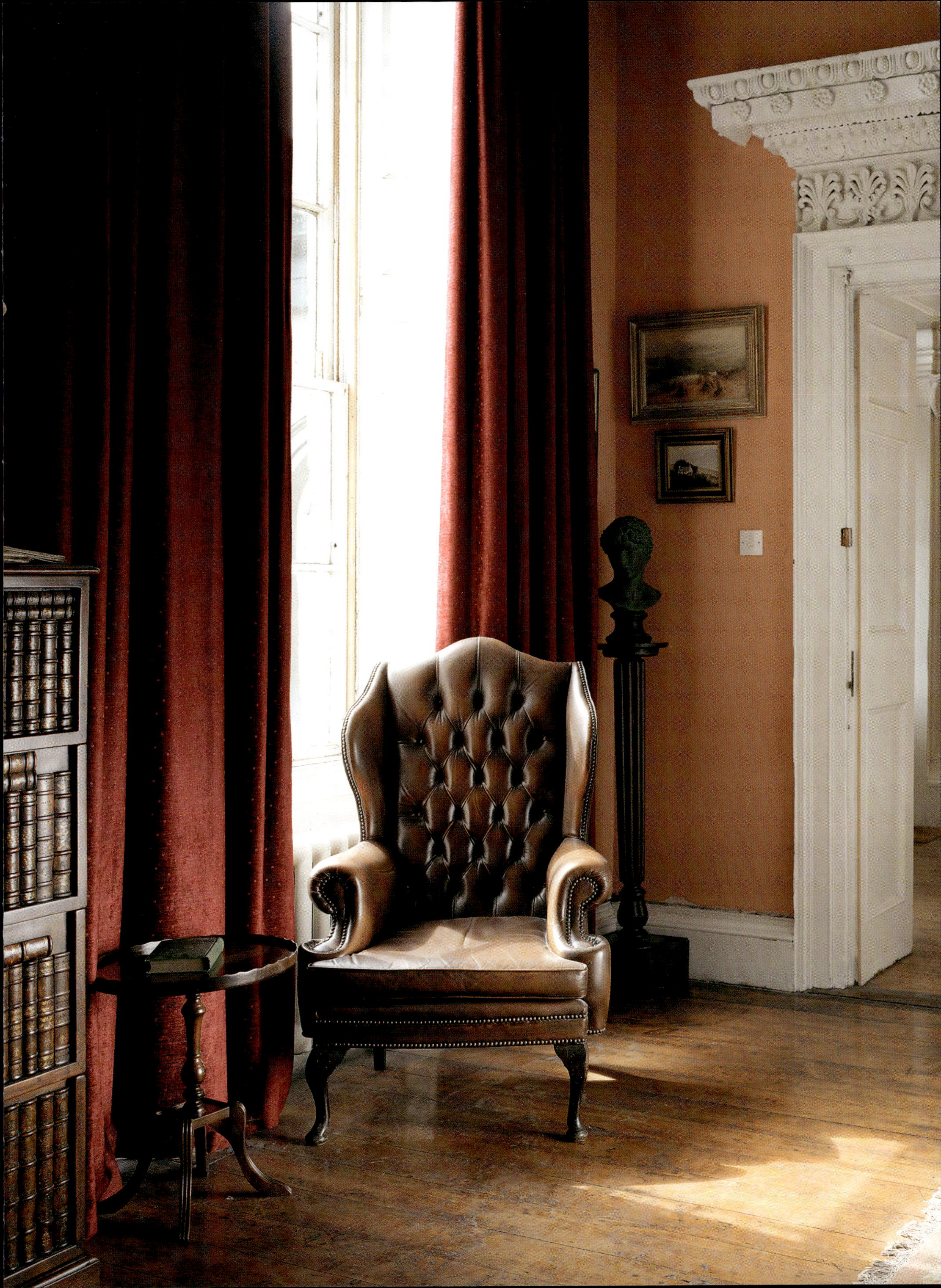

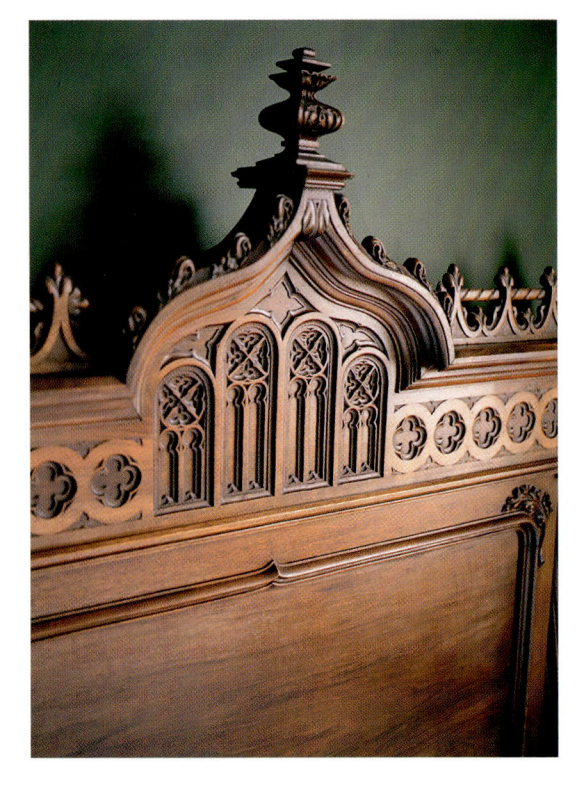

house is restored. The huge basement, the field and whether or not to recobble the yard are going to keep Michael, Laura and their family members happily busy for the foreseeable future. Their work must be made lighter by the consciousness of what has been achieved here. A house of over 8,000 square feet, with six bedrooms, a hallway 60 feet deep from doorway to stairs with five high, richly-embellished pedimented doors is a tall order by any standards, but here it has come together in an exercise which combines symmetry with ebullience. Laura and Michael have kept things calm; they have gone for book-filled cabinets, log fires under the marble mantelpieces, rugs on the polished floors. The house speaks of style, but quietly.

No known architect is recorded, but Michael and Laura give credit to the O'Regans of Doneraile

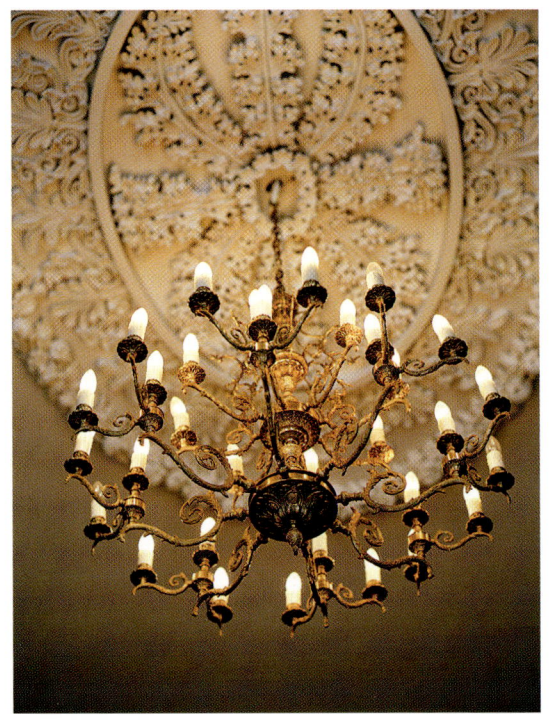

Doors, ceilings and even bedsteads are richly embellished.

ABOVE: *The overmantel in the dining-room and (below) detail of the dining-room plasterwork.* (images courtesy of Laura O'Mahony)

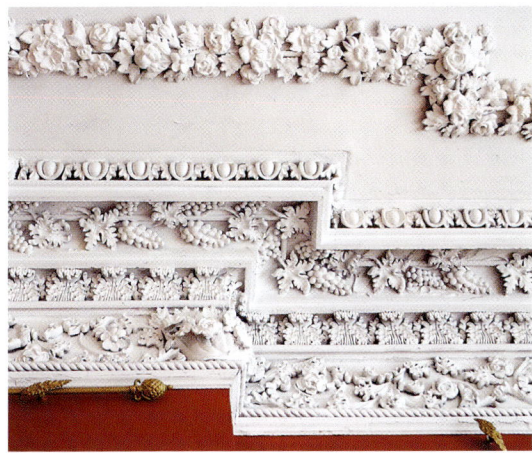

as the builders of a kind of fortified town house for Arthur Gethin Creagh and his wife Isabella in 1837. Their granddaughter, Isabella Creagh Shaw, married William Makepeace Thackeray; the house is also associated with Daniel O'Connell, who defended the accused in the Doneraile Conspiracy of 1829, and with Edmund Spenser, the poet whose Irish estates included the town of Doneraile and his home at nearby Kilcolman Castle. The Doneraile demesne and mansion were sold to Sir William St Leger by Spenser's son Sylvester; a younger son had died when the castle was set on fire and the family was driven from Kilcolman in 1598. In its history and its splendid presence in the town, Creagh House brings all these strands together.

Creagh House,
Doneraile, County Cork
Tel: 022 24433

Curraclone: St Peter's Church

Curraclone, County Laois

Who knows what makes a place special? What draws us back to it time and again as if to find there something otherwise missing from our lives? In this case it is a church seen from a distance and so long ago that for years, thinking of old churches, I thought this had its substance merely in a dream, an image of a red door in a tower backed, as if in a fairytale, by a wooded hillside.

Then a trip to Dublin was diverted at Abbeyleix for Stradbally and Athy. And there it was: the woods, the grey belfry, the crimson door. In Athy it was identified as Curraclone, so here I am, in the windy sunlight of late summer, with the red door of St Peter's church opening inwards on the small silent space of nave and chancel and outwards on the narrow rampart of headstones and beyond them the drowsy golden pastures of the valley.

What looks like a by-road now was once the main road. It formed a direct line from the farmhouse of the Walsh (now Walsh-Kemiss) family, which in 1804 gave the land on which the church was built. It was a replacement for Old Curraclone before that parish was amalgamated with Stradbally. We look out now on Kylebeg and Oakvale and the townland of Ballykilcavan; close by the flowering grass is ripe with scabious, corn cockle, ox-eye daisies and clover and the great trees of the churchyard sweep the ground, the beeches laden with mast and the low branches crusted with lichen. This is a church of the countryside, quietly enriched with both the incidental and the deliberate symbolism of its locality.

Peter Walsh-Kemmis, whose family have been here since 1639, turns the key to let me in, and it is the rector, the Revd Nancy Gillespie, who shows me the report on the building commissioned by the Heritage Council from Lindsey Conservation Architects. The church was designed in 1804 by George Joyce in a style synonymous with the patterns of the Board of First Fruits and built in local limestone. A vestry was added in 1869 and the windows were altered later in the nineteenth century with the insertion of granite ribs dividing them into two lancets with metal diamond-panel frames. The interior of the church was remodelled first in 1899 by William Hague, who had earlier designed the Catholic church in Stradbally, and then in 1905 with the installation of the reredos designed by Frances E. Johnson-Walsh.

These influences are evident in the Celtic Revival flourishes which decorate the stonework and fittings, even the roof beams springing from chevron-carved limestone corbels. But the big oak reredos is an astonishing piece of work to find in any Irish church, telling the story of the Redemption through a succession of interwoven but coherent mystical numbers. The carving, intricate and precise, was carried out from 1905 to 1913 by pupils of the Stradbally woodwork school established by Miss Jane Perceval (who died in 1895) and subsequently run by Miss Kathleen Shaw (1875–1962). If you seek their monument, come to Curraclone. Deciphering these panels must have diverted generations of parishioners – especially the young ones – and still offers a challenge even to casual observers of this beautifully created evidence of the skills and probably devotion of the young woodworkers of Stradbally.

The parish of Curraclone is in the diocese of Leighlin and there is a record of incumbents since 1612 and of curates from 1663. When I ask Peter Walsh-Kemmis about the line of headstones set on a low plinth and stretching across the churchyard, he tells me that these are Walsh family graves: his mother and father and several grandfathers are buried here under the nine crosses, that in the middle the largest in a mildly Celtic style. Other local families still use the churchyard, although space is harder to find now as so much of the land under the meadow grass is solid rock.

We muse over the future of this little church on Bawn Hill, so similar in many outward ways to other little churches in other townlands, yet inside so extravagantly different to anywhere else. Although few travellers now come off the curve in the main road leading to Stradbally, I remember that this is a district of extravagances: not far away is the rocky mound of Dunamase, and at Curraclone we are in the heart of Leinster, which for so many centuries was the heart of Ireland too.

RIGHT: *St Peter's Church at Curraclone, seen from the old road near Stradbally and (below) the reredos carved in oak 1905–13 by pupils of the Stradbally woodwork school.* (images courtesy of James Flynn for the *Irish Examiner*)

CURRACLONE CHURCH

Delphi Lodge

Leenane, County Galway

Time is what you need most for any journey through Connemara and south Mayo. Time is also a crucial factor in the safe navigation of these winding roads, which offer heart-stopping views seducing even the most dedicated drivers to sudden pauses or halts or long study of the rear-view mirror. Sheep graze among the lilies in the gardens and crop undisturbed where the road signs say 'No Verge'. Believe this. When they say 'no verge' they really, really mean it. Really. Falling sheep are another hazard, or else rocks dislodged by falling sheep. This route from Leenane to Westport lies along the north wall of the Killary and cuts through the pass where the Bun Dorcha River enters the harbour. The hills mount in green escarpments above Finn Lough and eventually enclose the sudden, dense woodland which surrounds Delphi Lodge. Here in this amazing wilderness a fine country house has been restored to life through the inspiration, addiction and determination of a young couple who, at the time, were more or less unaware of exactly what it was they were doing.

This, at least, is how Peter Mantle explains it

OPPOSITE: *Delphi Lodge, a unique mix of the well-kept Irish country house and a Mayfair hotel, with a touch of the Georgian ethic.* ABOVE AND RIGHT: *Be prepared to fish hard at Delphi.*

now. The addiction was his; as a freelance journalist working from America for the *Financial Times* in London, he was indulging his Irish loyalties (he's half Irish and spent much of his life here) and his passion for fishing in the west when he discovered the near-derelict retreat built in the 1830s by the Greece-loving Marquess of Sligo. And even then it wasn't so much the house, despite its startling location in the heart of this unspoiled and remote valley, as the promise of the lakes and the river. But the house was part of the deal and in 1985 Peter and his wife Jane set about restoring it. 'But we were quite naïve when we bought it; we had no idea what it would take. And I have to admit that it was very difficult to get motivated about the issues of the financial world at the time. That plan lasted for about a year …'

They were young, and precarious economic circumstances weren't so terrifying then as they might be now. So they concentrated on doing as well as possible what they really wanted to do; they have succeeded to a degree which has set the standard for other similar ventures. The house, a large, ivy-clad and unpretentious square backed by the mountains and fronted by the lake, is serenely comfortable. My notes say that the décor is a unique mix of the well-kept country house and the Mayfair Hotel with a touch of the Spartan ethic thrown in, but that is before I find the delightful library (well, apart from the billiard-room, there has to be something else to do when the fishing is off) with its predictable concentration on fishing and other country pursuits. The dining-room can seat twenty-six people at the kind of pinch guests seem to love to make. The table to accommodate them is so big when fully extended that, in order to stand back to admire one of the several excellent landscapes by Neil Holland (Frank Eggington is another marvellous presence), I have to walk right down to the other end of the room and come back up at the far side of the table. This kind of wackiness is reassuring in what has become a tightly knit and highly organised operation which now includes self-catering centrally-heated cottages across the road.

The library offers an alternative when the fishing is off. (images courtesy of The Hidden Ireland)

Delphi is a quiet wonderland: as a fishery it does not claim to be the most prolific in the world but it is certainly one of the most beautiful. And rewarding: 'be prepared to fish hard in bad weather over several days', warns the brochure. Delphi Lodge has also stood the test of time. Just when the Mantles thought they had got things right, it looked as if everything was going to disappear into a proposed mining development on Mweelrea. The developers listed Croagh Patrick as part of their operation and ecclesiastical intervention saved the day – so far. Then came the explosion in intensive fish farming, with the consequent exaggerated population of sea lice and the almost total eradication of the natural wild fish stocks.

Yet the Mantles have survived these shocks. When they began to transform Delphi Lodge they saw it as a way of putting life back into this bewitching valley. They realise that others can do the same: the adventure centres, if the numbers could be controlled in some mutually advantageous way, and the government takeover of the Erriff Fishery are examples of industries which can co-exist in a given landscape. 'It's not that a place should be a theme park,' muses Peter, 'but planning must be sensitive to the nature and character of a location. We're only custodians for a time, and there simply are not many valleys like this one left in Europe, not to mind in Ireland.'

Peter Mantle has now developed the Delphi Club fishing resort on Abaco Island in the Bahamas. Delphi Lodge at Leenane is managed by Michael Wade.

Delphi Lodge,
Leenane, County Galway
Tel: 095 42222
www.delphilodge.ie

Derrynane House

Caherdaniel, County Kerry

The first thing to be done on getting to Derrynane is to fall on one's knees in gratitude for a safe arrival. The road from Sneem (or, in the other direction, from Cahirciveen) clings like a vine to bare rock, winding and twisting and providing views of marvellous distance, clarity and beauty at which the driver dare not look for a second. To take one's eye off the road in parts of this route is to indicate a strong desire for death.

Daniel O'Connell was brought up at this fine old farmhouse close to the shore of Derrynane Bay. Apart from absences at school (first at Fr Harrington's Academy at Cobh, then at St Omer and Douai in France), he and his brother Maurice spent their childhood at Derrynane House, the home of their childless uncle Muiris. As the two eldest of ten children, the old Irish custom of inter-family fosterage allowed these two boys to live with Muiris, known as 'Hunting Cap', the son of the merchant Donal Mor O'Connell. This was an important family, one of the few surviving clans of the Catholic Irish upper class. Daniel's aunt Eileen was the poet who, married to Art O'Leary, won her enduring place in Irish literature as the author of *Caoineadh Art Uí Laoghaire*. It is through Eileen's description of the people from whom she came that we can get some idea of the cultured background to O'Connell's youth – although it was well known even then that much of the family status had been built on nothing much more than successful smuggling.

Indeed there is something of the smugglers' cove about Derrynane. The road from Caherdaniel seems to lead deeper and deeper into woods, which are unexpected given the rocky headlands on all sides. Then a clearing provides a car park and a gravel path announces the house with its slated front and battlemented wing. The roofline to the front is pierced by those dormer windows which are so typical of the vernacular architecture of the area – although, to judge by the modern or remodelled houses all around, Kerry's planning authorities have no respect for the county's own particular house-building style.

The first house here was built in 1702 by Daniel's great-grandfather, John O'Connell. The south and east wings were built after O'Connell had inherited the property from Muiris in 1825. In effect he turned the house back to front, introducing narrow sash windows so that the view from the dining-room and drawing-room would be towards the long stretches of dunes, headland and sea. The woods cluster behind the house and must have been something of a problem to Derrynane's gardener James O'Shea, although they provide cool meandering walks for visitors and here and there open into glades and lawns.

The house is not grandiose yet gives the impression of a particular kind of elegance. A French kind, I

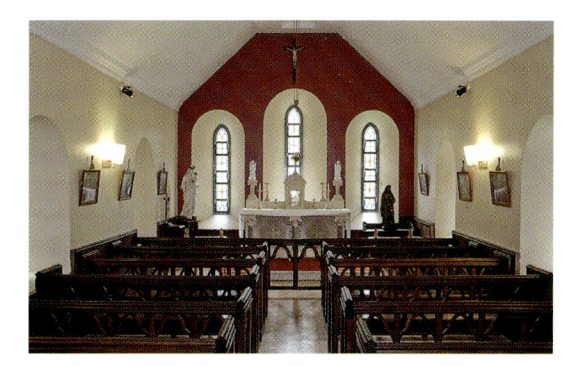

Left: *The portrait of Daniel O'Connell at Derrynane House is by J.P. Haverty.* Above right: *The oratory and (below) the chariot of gold in which O'Connell rode triumphantly through Dublin after his release from prison in 1844.* (images courtesy of the National Monuments Service, the Department of Arts, Heritage and the Gaeltacht)

think, and my guide Evelyn Breen reminds me that O'Connell's ideas of proportion and décor may have been influenced by his years in France. That style is light and graceful rather than ornate, and most of the furniture is that used by O'Connell and his wife Mary. The death-bed brought back from his collapse in Genoa still has its poignant significance, as do items such as the christening bowl in a brass-bound box which was made from the outer coffin in which O'Connell's body was brought home from Italy. Behind the door in one room is the rough wooden lectern which went with him to the meetings on which were built his successful campaign for Catholic Emancipation.

To stand here, to think of the battered old desk and its times, to think of the court cases, of the Doneraile Conspiracy, of his wealth and of his debts, and then to look out of the window and see the holiday people walking along the dunes, their dogs electric with the hope of rabbits: this is to find oneself strangely in touch with the past and to sense its compelling relevance to the Ireland of today. This facility enhances Derrynane as a tourism venue but also emphasises the care with which the different elements of the whole operation – gardens, guides, display and refreshments – function together.

The shared, relaxed and knowledgeable competence is as welcoming to the casual visitor as it is helpful to those who come, as many do, seeking that sense of contact with an extraordinary Irishman who never turned his back on this beautiful, exhilarating and cherished demesne. ♣

Derrynane National Historic Park is in the care of the Office of Public Works.

Derrynane House, Caherdaniel, County Kerry.
Tel: 066 947 5113   www.derrynane.com

Desmond Castle

Adare, County Limerick

If ever a village needed a bypass then it is Adare, an ancient ford over the River Maigue and a hub for major routes through Kerry, Limerick and Galway. It is shaking to its foundations. Yet with its embarrassing wealth of priories and abbeys and that picture-postcard row of cottages with overflowing gardens, it's as if Adare spreads an aura of taste and environmental sensitivity all over its neighbourhood.

Something of this stemmed from the Quins at Adare Manor, especially when the family took on the surname Wyndham Quin and later the title of Earls of Dunraven. As 'improving' landlords, through several generations the Dunravens have had a lasting influence on the whole district and, even when the international sporting spotlight falls on the manor – which the family sold in the 1980s – and its golf course, there is a sense that this fame emanates from much more than the demesne itself.

Modern Adare began in the early thirteenth century with the arrival of the Norman knight Geoffrey de Marisco. Perhaps there was already a fortification near the ford where de Marisco, funded by Henry III, began to build, but certainly what is there now signals the evolution, and gradual dominance, of the great FitzGerald clan as it swept its way through the history of the south of Ireland from Kildare to Kerry. That clan divided itself into the Earls of Kildare and the Earls of Desmond, and it is with the fortunes of the Desmonds that the castle buildings rose up along the banks of the Maigue and, with the final help of Oliver Cromwell, fell.

Now restored by the Office of Public Works, the castle could be said to be one in a Desmond chain of Newcastle, Askeaton and Adare. It is part of a linked plan of restoration and conservation undertaken by the OPW in which Newcastle was first restored, now Adare, and the team is already working on Askeaton. Grellan Rourke is the senior conservation architect on this project and, although I resist his invitation to inspect the inner mechanisms of the portcullis suspended above the main gate, it is impossible to deny his enthusiasm for a vast chapter of Irish history revealed through the rescue of this castle.

When the Dunravens left Adare Manor they offered the castle and its surrounding parkland to the OPW, which regarded it as one of the most important sites in Limerick, a ruin with a gentle majesty. Everything that has been exposed has a historical and archaeological coherence: the ancient yew trees in the circular courtyard, the steps set into the walls to reach the battlements which gird the entire enclosure, the high keep set within its own walled precinct, the two great halls with their service buildings, ovens, wells and polished windows looking on to the river. Grellan Rourke explains the defensive purposes of much of this design, the way in which

A vast chronicle of Irish history is revealed through the rescue of Desmond, or Adare, Castle. (image courtesy of the National Monuments Service, Department of Arts, Heritage and the Gaeltacht)

the main gatehouse would lead on to inner gates, and how different elements of the surviving building succeeded one another from the thirteenth to the fifteenth centuries.

The sense of discovery adds to the visual and atmospheric excitement of the place as we see where the moat continues inside the curtain wall, where the passages gave access to towers and ramparts and vaulted undercrofts, where the garderobes or lavatories were, how the loopholes and arrow-slits could be reached and how the square slots in the walls show the mighty dimensions of the timber joists holding up the floors. Niches in the arched gateways explain the technology of medieval security, how the drawbridge was operated through weights and balances and how doors and gates were barred from wall to wall. There would have been domestic timber houses and sheds sheltering people and animals within the enclosure, and at the riverside there is evidence of a little quay to make use of the tidal waterway.

The OPW is adept at finding bushels under which to hide its lights, so we may not always appreciate the way in which an achievement of this kind is not just a recovery of what was almost lost but is a gift to the nation of our own history. The story may be told in stone, place by place as in chapter by chapter. Askeaton on the Deel was the last home of Gerald, 14th Earl of Desmond, Newcastle and Adare among his many refuges and gathering-places. Now the high road to Tralee passes the gatehouse through which he and his countess must have ridden long ago, exits and entrances recaptured here in the towers in which the Desmonds must once have felt invincible. ♣

Desmond Castle,
Adare,
County Limerick
Adare Heritage Centre: 061 396666
info@adareheritagecentre.ie

Dromana House

Cappoquin, County Waterford

In the kitchen at Dromana the talk is of bailiffs and beats as Nicholas Grubb turns the pages of a logbook recording former events at this ancient house on the Blackwater. Now that Nicholas and his wife Barbara have moved in with Barbara's mother, Emily Villiers-Stuart, fishing is becoming an important part of life here once again. 'What we are doing is building on what we've got,' explains Barbara Grubb, 'and in our long-term plans fishing will be one of Dromana's attractions for visitors, along with the rods we can provide at Ballyduff.'

This is Dromana reborn. Renewal is the theme, with rental accommodation elegantly fitted into one end of what is now a long rather than a large

OPPOSITE: *Emily Villiers-Stuart and her daughter, Barbara Grubb, at Dromana House.* ABOVE: *The house on its crag over the wooded bastion on the Blackwater.* BELOW: *The Hindu-Gothic bridge (right), built to celebrate a Villiers-Stuart marriage.*

house. When visitors come, they can ramble through 600 acres of woodland outside the door or find a nook in the 30 acres of lawn and shrubberies and winding paths. They can walk to one of Ireland's most attractive villages at Villierstown, or turn left to wander down to the ceremonial Hindu-Gothic gateway built over the Finisk River to celebrate the marriage of Lord Villiers-Stuart to Pauline Ott (even the family portraits hint that this was a marriage made in haste and repented at leisure).

Dromana was a mainly Georgian mansion when Emily married her late husband, James Villiers-Stuart. The first Dromana began in 1215 with the ancestors of the FitzGerald Earls of Desmond. Preserved with dedication by James Villiers-Stuart, the archive of 16,000 items now at University College Cork (thanks to the Australian entrepreneur and philanthropist John FitzGerald) includes records dating from 1400. James Villiers-Stuart was a child of Dromana, growing up here when it still contained its vast ballroom and

DROMANA HOUSE   III

ABOVE: *The floor of Dromana House's drawing-room includes timbers from the old bridge in Waterford city.* BELOW: *The sitting-room in one of the self-catering apartments.* (images courtesy of Bill Flynn)

of the Decies for, as the tablet inside announces, the accommodation of his mountain tenants. This was Henry Villiers-Stuart, commemorating his victory as the parliamentary candidate supporting Catholic Emancipation in 1826.

At Dromana we stand under the portraits of the Grandisons, of the Villiers-Stuarts, of that famous Countess of Desmond who fell from a cherry tree at the age of 140. Here is the serene sitting-room where Lord Barrymore shot himself after gambling away his estate in his last game of cards. We haven't even mentioned Barbara Villiers, Duchess of Cleveland as a result of her long reign as mistress of Charles II.

'We are only tenants for life,' says Barbara Grubb, walking into the drawing-room where the floor contains timber planks from the old bridge in Waterford, while Emily remembers that the silk curtains of the boudoir were bought at the auction of Dorchester House in London before it became the Dorchester Hotel. There aren't many houses in Ireland in which you can stand on the Waterford Bridge and admire the curtains of Dorchester House.

There's an account of the Battle of Affane down below the bridge. When the Butler Earl of Ormond defeated the Earl of Desmond there in 1565, the injured Desmond was borne from the field on a litter held high by the Ormond troops. As a jeering soldier shouted: 'Where now is the mighty Earl of Desmond?' the reply came from the litter: 'Where but in his proper place, on the necks of the Butlers!'

Oh well, it's only reportage, and they all came to a sticky end. But the woods still shadow the river on either side. A boat purrs up to the slip and, as we wave from the great bastion, medieval Ireland seems somewhere just beyond the ferry-woman's cottage on the shore. ♣

Dromana House,
Cappoquin, County Waterford
Tel: 086 8186305

when the grounds included coach houses, stables and kennelling for the hounds of the West Waterford Hunt. But both his parents died while he was still a minor and the trustees sold the farmlands to the Land Commission. Trained in estate management but now with nothing to manage, James moved with his wife and family to work elsewhere and the house was taken over by a relative who eventually had the entire Georgian section removed.

The Dromana to which James and Emily returned thirty years later is a Jacobean manor and guided by Emily, a tour of the house provokes a suspicion that if you take a wrong turn you may end up in the Blackwater, surging immediately beneath the crag on which the house was built. To the north the Knockmealdown Mountains curve into the further slopes of the Galtees and the Comeraghs loom to the east. Downstream there is a glimpse of the pier at Villierstown and further down again, near Aglish, is An Túr, the church of St Patrick in the Drumm Hills. Approached by a rising double avenue of splendid beeches, the church, simple and sturdy, is no relic but a place of active worship built by Lord Stuart

Dún na Séad

Baltimore, County Cork

The ruins of the castle, on the summit of a lofty rock over the pier, and commanding every part of the harbour, are extensive and beautifully picturesque.

That description by Samuel Lewis in his *Topographical Dictionary of Ireland* still applies to Dún na Séad, with the exception of one word: 'ruins'. Instead Bernadette and Patrick McCarthy have restored this old castle as their home and as a tourist attraction for Baltimore. It had been a ruin for 350 years; the MacCarthys can trace the long trail of ownership to the present day.

Baltimore, with its harbour and rich fishing grounds, was originally an O'Driscoll holding. The Irish were remarkably nasty to one another when they only had each other to fight and, although the first castle here is that of the Norman adventurer Sleynie in 1215, the most dramatic events at Dún na Séad seem to have taken place in the fourteenth century. By then Sleynie was gone and the O'Driscolls had ousted the usurping MacCarthys.

According to James N. Healy's *The Castles of County Cork*, the rivalry between Baltimore and Waterford arising from claims to fishing rights off the Munster coast took a particularly drunken turn in 1537 when a Portuguese fleet on its way to Waterford with a cargo of wine was captured by the O'Driscolls. The retaliatory raid by the men of Waterford brought about not only the destruction of castles, forts and friaries in the harbour but it would be nearly another hundred years before this legendary competition in deception and avarice took its most famous toll on Baltimore. In the meantime the rebuilt Dún na Séad was surrendered to the Crown forces after the Battle of Kinsale. However, its proprietor Fineen O'Driscoll somehow managed to hold on to the fortress until he ran into a complicated series of arrangements, of which the main beneficiary was Sir Walter Coppinger.

There is a thread of history and folklore uniting these west Cork names, properties and families which seems to merge in a gory narrative of agreement, deceit, ambush, arson, pillage and siege. Visiting Dún na Séad today as the evening darkens and the sea glistens beyond its rim of coastal lights, it's hard to resist the insistent rhythms and imagery of Thomas Davis:

> *So still the night, these two long barques*
> *round Dunashed that glide*
> *Must trust their oars, methinks not few,*
> *against the ebbing tide.*

As it happened on that night in 1631 the barques were guided into Baltimore by a Waterford skipper (subsequently hanged for this crime); the Algerians aboard raided the village and kidnapped 200 of the

ABOVE: *A light touch allows medieval resonances in the living-room at Dún na Séad.* RIGHT: *Bernadette McCarthy and the family's dog, Rí.* (images courtesy of the *Irish Examiner*)

English settlers brought in twenty years earlier by Sir Thomas Crooke. Only two of them were ever to return to Ireland. Thomas Davis, in 'The Sack of Baltimore', imagines, probably with some accuracy, their eventual fate.

One might think that resonances of this kind must now be far from Dún na Séad, given that its well-polished floors and well-chosen furniture with their light touch of the medieval speak clearly of family life. Yet the display of armoury above one of the two fireplaces in the great hall reminds us that in a census taken in the sixteenth century MacCarthy of Carbery had under his command sixty horsemen, eighty gallowglasses and 2,000 kern soldiers. High on a beam is a gallowglass sword, a massive weapon suggesting the need for mighty muscle power if it were to be efficiently wielded. Eighty of those would be something to be avoided, unless, perhaps, one had ninety on the other side.

It was in 1997 that Bernadette and Patrick decided to tackle Dún na Séad. It took eight years and five architects to get it right, from the gallery in the roof space to the downstairs bedrooms, from archaeological surveys to plumbing, from conservation to a modern kitchen and room for the four children and the large dog. 'It's not guesswork', explains Bernadette, a language teacher and historian. 'The building gave us the answer at each stage; for example, the gable ends were intact, so that gave us the pitch of the roof, the remaining corbels inside showed the ceiling height, and the old lime mortar left traces on the walls, so that's what we used too.' Authenticity matters to Bernadette in her involvement in local campaigns such as the heritage trail created to mark significant features of the village. Baltimore is a place offering serenity, adventure and beauty as well as the fascinating history of which Dún na Séad is still a part.

Dún na Séad,
Baltimore, County Cork
Tel: 028 20735

AT HOME IN IRELAND

Dunbrody Country House

Arthurstown, County Wexford

The December night seems to have come down too quickly, yet, as the signposts drift past, history lurks in the names of the crossroads and junctions: Bannow, Shelmalier, Duncannon, Hook Head, Wellington Bridge and, at last, Arthurstown and the sharp turn into the avenue for Dunbrody House, where the lights shimmer through the dark.

The belated afternoon tea is brought to my suite in Wedgewood china; an orchid spray decorates the table, the bed is bolstered like a galleon and in the bathroom a fleecy robe is warming against the towel rail. And on the edge of the bath sits a bright yellow plastic duck. It is this mixing of elegance, warmth and fun which makes Dunbrody House such an experience, although proprietor Kevin Dundon might not thank me for not including immediately his achievements in the dining-room. But I'm getting to it, after a detour to chat with Catherine Dundon in the sitting-room.

It's no surprise that Dunbrody is in Ireland's prestigious *Blue Book*, even though Catherine (from Dalkey) and Kevin (from Malahide) only found the house in 1996. But their approach to any challenge can be gauged from the fact that, although they began work on the house in February 1997, they were able to open for business – beginning with the restaurant and five guest bedrooms – in May of that year. With Kevin a certified *chef de cuisine* and Catherine's job as export sales manager for the Boyne Valley group, together they made up the most expensive elements of a hotel organisation – chef and manager.

'There were some things we had to do immediately, like getting in a good kitchen and a good heating system, and eventually we also rebuilt the wing which had been demolished years before, when the house had more or less been turned back to front.' So settled is the atmosphere now that the change to a nineteen-bedroom country house hotel seems almost imperceptible. The Dundons and their dedicated staff have got it right. They used local labour as much as possible, overseen by builder Seamus Howlin, so everyone in the neighbourhood knew what was going on. They are also blessed with a housekeeper whose mother and grandmother had worked for the Chichester family, previous owners of the house.

Situated in a wooded estate close to the sea and bordered by the lovely estuary of the river Suir, Dunbrody Park was built first for Lord Templemore in or around 1860. The Chichester–Templemore estates included Dunbrody Abbey at the other side of Ballyhack. The Chichesters, Earls of Donegall, inherited the Itchingham estates through marriage and began to build Dunbrody Park in the early nineteenth century. Lord Spencer Churchill, third son of the Marquess of Donegall, was the first of the family to live in the original house here, at a time when

A combination of grace and practicality gives Dunbrody Country House Hotel immense personality. The attractions of Dunbrody are enhanced by a sympathetic sense of style. (images courtesy of Ireland's Blue Book)

his family owned more than 11,000 acres of County Wexford. Dermot R.C. Chichester, 7th Marquess of Donegall, still lives on the Dunbrody estate.

Alterations to the house in the last couple of centuries included those by Lady Templemore, who had lived in France and who introduced the long façade of French doors opening into the formal gardens. This and other changes give the house immense personality and its combination of grace and practicality has been enhanced by the colour schemes, fabrics and furniture and a sympathetic sense of style. 'We're serious about the quality we offer,' says Kevin as we walk the land through the morning fog. 'We didn't come in with lots of money and blitz the place but went from room to room. We got revenue going through the restaurant, but the really hard work on the house has been done with the help of our families and of our fantastic staff and, although it has been very hard work, we're not phased by any of it.'

Instead they are making their mark: already the organic kitchen garden is supplying seasonal fruit and vegetables, already the kitchen is winning international as well as national accolades. Taking up part of the former ballroom, the dining-room in winter is a red-walled cocoon of warmth and plenty, with those long windows looking out over lawns and fields and eventually the sea. While this is not the place to go on about the menu or wine list, I can't help but remember dining on the parcel of smoked salmon with crème fraîche topped with a scallop and forest mushroom spring roll, followed by the roast loin of bacon on a bed of braised cabbage leaves with a potato cake, followed by raspberry torte. And as for breakfast! Oh – just go to Dunbrody.

The 7th Marquess of Donegall died in April 2007.

Dunbrody Country House Hotel,
Arthurstown, County Wexford
Tel: 051 389600

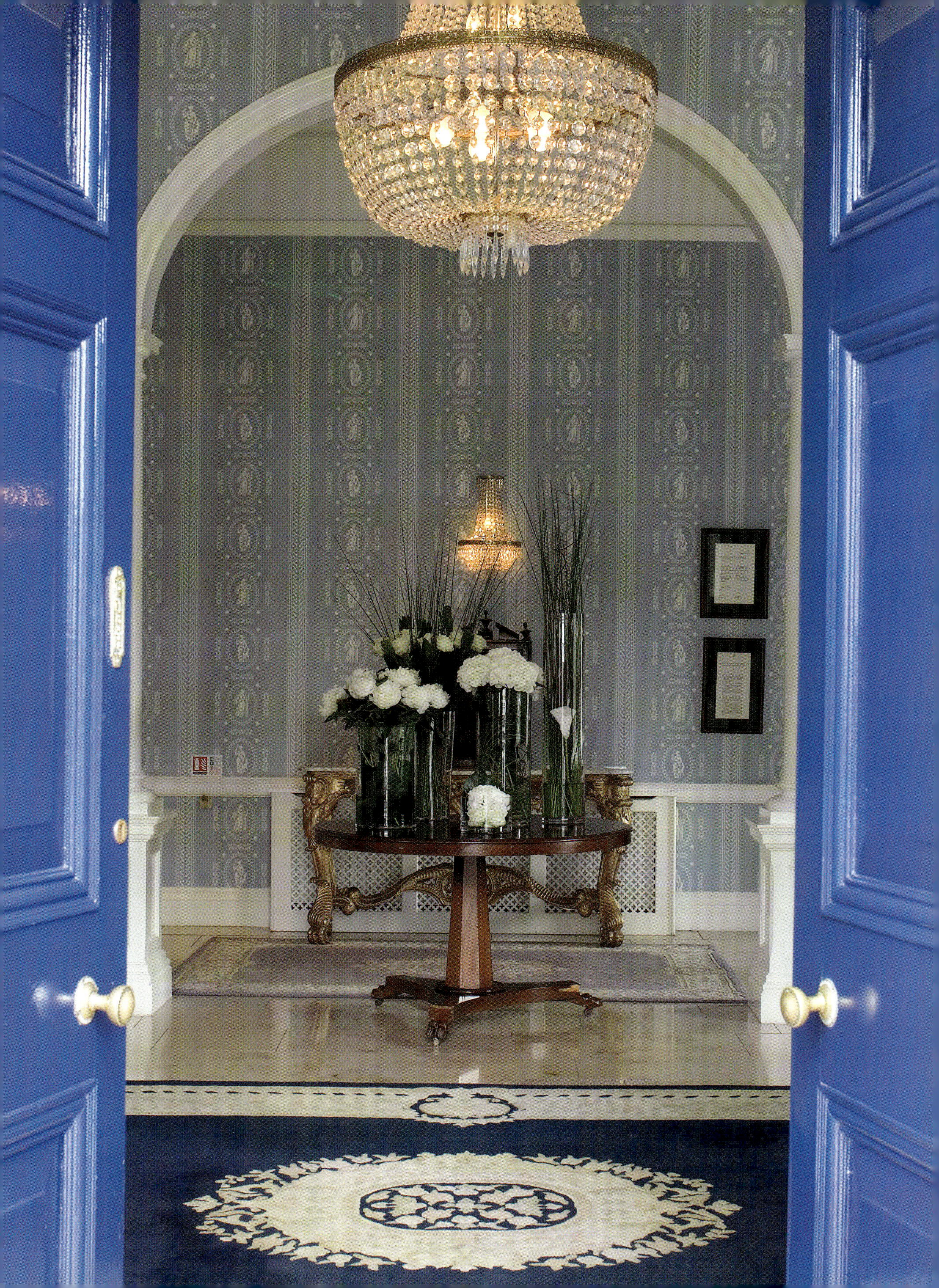

Dysert

Ardmore, County Waterford

'When we came it was nothing like it is now; there was nothing here but the bungalow, a windswept bare hill, red-hot pokers and a hebe hedge.' Virginia Brownlow stands on a flagged terrace which leads on to another slightly higher terrace above the sea, with steps at the side which lead on to another terrace again, which is merely an overture to yet another terrace hidden among the sheltering trees and shrubs. 'My mother thought it would be a great place for us to grow up – and it certainly was.'

Virginia is remembering the arrival of her sister Sally, herself and her mother Molly Keane at the small house in Ardmore in 1950. For this is Dysert, the place in which, as Sally Phipps recalls, Molly Keane spent many hours writing, 'sometimes furiously, sometimes happily, always diligently and frequently with brilliant results'. Both sisters hope that some residue of that working life remains in this delightful house so that it may find a new life as a writers' retreat. 'It's a house that has to earn its living now, but I think it's a place which will foster creativity.'

Born Mary Nesta Skrine, Molly had been a writer when she met Bobby Keane of Cappoquin, having published her first novel at the age of seventeen; the proceeds went to fund her social life, in which, paradoxically, to be known as a writer at all would mean exclusion. That's why the early pseudonym 'M.J. Farrell' was born, the name seen over a pub on her way home from a hunt. The young Molly was something of a free spirit, no easy attribute given her background of the big house, the hunting field and hunt balls. These were the stuff from which she wrote her novels and wove the plays which were performed in London and usually directed by Sir John Gielgud.

Her married life with Bobby and her two daughters was settled at Belleville, near Cappoquin, but she left that house after Bobby's early death. That shock and sadness (he was only thirty-six), and the realisation that her kind of social comedy was out of step with the new theatrical generation of 'angry young men', meant that she laid down her pen. 'But she came from the big house,' says Virginia, 'so she did big house things: she loved hospitality, she was keenly interested in people, she was a talented home-maker – really, it was wonderful growing up here.'

Transforming this house was how, without writing, she expressed what Sally describes as her complex, generous and paradoxical personality. 'When someone asked her later what she might have done if she had not been a writer, she replied that she would have been a housewife – and that she would much rather have been one anyway but that it didn't pay.'

Molly lived at Dysert for nearly fifty years and Virginia Brownlow remembers the people who worked with her mother to create this atmosphere of

A place which will foster creativity, Dysert is a house made by a writer: everything has been worked out. (images courtesy of Deborah Trentham)

hospitality. 'Jack O'Brien wrote the plans on the back of a cigarette packet,' says Virginia. 'He was an artisan builder and was assisted by his sons, and together they did all the stonework, digging out the soil which was then barrowed out; I was about four then and I got to ride home in the empty wheelbarrow.' The same Jack O'Brien copied the elegant timber fireplace in the sitting-room from a sketch of a fireplace in Clonmel; the bookcases too were copied – there are well-filled bookcases all over the house – and when we go downstairs Jack O'Brien's name is invoked once again for the greenhouse and the outdoor safe built into the rock outside the kitchen door. Indoors the thick curtains of double-lined ticking are the work of Josie Morrissey, responsible for all the curtaining and upholstery, for clothing the children when they were young and later for assisting Virginia in the management of the house.

In Molly's bedroom a butterfly casts a tiny shadow on the white walls. It's a house made by a writer: everything was worked out, the trees screening the plot of mobile homes at the distant beach and yet opening out to frame the vista of the bay, the wave-lapped headlands, the village roofs. Dysert holds traces too of its many noted guests. The actress Peggy Ashcroft was the visiting friend who discovered the manuscript of *Good Behaviour* in 1980 and whose encouragement spurred Molly out of her relative obscurity and reminded the world of the presence of a fine, acerbic and entertaining writer. ♣

Tel: 086 4071811 or
(UK) 0044 (0) 2075863479
www.dysert.co.uk

Enniscoe House

Castlehill, Ballina, County Mayo

Driving away from Enniscoe I stop and look back along the avenue. Behind the woods rise the slopes of Mount Nephin. In front lies Loch Conn. It is no wonder that this was once known as Prospect House, an architectural descendant of the fortified mansion built on the shore of the lake some time in the seventeenth century by the Jackson family. And prospect, apart from the view, is still one of the elements of what has in recent years become something best described as a small business community, emulating the activity which once would have been created by any self-respecting and self-sustaining country house in Ireland.

Enniscoe was, and remains, a relatively modest building, expressing the accepted architectural beauty of the later Georgian style. This has been both revealed and enhanced by Susan Kellett, whose mother came from this neighbourhood and who spent many a childhood summer at the family house near Pontoon.

OPPOSITE: *Enniscoe House is a classic Irish heritage house of medium size.* ABOVE: *The rare attributes of Enniscoe's earliest years are embellished by its soft-focus comforts.*

When Susan, a social worker, and her brother, a fine art specialist, came back to the rundown farm and house which had been the property of their father's late cousin, they decided to make the effort to keep it, without quite knowing what that effort would entail. But even allowing for the decline in farming along the western seaboard, Susan felt that there had to be a future for a house on a lake in the west of Ireland.

'Taking guests was the obvious way that the house could earn its keep, and also I'd had the experience of a few fishing parties and shooting groups,' says Susan, who now runs the property with her son Dj. 'And the house itself is so attractive: originally it was three storeys over basement, tall and narrow on towerhouse lines until the family wanted something a little grander. By the time that the Jacksons had become the Pratts, the two grand reception rooms, staircase

ENNISCOE HOUSE

hall and oval landing with its domed lantern had been added.'

Because the Famine bankrupted the family, there were very few later changes in what has been described as a classic Irish heritage house of medium size. So Enniscoe now offers its guests the rare attributes of its earliest years embellished by modern, soft-focus comfort; light, reflected from the lake, permeates the house like some mild interior sun. Meals follow the country tradition of gracious sufficiency, boosted to suit modern palates by a skilful kitchen staff.

At the time of her arrival (after the Pratts had become the Nicholsons) the Victorian gardens, says Susan, were not dead, merely sleeping. In 1996 they achieved recognition from the Great Gardens of Ireland restoration programme and, with that support and the help of FÁS and Meitheal Mhaigheo, Susan set about reclaiming the one-acre walled flower garden now in the care of head gardener Annette Maughan. Advised by architect Jeremy Williams, Susan also set about restoring the coachyard and farmyard buildings as several cottage-style apartments, now available on self-catering terms throughout the year.

And then there is the heritage centre behind the house and for many hundreds of people the place that makes Mayo the centre of the world. 'When I came back here, people were searching for something that might generate local employment,' remembers Susan, 'and we realised that as well as coming for the fishing and the walking people came to search for their family connections – invariably ending on the doorstep of the parish priest or rector. Our local society helped establish the Irish Family History Foundation, a research service which has become enormously significant.' Now the Mayo North Heritage Centre has taken on an independent life of its own. 'There was so much here to begin with. Church registers, in our case for twenty-nine parishes in Mayo, school roll books, census records and a great depth and range of local knowledge. We built a terrific database, and

Enniscoe. There had to be a future for a house on a lake in the west of Ireland. (images courtesy of Dj Kellett)

we can offer clients a service in which they can have complete confidence: it's much, much more than just a pretty certificate!'

Equally, Enniscoe is more than just a pretty house. It was along French Avenue, after all, that General Humbert marched his men away from Ballina in 1798. And yet, within the house itself, there are no intrusions. Life may be thundering away beyond the walls, but in these passages and light-filled rooms there is nothing to disturb the calm of a quiet country house living its productive life to the full.

Enniscoe House,
Castlehill, Ballina, County Mayo
Tel: 096 31112
E-mail: mail@enniscoe.com

Ennismore

Montenotte, Cork

Someone, someday is going to have to make an audit of what remains of the fine houses of Montenotte in Cork. To pass the great remaining gateways is to realise that this area is something of a continental shelf on which were perched the homes of the wealthy, a catalogue in stone of what was once Cork's élite. From here a few mighty generations surveyed their city, which in several cases has responded by annihilating all trace of them.

But not Ennismore, a house which has been given a new lease of life by the Dominicans. Up here, about 18 acres of the grounds are still rented out for corn, the protective timber still stands and the gardens, even in winter, glow under the caring hands of Brother Tom Casey. The Dominicans came here in 1952 when the estate was sold after the death of Mrs Helen Leycester, the last to live here of the family which built Ennismore between 1835 and 1837. William Leycester was a mayor of Cork when he built neighbouring Vosterburg, a house of considerable status; his son Joseph was also a mayor of Cork and moved a few yards uphill to build Ennismore. From here he could observe the comings and goings of the river port below, a matter of some importance given his prominent role in the foundation of the City of Cork Steam Packet Company, although the records suggest that in fact Ennismore was built for his son, William Wrixon Leycester.

Shipping was always a notoriously uncertain way of making a fortune and the house remained more modest than originally planned. Its façade (and the long, skylighted hall which is one of the main features of its interior) has a gently ornate, almost cottage-style design, decorated at one side with a wrought-iron tracery. To this the Dominicans were allowed to add modern buildings at the back, capacious enough to meet the demands of the popular retreat house. Ennismore was never going to be an easy house to adapt, but the Dominicans have kept its core identity intact, the main rooms retaining their fireplaces of green or white marble, the Bow Room its shuttered French windows giving on to the lawn from which signals from passing ships could be observed and answered, and the shipping bell in the farmyard which alerted the coachman to the approach of visitors from abroad.

Brother Tom Casey is not an easy man to track down. 'He's in the garden', the receptionists would reply, even on one of the coldest, wettest, dreariest days of the winter, darkening early, bitterly cold with a vengeful gusting rain. But Tom Casey is a man who believes he has been given 'a special grace' in being allowed to care for the gardens at Ennismore. As he walks the paths through the woodland, itemising the blossoming or fruiting or leaf-colour habits of the borders and the several fine old trees, naming and ageing the splendid specimens surviving from what must have been the very first gardens up here, from the warm brick walls and box-edged parterres to the arched gate into the 'wilderness' to the towering, full-skirted lime tree and the horse chestnut which Tom Casey, applying accepted ageing techniques, has dated as planted in 1690 (chestnuts it appears, first arrived in Ireland *circa* the end of the seventeenth century), from all of this to the alcoved brick-built shelter for the donkey which pulled the lawnmower – the ground is in Tom Casey's care.

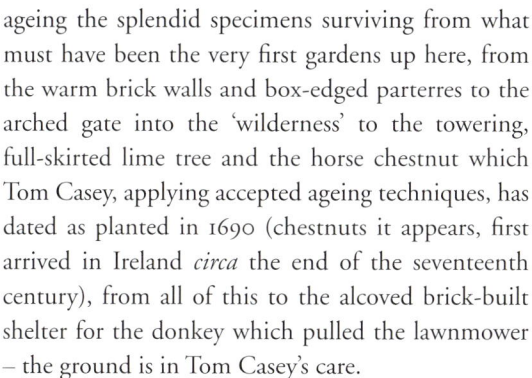

A Kerryman who played in the Kerry county final at nineteenth, he was brought up to work on the land. 'I like the work, it's been my life. At night I would go into fields I could name one by one, watching the badgers come out, hearing the last bird-calls. I can still do that here – weather is no hardship to me.' No hardship, because he can find continuity not only in the plants and trees brought back from

LEFT: *Brother Tom Casey in the greenhouse.* RIGHT: *The long hall with its skylights is one of the main interior features of Ennismore* (images courtesy of the *Irish Examiner*)

the many Leycester travels but in the newly revealed stone walls built, like the house, from the remains of an old church at Vosterburg: he says of this discovery that he stood there for a while and 'thought about the men who worked here long before my time … they watched the sun rise and set, heard the dawn chorus each passing spring and, perhaps, worked under the beautiful lime tree.' Just like himself.

The retreat ethos at Ennismore is based on a combination of environment and events examining the Christian tradition.

St Dominic's Retreat Centre,
Ennismore, Montenotte, Cork
Tel: 021 4502520

Fair Green Cottage

County Cork

The castles of east Cork are numerous and intriguing. Ightermurragh's gaunt ruin still hoists its Tudor chimney stacks into the sky near Ladysbridge. Beyond lies Castle Richard, a reminder that these level, coastal acres have been home to the Imokilly FitzGeralds, who left these fortified houses as their legacy.

It is in one of those ancient townlands that John Ahern and his wife Sue have created their home from the wreck of a derelict building. Fair Green Cottage was last inhabited as a card-school and before that was locally notorious as a Famine soup kitchen. When the scrub was cleared away, John found traces to explain an old map's depiction of six cottages and a house built in a semicircle and facing on to a hidden road. This, he thinks, must have been the original hamlet of Ballymacoda, for on the other side of the road stood Cooledera Castle, and a few hundred yards seaward is Ballykinealy, once the family holding of the eighteenth-century poet Piaras Mac Gerailt.

These were the names and places of John Ahern's childhood, names he carried with him when he left for London in 1960. It was in this very house – then owned by a tailor and quilter – that his uncle Tom Ahern served his apprenticeship before setting up his own tailoring business in Cork city. When Sue bought the land as a gift for John's fiftieth birthday, they created together this thick-walled, tiny-windowed, half-doored and deeply thatched cottage, snug as a fairytale and surrounded by lawn, field, orchard and rose-bowered fences.

Although Sue is a Londoner born and bred, she agreed to leave her work in the clothing industry when John decided to take early retirement and move back to Ireland. That meant three years in a mobile home under the cliff against which the cottage was built. Faith kept them going: faith in the integrity of the little house and faith also in John's own ability to fashion ceilings and shutters, dressers and casement windows, doors and lintels and timber flooring with his hands. In this he was helped by his brother and by what he thinks of as a family tradition. His father, after all, was a stonemason, and his uncles were, he says, 'all handy'. They were supported too by the enthusiasm of their two sons who, having listened to bedtime stories about Ballymacoda, found as young adults that the stories were true, the people in them real.

But here in the house the only real things were the walls and the fireplace. Two rooms downstairs form the kitchen (with a solid Austrian range) and living-room (with an old Cornish firebox and oven sitting into the original hearth); the ceilings are lined in tongue-and-groove, the floors are one-ton slates and, in the corner, the panelled, steeply pitched staircase leads to two bedrooms and a bathroom set deep under the eaves and created by raising the gables by

ABOVE: *John and Susan Ahern outside their thatched cottage at Ballymacoda and (right) Sadie in the cottage paddock.* (images courtesy of the *Irish Examiner*)

five feet. The walls were finished with distemper on stone, according to guidelines John picked up from the Society for the Protection of Ancient Buildings. The house is as dry as a bone, the gable walls three feet thick and heated by the ranges downstairs at each end, with the thatch, according to John, acting like an eiderdown.

Authenticity is always a challenge and there is something about the thatch which evokes not so much an Irish reference as, perhaps, an English one. 'It's the shaped eaves,' explains John, when I ask about the difference between this and the few other thatches in the vicinity. Thatching is not just a skill or an art: it's a whole other world. In this case the work was done by Trevor Dogherty, of The Thatch Company in Dungarvan, using Scottish reeds at the back and Turkish reeds at the front.

Scotland? Turkey? What's wrong with Irish reeds, I wonder, thinking of the bronze stretches near Youghal, or the pyramids drying on the banks of the Blackwater near Lismore. 'There aren't enough reed beds being managed, although in some places they are getting more attention now. The market is developing, but at the moment Irish reed is either too thick or too bent for roofing; it's not like long ago when there were sheaves left after the threshing – we even had to import the wheat reed for the skirts up there."

We look up at the embroidered roofline, at the deep flanks around the little windows, the thatch as thick outside as the walls within. This dream cotttage is a testament to an awareness of the old home-making crafts which have not quite disappeared. Cottages, like castles, can be a legacy too.

FAIR GREEN COTTAGE   127

Flemingstown House

Kilmallock, County Limerick

There are two reasons why I have to be very grateful to Imelda Sheedy-King. First, that she introduced me to a wonderful Irish farmhouse cheese and, second, that she didn't eat me without salt when I wondered what might bring people to Kilmallock. Produced by the Keatings at Clogheen, County Tipperary, the cheese is Bay Lough, a semi-soft unpasteurised product with a ripe, golden, Cheddar-like aroma and a lingering taste. Eaten with an apple tart in the sunlight of Imelda's kitchen, this seems to express all the very best of the fruits of the earth: Irish milk, Irish cheese, Irish apples and Irish artisan skills.

Imelda's home is the centre of a thriving farm now run by her family; the windows overlook paddocks, lawns and pastures under the hills which frame this valley, lying as it does between the Ballyhoura and the Galtee Mountains. Although the house itself has been restored and refurbished through the years,

ABOVE: *The old country furniture gleams as part of a true picture of Irish hospitality. Flemingstown is an honest-to-God farmhouse influenced by generations of people who understood comfort.*
(images courtesy of J.J. Mortell)

Flemingstown remains an honest-to-God farmhouse, solid and substantial and layered with the influence of generations of people who knew how to make a house comfortable.

I suspect that Imelda, who married Martin King after the death of her first husband Seamus Sheedy, has never known an idle hour in her existence. The old country furniture is polished and gleaming and, like the house itself, part of a true picture of Irish rural hospitality. The guest sitting-room is closely carpeted and has a big, well-stacked fireplace. Here and in the dining-room the hearths gleam with firedogs and brasses; old family photographs hold their place with prints and samplers and in a landing alcove an urn blazes with daffodils. Light from the fields spreads across the south-facing rooms; in the modern conservatory, stained glass by the late Bill Malone links the new with the old.

The rooms are enhanced by Imelda's own curtain-making (she uses interlining so thick as to be almost like sheepskin) and by her attention to detail in fabric and décor. Outside, the white-walled house is host to ivies and vines; inside, the fires hum, the beds have their electric blankets, there are concealed television sets and, in the arches which close the corridors, shelves of books and magazines.

As we talk about her dinner menus, her Galtee award for the best breakfast in Ireland and her designation as the 'Little Gem' winner for 2002/3 by the RAC, I dig eagerly into the Bay Lough cheese again. To justify indulgence at her table, she sends her guests to Cashel, to Blarney, to Killarney and Killaloe, to Bunratty and the Burren and to Annette O'Donnell's stables in the Glen of Aherlow. St Saviour's Dominican friary at Kilmallock, begun as a FitzGerald foundation in 1291, still has its choir, cloister garth and exquisitely carved thirteenth-century reticulated window. From this flat greensward around the friary, the loveliest sight is that of the steepled Gothic-Revival Catholic parish church of SS Peter and Paul, built in 1879. The broken outlines of the

FLEMINGSTOWN HOUSE

Church of Ireland collegiate parish church, also SS Peter and Paul, date, like the friary, from the thirteenth century. There is a belfry, built like a round tower, which is reputed to be of pre-Norman origin and, although the poet Seamus Ó Cinnéide lived in Kilmallock, it is another eighteenth-century poet, Andrias Mac Craith (known as An Mangaire Sugach), who is buried in this churchyard.

It was in 1600, at this church of SS Peter and Paul, that the FitzGeralds of Desmond ended their convulsive odyssey through the sixteenth century. Although James Fitzthomas FitzGerald had stayed aloof from the Desmond Rebellion of 1583, he joined Hugh O'Neill's campaign in 1598 and took the title of Earl of Desmond as if to replace the clan's lost leader. The English, and subsequently the Irish, dubbed him the 'Sugán' earl, a man of straw, and despite his command of 8,000 clansmen he was forced into hiding and eventually discovered here. He died in the Tower of London in 1608.

What a scene it must have been, that mustering of the English force that led to this place, that wandering away of the Irish followers, that lonely submission to a queen he would outlive by only five years but to whom, even at this point in his bewildering life, he would not betray his countrymen. Only the little river separates this ruined church from the ruins of St Saviour; over there, on the other side of the river, is the broken monument to Edmund FitzGibbon, the last of the legendary White Knights, the man who led Lord Carew to FitzGerald's hiding place at Kilmallock.

Flemingstown House,
Kilmallock, County Limerick
Tel: 063 98093
E-mail: info@flemingstown.com

Fortwilliam House

Lismore, County Waterford

As I close the bathroom door, the window rattles in the opposite wall and I feel a small mean thrill of relief: at least one little thing is askew in this otherwise impeccable house. Loyalty, love and cash, like a recipe for a Victorian marriage, are a rare enough architectural combination, but in its latest stage of life Fortwilliam House got an injection of all three together in the person of the late Ian Agnew, a London businessman devoted to fishing.

Not a man to do things by halves or even three-quarters, Ian Agnew restored this house from roof to basement, parkland to coachyards, with evangelical commitment and an eye for authenticity.

All is in order: the stone-floored basement corridor,

BELOW: *Fortwilliam was once the Irish residence of Bend'Or, 2nd Duke of Westminster, and his fourth wife, Nancy Sullivan from Glanmire, Cork.*

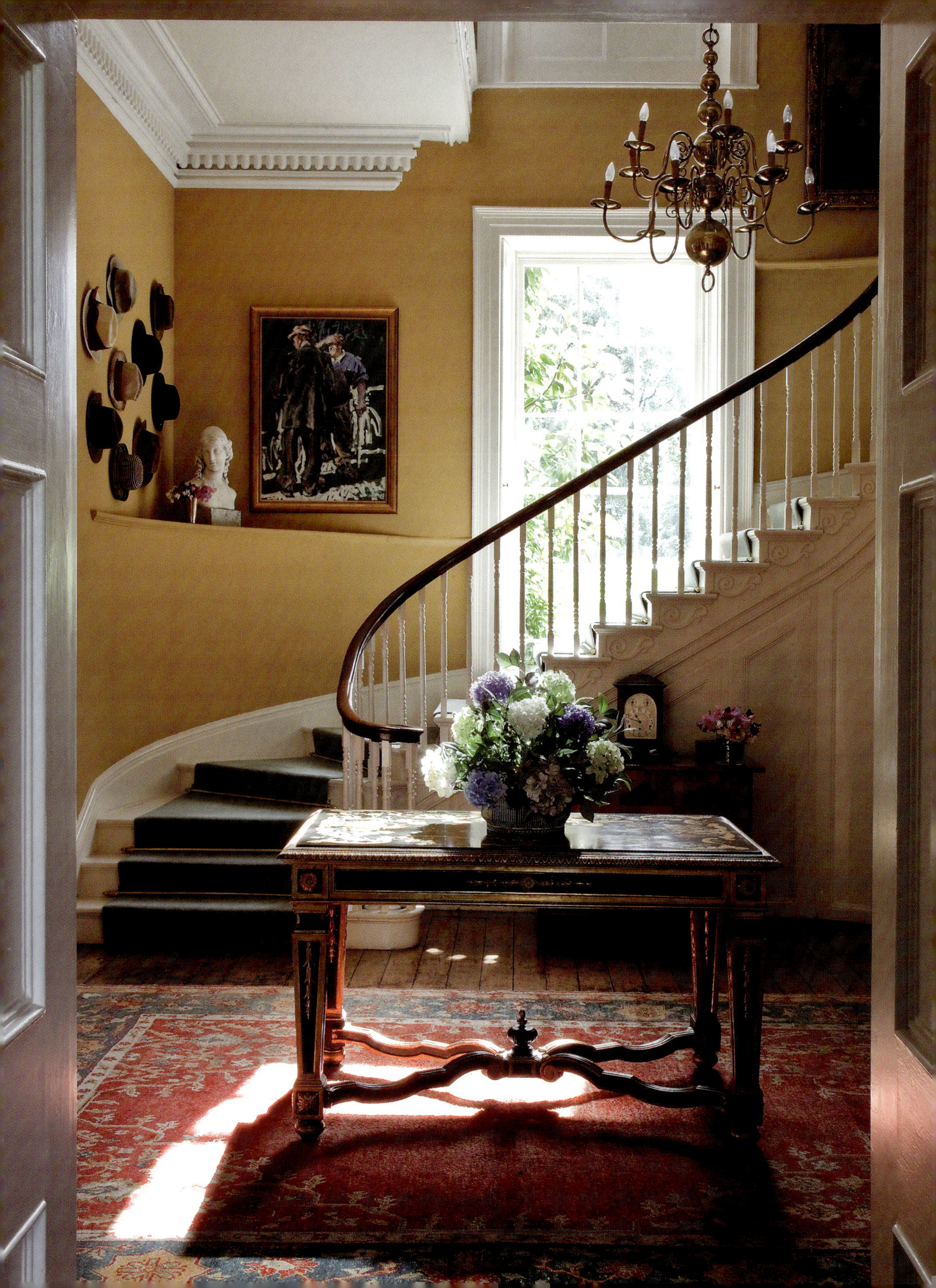

ABOVE: *The Louis XV gilded panelling distinguishes the drawing-room at Fortwilliam House.* BELOW: *The atmosphere of the dining-room has a quiet contemporary tone.*

the kitchen units made from the timber of fallen trees in the parkland, the Louis XV gilding and panelling in the drawing-room, the décor echoing the Georgian and early Victorian provenance of the house, the clean curved sweep of the cantilevered staircase, the farmyard down the avenue with its blue-painted numbered looseboxes, its lambing sheds, its farmhouse and the long track of the gallops, the paths through the riverside woodland leading to the garden framed in walls of red brick and presided over by a flock of chauvinistic hens. In summer the greenhouses are packed with grapes and sweet peas; from the north-facing windows of the house the inches, where the Blackwater floods from time to time, are mown by sheep, and the 400 acres of farmland are managed productively for both grazing and tillage.

'It's not a grand house,' says Sara Agnew, 'it's what I call a baby grand.' Yet, within and without, all the proportions are well defined in this design by the brothers James and George Richard Pain. Although Sara and her family keep Fortwilliam as a property available for private rentals, it does have its public moments, including the annual West Waterford pony camp. Because Sara, a jewellery and textile artist with a special interest in the tribal narrative embroidery

FORTWILLIAM HOUSE   133

of Gudjarat, is also a painter, and because the size of Fortwilliam makes it a suitable depository for the pictorial residue of other family homes, a quiet contemporary hum lightens the air.

Built in 1836 for John Bowen Gumbleton of a family of significant landowners in west Waterford since 1695, the house can be traced through the generations to the sale in 1932 to Patrick Dunne of Dungarvan. After that, it had been leased to tenants including Adele Astaire, widow of Lord Charles Cavendish of Lismore. When Bend'Or, 2nd Duke of Westminster, married Nancy Sullivan of Glanmire as his fourth and final wife in 1947, Fortwilliam became their Irish residence. Bend'Or was named for his grandfather's favourite racehorse and Nancy was later renowned as the owner of Arkle. They bought the property with its furniture, effects, Hereford herd and farm stock for £10,000, redecorated it as a seasonal home (they had several others) and kept it until Bend'Or's death in 1956.

Sara Agnew believes the elaborately floral French gilding and painted medallions in the drawing-room were installed by the Westminsters, who are also thought to have panelled the dining room with wood from the duke's yacht. Then came the Drummond-Wolffs from America, and after them Mr and Mrs Murray Mitchell. 'When I arrived, all the hard work had been done on the house,' remembers Sara. 'That meant that Ian and I had the greatest fun together, finding furniture, discovering things, going all over the country. He had already engaged Daphne Daunt in Cork to choose the interior finishes, from curtains and carpets to wallpaper and paint, and the result combines the pristine with the traditional.'

Her own sturdy paintings of local events sit happily here with the work of other Irish artists. Fortwilliam may be a house which gives up its secrets slowly, but Sara says now that she and Ian were 'incredibly happy' here in this friendly house. She is not morbid, and to see Ian's beloved rods stacked in an angle of the hall is only to realise that his is a real, enlivening and enabling presence still. 'He was mad about fishing and saw the house advertised in *Country Life* while in the dentist's waiting-room. A couple of years later he was fishing in Waterford and asked the ghillie if the house was still for sale. It was. That was one of those amazing moments, the moment that transformed his life.' And the life of Fortwilliam too. ♣

Information on Fortwilliam Fishery is at info@fortwilliamfishing.net
Tel: 087 8292077

'Not a grand house. But a baby grand.' (images courtesy of James Fennell)

Foxmount Country House

County Waterford

Foxmount Farm is a haven of rural tranquillity and one should expect nothing less, given that this is the home of Margaret Kent, who has become the standard-bearer for the reputation of farmhouse hospitality in Ireland. With its back to the farmyard and to the long kitchen garden, creeper-clad Foxmount looks across a close-cut lawn and blossoming shrubbery to verdant fields roamed by a couple of glossy horses and shaded by copper beeches, oaks and limes.

Picture perfect, in fact. Recognising it as a lovely place to stay, I also realise that it must be a lovely place to live. And that's how it began: a lovely place to live for Margaret and her farmer husband David, a lovely place in which to bring up their three children, and now a lovely place to share with guests who appreciate what the Kents offer. When David and Margaret first came to this house as a young newly-married couple, it was in a condition which David now describes as 'absolutely frightening'. In 1960, when it was bought, no one had lived in it since 1947. There was no ceiling in the drawing-room, no fireplace, yet even when they had to live in the two habitable rooms they knew that this was going to be a fine family home once, as Margaret says, 'we had put manners on it'.

Through the years of this transformation, Margaret grew in confidence from the early days when she apologised to guests for 'only having free-range eggs!' At that time 80 per cent of her business was Irish, her emphasis was on a farm holiday and the Kents offered ponies and tennis and lots of space for play. 'Our family enjoyed all that and so did we, and now we have those visiting children coming back here with children of their own.'

But times change, and Margaret decided to change with them. Supported by David and their children and by her long-term housekeeper, farm staff and the gardener, she upgraded with purpose and retained not just her existing guest list but expanded it.

Although she is now widely regarded as a mentor, Margaret admits to mentors of her own. There is Myrtle Allen, who 'made it fashionable to be of the country'; there is Darina Allen, who taught a new generation how to do country things. But those things – scones and homemade jams and bread and hand-picked fresh fruit – were all the ordinary stuff of life to Margaret. And so it is to Monica Sheridan that she gives the greatest credit: as a guest at Foxmount, Monica encouraged her, as she encouraged so many women throughout the country, making them proud of what they had to offer. A clever cook herself, Margaret says also that she retained so much from her own mother, a farmer's wife who reared thirteen children and still found time to make grape chutney.

'Monica told me just to keep doing what I was doing, because what's good and fresh and the way

At Foxmount Country House, years of transformation have resulted in a haven of rural activity and tranquillity. (images courtesy of Mrs M. Kent)

it's used can never change. Here we have our own beef, our own lamb, fish from the harbour and the river, fruit and vegetables from the garden and local cheeses. But there's still a gap, people are still not confident enough to feel these are good things in themselves; they're holding courses now on how to be friendly, how to be hospitable! I ask myself – what are we doing? Where are we going?'

If Margaret ever asked herself that question, she found the answer quickly. More than thirty years ago she realised what she was good at and is sticking with it. Her experience, coupled with innate taste, has led her to help others. She has a special kind of gentle authority, and she makes adaptation look not just possible, but easy. Foxmount itself has a lot to do with this. It is a house with a history, beginning, they think, in 1741.

Generations of Waterford grandees and farmers, through a lease of lives renewable forever for the town and lands of Cross in the Barony of Gaultier, through Woodstown House, the Wilkinsons, the Maddys and the Lynns, finally reach the marriage of Eleanor Lynn to William Maine Fox in 1807. They emigrated to America in 1832, followed by their son Mathew. But Foxmount survived until it came into the remarkable hands of David Kent and his wife Margaret. ♣

Foxmount Country House,
Passage East Road, Waterford
Tel: 051 874308

Frewin

Ramelton, County Donegal

Regina Coyle isn't afraid of white. In my bedroom, walls, ceiling, windows, lamps, both of the two fireplaces, all the bed linen and coverlet are in white. A carpet of ecru wool, a fern in the black coal bucket, the poppy-strewn throws on the armchairs and the rattan day-bed are the only colours. Were it not for the book-packed study downstairs, Thomas Coyle's promise of a visit to his Dun, Tory, Dexter and Moiled cows and the glimpsed suggestions that the town of Ramelton in Donegal is somewhere to be savoured, I might well stay as long as possible in this sunny room overlooking Frewin's lawn and shrubbery.

However, Regina explains that it was Thomas who was responsible for the restoration and décor of this friendly and distinguished old rectory. As we talk about conservation and preservation in Donegal, I mention that on the way here I took a detour around Fanad Head, and found near the lighthouse a beautifully restored thatched cottage which put to shame all the largely deserted modern holiday homes on the peninsula. This cottage too was the handiwork of Thomas Coyle, who has made specialist building and reconstruction his livelihood. Frewin itself is predictable in design but keeps on springing surprises. When the pebble-dash façade was stripped back, the stonework was revealed with brick trims and marked string courses. Its shape too extends into an unexpected two-storey bow and a couple of unusual windows are thrown in as a kind of architectural diversion.

It's the kind of thing, I realise, which delights Thomas Coyle's heart, although Regina must have quailed a little during the four and a half years it took to achieve the finish they wanted. 'He's the one with the flair for design and colour and texture and craftsmanship – and for seeing what a building is really like or really could become.' She accepts responsibility for the bed linen, for the bowl of old roses which scent my room and for the dressing-table dish of fruit complete with napkin and knife.

She's in charge of the kitchen too. The next morning we join the mob at the country market in Ramelton and I see the lengths to which she goes to be sure of her free-range eggs and her garden vegetables. She's also the one who manages the hospitality, with the inviting drawing-room an alternative to the study (fires, a tray of tea and homemade biscuits for arriving guests, and all those books). Regina moved around Ireland during her childhood as her parents worked with the Vocational Education scheme. Four years were spent in Letterkenny and it was when she went back to work in the town some time later that she met Thomas, a farmer's son who had come home to his native Ramelton from a stint in Australia. Thomas did a lot of stints; his career has taken him from England to Austria with America somewhere in-between.

Were it not for Frewin, I might never have heard of Ramelton, even though the shores of Lough Swilly on which Ramelton has grown always retained an elusive historic glamour. A thriving town beautifully situated on the bank of an inlet of Lough Swilly, when freight was landed here for transport into the hinterland, Ramelton supported no fewer than nine churches, even though the population is said never to have exceeded about 1,500. One of the town's most famous fathers was the Revd Francis McKeamie,

OPPOSITE: *The study in this friendly and distinctive old rectory.*
ABOVE AND RIGHT: *Bedrooms and the bedroom corridor at Frewin.* (images courtesy of The Hidden Ireland)

who was born in Fanad in 1658, converted to Presbyterianism and worked on the mission field of Maryland, and as the first moderator of the First Assembly in Philadelphia in 1706 is regarded as the father of the Presbyterian Church in America.

I learn all this when Thomas Coyle lures me away to the fields where his cows graze, incurious and content. We talk – well, he talks and I listen – of his hopes of reviving the old Donegal breed of Dexter. It is a still evening, the clouds have lifted and a sunset spreads itself across the sky, illuminating the distant headlands and the hills beyond Lough Fern. Back at the house and laden with purloined books, I realise in my bedroom that Regina Coyle understands that a bed isn't a kind of straitjacket: the quilt has been turned down and the sheets loosened at the edges. The blinds are lowered, the lamps glow and in the bathroom the pipes are heating the towels and bathrobe. Bliss.

Frewin House,
Ramelton, County Donegal
Tel: 074 9151246
www.frewinhouse.com

Gaultier Lodge

Woodstown, County Waterford

The popular translation of Gaultier in Waterford is 'the land of the foreigner'. Strangers have been finding their way to the long strands of the estuary of the River Suir for what seem like millennia, and it could be said to be totally appropriate that Sheila Molloy, artist and former joint master of the Waterford Hunt, is still welcoming visitors to Gaultier Lodge.

This is a real wind in the hair place: sand in the toes, a salty mist sighing inland from the sea and, if one is staying with Sheila Molloy, the promise of a drawing-room laden with books and magazines and flowers, of a good dinner, a delightful bedroom with views suggesting that the golden strand is part of the house and, in the morning, a breakfast feast which includes homemade muesli, jams, breads and yogurts, as well as Irish cheeses which, Sheila says firmly, are really better than any other cheeses anywhere.

The 'wind in the hair', incidentally, is only true once one gets on to the beach. The house itself,

Designed by John Roberts and built in 1779, Gaultier Lodge was initially a hunting lodge and later a dower house.

GAULTIER LODGE

The mouldings, friezes and fireplaces of a typical Georgian interior.
(images courtesy of The Hidden Ireland)

built in 1779 to a design by John Roberts, began as a hunting lodge, where the Gaultier hounds were kept for many years. Later designated as the dower house for the Ballyglan estate across the road, it is set like an egg in a nest below the dunes and behind a rampart of wall, ditch and hedges. Something of this careful sheltering from the prevailing elements characterises the house now that Sheila, widowed by the death of her first husband Dr Jim Molloy, has raised her two children here and is making wider use of the premises.

The entrance hall with its coved ceiling is slightly later than what might be called the staircase hall if there were a staircase, which there is, of course, but it is set away from this split-level arrangement and it goes down rather than up. Sheila has an artist's appreciation of colour, texture and, it has to be said, although she might wince at the word, charm. While her own work ranges from fine, acutely observed drawings to assertive studies, her décor is attuned to country-house style. What she and her husband found when they bought Gaultier Lodge from the Mathews family (Charlie Mathews of Royal Showband fame) they enhanced lightly and not at all at variance with the mouldings, friezes or fireplaces of a typical Georgian interior.

This confident touch also allows for a sense of fun, not least in the proliferation of trophies from the equestrian world, including the brush and mask of several foxes or the antlers used as a hat stand. But these are evidence of the hunting, shooting and fishing era for which the house was built, and in the entrance hall Sheila herself put up a decorative frieze to carry on the theme so familiar to her and to many local people (there are still five hunts operating in the district). 'Vegetarians,' Sheila notes, 'don't seem to mind all that. I think they just like my food.' This is served in the dining-room, which like all the others on this floor looks directly over the beach and which is also distinguished by the wide wooden fireplace which came from Corballymore House in Dunmore East.

Gaultier Lodge is full of such references to other houses and other owners, and some portion of the land bordering the great beach was owned by the Wadding family, forebears of the Franciscan historian and theologian Luke Wadding. But the 'foreigners' who gave their name to the Barony of Gaultier were probably the Vikings who displaced a pre-Christian Irish settlement uncovered in the Woodstown excavations of the last ten years. The dig unearthed items of stone, bone, silver and amber and coins from Byzantium, and a single warrior grave whose inhabitant had been eroded to extinction by the salt soil but whose full battle array remained where he had lain.

Such archaeological and historical treasure-troves may draw people to this house, but Sheila Molloy, assisted by her daughter-in-law Alieda, has ensured that the predominant reason to visit Gaultier Lodge is the quality of the hospitality and the environment she has achieved here. So much so that the house was included recently in the best 1,000 bed and breakfast premises by the *Guardian* newspaper. I should add that dogs are accepted by arrangement and for an extra €5; it's worth it, to see the mutt enjoying every glittering yard of that shoreline.

Gaultier Lodge,
Woodstown, County Waterford
Tel: 051 382 549
www.gaultier-lodge.com

Ghan House

Carlingford, County Louth

'We had always had a special feeling for Carlingford,' says Joyce Carroll, who describes her role now at Ghan House as the 'go-for', a role with which she appears to be perfectly contented. So well she might be, given that this old house in this unique old village has risen to its current status in the world of international hospitality initially through her own dedication and, latterly, while supported by her whole family, through the inspiration and commitment of her son Paul. The Carroll family lived in Carlingford before moving to England, and then returned every year for summer holidays. Trained in hotel management, Joyce had run a ten-bedroom country-house hotel in Somerset, so it made sense on coming back to live in Ireland that she would set up a business here. And although when they saw it again Ghan House was somewhat less than perfect, it seemed the ideal place in which to establish a cookery school and to lure Paul home from his career as an advertising and corporate photographer in London.

Working to a schedule of special restaurant menus, from Georgian banquets to medieval feasts and gourmet nights based on stories from the Táin, Paul is cheered by the fact that Ghan House is developing an international reputation for the quality of its hospitality and accommodation. 'But it's a controlled business. We're more of a special destination rather than a routine seven-nights-a-week operation, so we can offer private dining facilities and attract corporate clients and small celebrations as well. But it's not a hotel – it's a very different business.'

It's different also to what Joyce had envisaged: 'I liked this house, and I was more than happy to work. When Paul joined me he was able to grow on aspects of the business. We have great ideas about what we'd like to do but really my feeling now is that I can safely let development in Paul's hands. So, while I still have a presence here, I'm mostly behind the scenes – and of course I bake the bread, and make the jams and chutneys. And do the go-for jobs.'

Both Joyce and Paul are well aware of their shared achievements at Ghan House, and prefer to steer the conversation towards Carlingford itself and the many attractions of the surrounding countryside. Beginning with Carlingford Lough, with the Mournes at one side and the Cooleys at the other, this is scenery changing from the dramatic to the serene, from ocean to small busy towns and villages to remote valleys. It was a fine evening as I arrived; earlier storm clouds had blown themselves out over the hills and before me was an ever-expanding panorama of sea and shore. Although afflicted two years ago with horrible agricultural troubles, this whole area has revived and Cooley lamb and beef figure prominently on the menu at Ghan House.

With Carlingford equidistant from Dublin and

An international reputation for the quality of its hospitality has been achieved at Ghan House. (images courtesy of Paul Carroll)

Belfast, even half-hour diversions can bring the visitor to Newgrange in the Boyne Valley or to Clermont Cairn behind Sliabh Foy. Time was against me and I did not travel over the Táin Way to Cairn an Mhadaigh, the grave – or so it is said and why should I argue – of Bran, the famous hound of Finn McCool. This is Táin country, its valleys and bogs laid over a wealth of passage graves and court tombs and all that remains of a race and a community which lived here more than 5,000 years ago. Legend wreathes around these townlands like a mist, and the vapour seeps into the more visible medieval Carlingford, with its tholsel, mint, town walls, friary and castles. Taking its name from its site on a strip of land beside the water, Ghan House stands at the edge of Old Quay Lane; on clear days you can see how, in the southern distance, Greenore and Greencastle almost meet, as if to block off the incoming ocean.

A plain white-painted two-storey building, Ghan House was built in 1727 for William Stannus, an agent of Lord Anglesey, and remained in the Stannus family (of which Ninette de Valois was a member) until it passed first to the Rutherfords and then to the Carrolls. Restoration rescued the shutters, the fireplaces and the decorated ceilings and now the house is alight and alive with welcome for all who take the trouble to find this fascinating part of Ireland.

Ghan House,
Carlingford, County Louth
Tel: 042 937 3682

Glebe House and Gallery

County Donegal

Standing under a painting by Edwin Landseer and looking at an inlaid table bought for £5 at Smithfield market reminds me that the essential magic of Glebe House and Gallery is a fusion of practicality and artistry. Left to the nation by the painter and writer Derek Hill before his death in 2000, the house was originally a Church of Ireland rectory in the parish of Gartan. Also known as Gartan Glebe, the house, which Hill believed might have begun as a fortified *rath*, was a small hotel from 1898 until it was bought by the artist in 1953. His adjustments resulted in a delightfully restored Georgian interior adapted for twentieth-century living. He converted the stable block into a studio, with a sitting-room for his housekeeper, Gracie McDermott, who had been employed earlier in the hotel and who remained with Hill when, years later, he moved to a smaller house on the far side of Lake Gartan.

The studio has been converted into an impressive art gallery, now in the care of Dúchas and managed by the curator, Adrian Kelly. The gallery, modern and bright inside, is not devoted to Derek Hill; the house serves that purpose, although Hill's work is a constant theme throughout the estate, along with that of the Tory Island painters whom he inspired and promoted. Painted a warm terracotta as it was when Hill first saw it, Glebe House has nine acres of garden subtracted from the 25-acre estate. Because Dúchas excavated the car park so that its bays are hidden by high grassy mounds, there is nothing to disturb the landscape. Long, mown stretches of greensward fall level by level to the water's edge; the house is shaded by mighty oaks, beeches, and limes with slender birches – Hill's favourite trees – for contrast.

Here and there little breaks, like hedges, are split by invading roses; these are the old roses, cabbage-layered, scented, dark and pale pink, in their element. Where it faces the lake, the building is draped in woodbine, jasmine, clematis and more roses, this time climbing tidily towards the eaves, with two wide-spreading tree peonies shadowing the terrace. Hill's personality, in so far as a person can be conjured from furniture, wallpaper, ornaments and shirts and shoes, still abides within the house. While those things evoke his physical presence, it is his spiritual being which presides. Even when enjoying the eccentricity of a bathroom, or the beauty of the dolphin tiles around the frame of the Victorian conservatory, there comes an awareness of the provenance of the artist's imagination, and with that the presence of his friends and creative forebears.

William Morris is here in fabrics, carpets and wallpapers. Laetitia Mary Hamilton is here; Nano Reid, Gwen John, Sidney Nolan, Mainie Jellet, Camille Souter, Mary Swanzy, Grace Henry, Augustus John, Louis Le Brocquy, Basil Blackshaw and John

A sympathetically restored house adapted for twentieth-century living. (images courtesy of National Monuments Service, Department of Arts, Heritage and the Gaeltacht)

Craxton, Evie Hone and the Tory Island painter James Dixon. Also, tiles by the novelist William De Morgan, a watercolour by the set designer Oliver Messell, and work by Derrick Greaves, John Bratby, Colin Middleton, Roderic O'Conor and Victor Pasmore. Hill's own portrait of Gracie McDermott is here, and so is his painting of his favourite dog, Caesar. The household dogs are evident in the kitchen, where their raised, padded box still stands in its corner, a heart-warming reminder of the affection for place and people emanating from this house.

There is sometimes a studied effect achieved by a man who once trained to be a theatrical designer and whose brother John was an interior designer of note. The house is an anthology of style, its personal grace notes found in things like old Beleek, hand-knotted rugs, lustre glass and lacquer cabinets, Irish spongeware, ceramics such as the plate designed by Picasso, the Tiffany lamp which puts all its imitations to shame or the collection of Wemyss ware built up in memory of a childhood breakfast set. That childhood began in Southampton and led to study, training and travel in Europe, Russia and the Far East. In Paris, Hill was encouraged by the couturier Edward Molyneux, in Italy he was befriended by the art historian Bernard Berenson. He also met Henry McIlhenny, who was restoring Glenveagh Castle near Church Hill, and it was while staying with him at Glenveagh that Derek Hill found this property beside its lake in County Donegal.

The Glebe House and Gallery,
Church Hill, County Donegal
Tel: 074 913 7071

Glenlohane

County Cork

There is nothing, I remind myself, like American bed linen. The heavy embroidered cotton spread, the padded comforter, the blankets edged with satin, the fresh soft lawn of sheets and pillowcases, the very abundance of pillows themselves. An electric blanket which does not have to be switched off so I can simmer all night long. When I draw back the curtains and open the shutters, the room is immediately painted with the night's frost. Outside, the striped lawns glow silver under the moon. The silence is deep and cold, the trees unmoving in the park, the dense sky coloured only by its own lights, its moon, its stars.

This is Glenlohane, near Kanturk in County Cork, where Desmond and Melanie Sharp Bolster have created the perfect blend of American comfort and Irish character. The house, lived in by successions of Desmond's family since it was built in 1741, has the typical grace of its period. Desmond is a fox-hunting man, bred to it from birth. Even his twenty years in America didn't dim his enthusiasm, so he and Melanie – who is American and also rode to hounds – decided that, if they were going to live permanently at Glenlohane, they would justify the expense of making it comfortable by inviting paying guests on hunting or simply country holidays. 'We've gained a great deal of confidence in what we do here,' says Desmond. 'We want to make our guests feel as though, for the duration, this is their home. It seems to work.'

Those who visit for a hunting holiday have their three outings a week with the Duhallow hunt. Then there are those who fish, and then there are those who want to ride through the countryside by day and eat in important restaurants nearby. As well as which, there's a lot to see and do in and near Kanturk itself. Desmond insists that Ireland is the best hunting country in the world and the Duhallow the best hunt in Ireland: 'excellent pack, wonderful huntsmen, gives very good sport'. The visitors are intrigued by the apparent informality of the meets, by the numbers of youngsters out on their shaggy winter-coated ponies (and by what those ponies will jump), by the centrality of the village pub and, above all – and for this Desmond and Melanie thank the local people – for the friendliness, the welcome they are offered.

This is one of the real bonuses for their guests, the sense that they can walk into the village shop and be remembered, that they'll be greeted on the roadway, that a farmer or a publican will take the time to chat. 'The Duhallow only allow three visitors a day and we have to have permission from the hunt secretary to bring our guests out. Our farmers don't like to see enormous numbers of people and if half of them are foreigners they like it even less. It's the farmers who

ABOVE: *The perfect blend of American comfort and Irish character and (right) history is remembered in the study at Glenlohane.*

own the land; people have to remember that without their goodwill there would be no hunting at all.'

The Sharp Bolsters offer a unique experience of Ireland at Glenlohane. The return to Desmond's home place had always been intended once their two children had grown up. 'Old houses can continue their working lives – it's a matter of understanding their different properties,' says Melanie. 'I like things to work and to be pleasing. Yes, the American preference is for the décor to be light and bright, but that was true of Georgian interiors too.'

After breakfast they decide to show me something of the country. With frosted mud cracking under the wheels, we swerve up Knockanuss, site of a terrible battle of 1647 which Desmond, with all the strategic appreciation of a former US Air Force pilot, recounts move by move, cannonade by cannonade, although, he says, it is a day forgotten by history. From the summit we can see the contour of the mass grave which was one result of the conflict. We pivot to take in the whole view: to the east the skyline is marked by the Ballyhouras, beyond them by the Knockmealdowns and the dim blue shadow of the Galtees. Before us the Boggeraghs sweep gently across the horizon and merge with the Paps, this morning snow-covered and brilliant against the bright sky. Further west again gleam the serrated icy spikes of the MacGillicuddy Reeks. This is winter, near Kanturk. ♠

Desmond no longer hunts but remains a follower and notes that the Duhallow includes a strong contingent of young riders. Hunting holidays are still very popular at Glenlohane. A pretty cottage near the house is also available for self-catering guests.

Glenlohane,
Kanturk, County Cork
Tel: 029 50014
www.glenlohane.ie

Glenville Park

Glenville, County Cork

I always somehow thought I was going to write – but of course I also thought it would be easier than it was, in fact!

All the same, Mark Bence-Jones admits that he was very lucky in having the friendship of Elizabeth Bowen in his early days as a writer. After school in Ampleforth, a history degree at Cambridge and a grounding in estate management at the Royal Agricultural College at Cirencester, his first book was read by Bowen, who sent it to her agent, who sent it to publisher Peter Davies. That was *All the Nonsense*; it was followed a year later by *Paradise Escaped* and another year on by *Nothing in the City*. Bowen gave a party for his first novel; Rosamund Lehmann came, and Antonia White. He lists these and other names with an amazement and gratitude which are still fresh. That was the time, he thought, to be in London. He wanted to meet girls, to have a good time, even though his proper place was back home in County Cork. And he did meet girls, the special one being Gillian Pretyman of Orwell Park, with whom he danced at a house party in Lincolnshire.

There was more to life than dancing and writing novels, of course. There was his budding career as a journalist, begun with Mark Girouard, who was the architectural editor of the magazine *Country Life*. Those were the days in which Bence-Jones began to develop his speciality, that of the origin, character and future of the great houses of Ireland and Britain, the economy on which they depended and the culture they harboured. Yet the signs of this commitment were there from early on, starting perhaps with his family house at Lisselane near Clonakilty in County Cork and his own home at Glenville Park near Rathcormac.

His first non-fiction title was *Clive of India*, which is still regarded as the definitive biography. This was also his first publication with Constable, which has remained his publisher ever since. Other books influenced by his life in India where his father had worked with the Indian civil service were followed by the source of his most prominent public expertise: *A Guide to Irish Country Houses*. This began with a new edition of *Irish Family Records* by Burke's Peerage, for which Bence-Jones was consultant editor. It became a separate volume instead, the first in Burke's guides to country houses and the nucleus of the comprehensive guide published by Constable in 1988. This features nearly 2,000 Irish properties, not all of them grand or very distinguished yet all recorded with respect and giving the history and lore of each family and the fate of each house.

This is also an elegy; time after time, entry after entry, the record shows 'burned in 1920' or 'later demolished' or 'now a ruin'. There is no escaping the fact that in a listing of this kind Ireland has been cruel to its great houses and country estates. Mark Bence-Jones appreciates this and does not minimise it. Yet it remains his subject: as a historian Bence-Jones has much of the objectivity of scholarly distance, assisted probably by the fact that his wife is related by marriage to that George Wyndham whose Act fatally divided the big house from its land and territory. Sometimes it can seem as if he were examining his own history. He has been a member of the Order of Malta for twenty years and is its current regent of the Irish Sub-Priory of St Oliver Plunkett. 'My religion means a lot to me, although I wouldn't like to say I'm devout – that implies a greater degree of effort or spiritual success than I can achieve.'

He is careful to correct misconceptions of the role of the great house in city and county. In his introduction to the *Guide* he says that while, during the struggle for Irish independence, many families

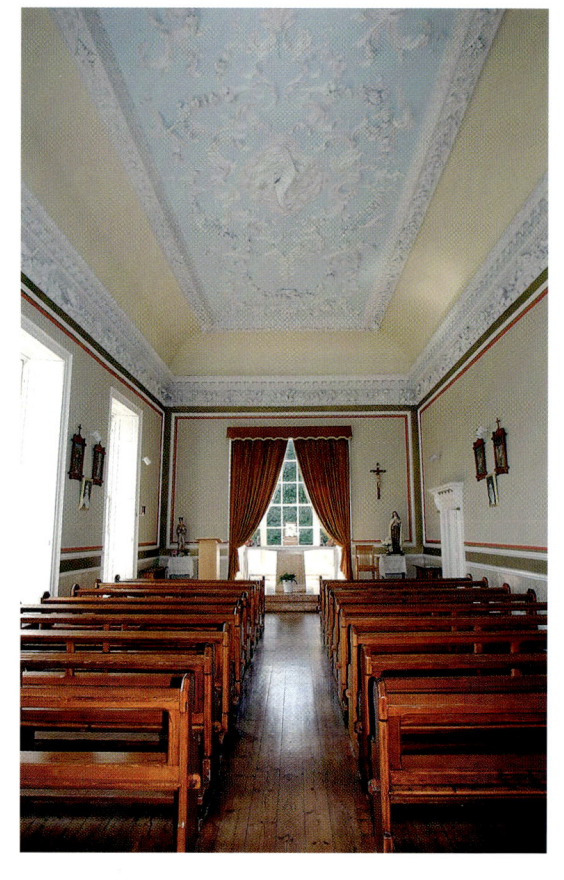

LEFT: *The late Mark Bence-Jones and (right) the oratory at Glenville Park.* (images courtesy of the *Irish Examiner*)

sold their ancestral homes and others left because of their political allegiances, most who sold their houses did so for the obvious reason that they could no longer afford to live in them. The house needed its supporting land-based economy to survive. Legislation is making life a little easier for many such homeowners. 'I think, happily, that the days when a house is likely to be pulled down are over; the remaining problem is that it hasn't been realised how much the surroundings of a house matter. A country house is not merely a building but an entity, with its demesne, furnishings and atmosphere making up a national heritage. What has to be preserved must be preserved together.' ♣

Mark Bence-Jones died in April 2010.

Glin Castle

County Limerick

'Is this part of the experience of staying here?' I ask weakly as I look up through the skylight at the commanding figure of the Knight of Glin, waiting for me to climb the timber ladder to the roof. I'm a groundling, happier with my shoes on the grass than with my head among the clouds. Or the battlements, if it comes to that. Earlier in the morning I had seen the wisteria climbing up the castle walls to the leads. Now the fragrant purple tassels brush my face. Lovely.

And lovely too is the vista – the Shannon at its widest disappearing beyond Tarbert, the distant smoke stacks slender as minarets, the slopes of County Clare across the water crusted with bold yellow gorse.

Of the twelve stone castles built by the FitzGeralds

BELOW: *Madam Olda FitzGerald and the late Desmond FitzGerald, 29th Knight of Glin, in the castle gardens.* (images courtesy of the *Irish Examiner*)

of Desmond around County Limerick, the one called Glin Castle isn't a castle at all. Desmond FitzGerald, 29th Knight of Glin, is disarmingly frank about the castellations which disguise what must have been an appealing Georgian house, plain, spacious and beautifully located, the home of John Fraunceis FitzGerald, perpetrator of this decorative abuse. Desmond FitzGerald and his wife Olda have continued to maintain the house along the lines set by his mother Veronica who, on her second marriage to the wealthy Canadian businessman Ray Milner, restored it with his encouragement and her fine taste. To this Desmond and Olda have added their own sensibilities, so that everything here has been treasured, bequeathed, restored and used through several centuries. It all belongs, and it is this sense of belonging, of fine things in their rightful place, which makes the splendour take on a human dimension.

In some ways the FitzGeralds were a rackety

Everything at Glin Castle has been treasured, bequeathed, restored and used through several centuries.

bunch, but they understood the relationship of house to land. Mark Bence-Jones thinks the service wing incorporates an earlier house which was itself a replacement of a thatched building. That in turn followed the castle in the village, which was besieged and broken in 1600. Although the need to fortify and watch the Shannon estuary diminished between then and 1780 – the approximate date of the present building – the location at the river's edge served the purpose of uniting the mansion with its landscape in the classical fusion of proportion, vista and function.

Indoors all this theory is softened into domesticity. The hall with its Corinthian columns has a ceiling of delicate paint and plasterwork, its motifs enlivened by personal emblems of the FitzGeralds as friendly reminders of the men and women who loved this place in their day. In the staircase hall two separate lower flights meet in a single – literally 'flying' – structure from the half-landing to the main landing. The imperial stairway is lit by a Venetian window, the spandrels decorated with floral ornamentation; even the beading on the handrail is inset so finely that it emerges only as a little detail.

In the drawing-room the light from the long windows fills a room finished in pinks and greys, so that even the portraits have a kind of pastel lustre. Vases of cherry blossom, branches of the snowdrop tree, azaleas and rhododendrons combine with family snapshots to enliven the arrays of formal portraiture. The whole house glows with welcome, from the open fires in their magnificent fireplaces to the helpful staff assisting manager Bob Duff in the arrangements necessary to accommodate guests., A native of New Zealand and a graduate of the Ballymaloe School, Bob insists that: 'This is a country house, and we serve the best possible version of country house food.' Which is true, if Meissen and Sèvres are country-house china and if, as at last night's dinner, the countryside includes a hare bucking around the lawn while a bronze sunset splinters the clouds over the Shannon.

Thinking later of the family rooms in what was the service wing, the kitchen adorned with biblical inscriptions rescued from the sale of Adare Manor ('Gather ye up the fragments that nothing be lost'), I ponder Desmond's decision to leave the Victoria and Albert Museum in London and turn himself into a farmer and conservationist (he is president of the Irish Georgian Society). I follow the road to the twelfth- century castle of the Norman FitzGeralds at Seanid. The tower stands on its earthworks; the plain opens out below towards Shanagolden. Although the view is beguiling, the tower is bleak, yet a few miles away in those attic rooms at Glin it is commemorated as the beginning of an adventure which has coloured and enriched Irish history for 800 years. ♣

Desmond FitzGerald, Knight of Glin, died in 2011. Glin Castle remains a family home.

Gregans Castle Hotel

Ballyvaughan, County Clare

Among the nicest aspects of north-west County Clare are the road signs warning of 'Walkers!' They are especially frequent on the twists and turns towards Gregans Castle Hotel, where brochures advise on free-range or guided walking routes endorsed by Simon Haden, manager of the hotel. Also encouraged are visits to the Burren Perfumery at Carron, a few very walkable miles away. Relaxation is the essential theme of Gregans Castle itself, despite the suggestion of such a wealth of activities in the locality that the unwary might regard this almost legendary hotel as merely a place in which to crash to rest at last. And it is a place in which to crash to rest, as I did, when I sat down to a lunch of warm lobster salad which, for the mighty sum of €19, provided me with a meal to fuel the rest of the afternoon's plans and to cancel dinner – almost. In a climate in which 'value for money' is regarded as a paramount criterion, I think it worth noting that in a hotel of renowned quality a meal of such excellence should be offered at such a price. Yes, yes, sandwiches can be had for a quarter of that charge: go off and have them.

Even as I write, I want to go back there. This would be no surprise to Simon and Frederieke Haden, who are used by now to welcoming guests returning year after year. This may seem strange, given the youth of the couple who now run the hotel, but Simon grew up here and remembers, and emulates, the warmth with which his parents greeted the people who time and again found their way back down or up Corkscrew Hill to this haven among the rocky landscape. Although its spreading outline has nothing of the castle about it now, Gregans' title evokes the O Lochlains, who were once the chieftains of these valleys and are remembered by the thirteenth-century tower house across the road from the hotel entrance.

The sections of the hotel are believed to stem from about 1750, but it was another one hundred years before Captain Gregory Martyn returned to live permanently at Gregans Castle. Gregans itself is more a place-name than a family title, except where it was once habitually used by the Martyns to style themselves as 'Martyn of the Gregans'. This mattered; Captain Gregory came to the property on foot of an inter-family lawsuit taken by his father, himself a lawyer, and the further re-establishment of the family status in Clare was enhanced by its Parnellite and Home Rule allegiances. There followed a swinging time for all concerned until Gregory's death in 1900. His widow departed to live abroad, leaving a son, Francis Florence Martyn, to work what was by then a much reduced estate. After his death, the house was sold first to the partnership of Alan McCorquedale and Edgar Taylor and then, in 1976, to Simon's parents, Peter and Moira Haden.

Peter had significant experience as a hotel

manager and, although a passionate hunting and sailing enthusiast, he found the time, with Moira, to build the hotel to a four-star rating. Now Simon and Frederieke are in charge. Both have distinctive backgrounds: Simon's obviously in the creativity and work ethic of his parents, enhanced by his own years at home and abroad, while Frederieke has

Gregans Castle. Relaxation is the predominant theme in this legendary hotel.

been influenced by the design and quality standards typified by her family's reputation as McMurrays, carpet-makers of Connemara.

'This is not a spa place,' says Simon. 'Our guests

Not a 'spa place', but contemporary management uses hunting prints and old portraits to keep the link with the best of what has gone before at Gregans Castle. (images courtesy of Ireland's Blue Book)

are not looking for that and that's not what we're about. But we are making plans for a library.' He has kept the hunting prints and old portraits which link all that he and Frederieke are doing with the best of what has gone before them, while also introducing the work of modern local artists. Frederieke has a delightful skill in bringing a picture, a bedhead, a fabric or a bowl of flowers together as if themed without being in any sense formal or forced. And then there's the kitchen where, with Simon's determined involvement, the hotel is moving to the forefront of an EU-funded promotion of Burren foods, beef and lamb from the local hills, fish from Carrigaholt and the Aran Islands: these are presented at Gregans Castle Hotel as part of the Burren Life Project (www.burrenbeo.com).

Gregans Castle Hotel,
Ballyvaughan, County Clare
Tel: 065 7077005

AT HOME IN IRELAND

Griesemount

Ballitore, County Kildare

Perched on its little rise above the river Griese in Ballitore, Griesemount is a house which has no need to pretend. Plain despite its vibrant yellow wash, square and unadorned except for the daffodils flowing from the front lawn to the distant water. This is spring-time and, even as I rejoice in the primroses sparkling through the wooded edges of the garden I'm reminded that the house is locally identified as the house with the snowdrops, so thickly do they flourish on the grass and thickets of the avenue.

Griesemount is a family house, given to nooks and niches and little stairs on to landings which turn into libraries and to windows which open on to a terrace. It's a place of faded rugs and fresh upholstery and paint, dimmed watercolours and radiant photographs, books and magazines piled under the glowing lamplight, a bedroom so joyous with rose-blown wallpaper that the cooler colours of spring outside are bleached to unimportance. Except in my room, where they have been made part of the décor, for here the walls are sprigged ivory and green and on the windowsill near the bed (closing these shutters for the night gives a lovely, old-fashioned sense of security and cosiness) the water jug reflects a vase of wild daffodils. Woven into this traditional pattern of a country house are the combined personalities of Carolyn and Robert Ashe, whose own taste insists on inventive solutions to the problems of old houses.

Ballitore is the only purpose-built Quaker village in Ireland, and the Friends' Meeting House stands just on its outskirts. A museum and library have been installed in the restored home of one of Ballitore's best-known earlier residents, the diarist and poet Mary Shackleton Leadbetter. Ballitore made its name a long time ago, when it was known as the Eton of Ireland thanks to the non-denominational school established by Abraham Shackleton, whose pupils included the MP and orator Edmund Burke as well as James Napper Tandy, Henry Grattan and Cardinal Cullen.

The 1798 Rebellion was a time of great horror and distress for the peace-loving Quakers, whose experiences were recorded by Mary Leadbetter in *The Annals of Ballitore*. Among its terrors were the unburied bodies dumped by the wayside. Indeed, a contemporary record remarks that 'For several months there was no sale for bacon cured in Ireland, from the well-founded dread of the hogs having fed upon the flesh of men.'

Shackleton, of course, is the big name in these townlands; the explorer Ernest was closely related to the George Shackleton who built Griesemount where he reared fourteen children). Here, however, all unhappy associations with unhappy times were shaken off, for this is a house whose connections include Duckett's Grove and Thursoe Lattin Mansefield of Morristown

Plain, square and with no need to pretend, the traditional patterns of a country house are given inventive solutions through the combined personalities and taste of Griesemount's proprietors. (images courtesy of Carolyn Ashe)

Lattin. We're not too precise about any of this as we sit in the friendly kitchen where Carolyn constructs a talkative, unending lunch – a soup, we think, and then just bread and cheese, but this somehow gets the added value of smoked salmon, and there's a paté, and a tingling salad and fresh rolls, and fruit for the cheese, and on it goes as I listen to the story of how Carolyn and Robert, back from Africa, found the house in 1983. 'It had been a very hot summer and when we came there was a glorious copper beech with the sun shining through it – we just loved it. We had no time then for the sensible things because this was the evening before the auction. So in we went the next day with our calculators in our hands and our hearts in our mouths!'

We talk as the haunting music of *Songs of the Auvergne* falls like a blessing on our laden table, on the sleeping dogs, on the birds at their feeder in the garden. It was from the estate of Sara Clucas von Stade, mother of Frederica, that the Ashes bought Griesemount. After years in New York, Sara came to Ballitore for a simpler life: 'Frederica used to visit her. One Christmas she sang at mass in Timolin – can you imagine, just going off to church on Christmas morning and hearing that voice?' We imagine; then Carolyn talks of the decision she and Robert made, once the children had left home, to welcome guests as a way of keeping the house busy and full. 'We decided we would do this to wrap around our lives as they were, not to wrap up our lives. That's the way we still feel about it; it's what we do here, but it's not all that we do.'

Griesemount,
Ballitore, County Kildare
Tel: 059 862 3158

AT HOME IN IRELAND

Hilton Park

Clones, County Monaghan

In terms of The Hidden Ireland, all roads lead to Hilton Park, and even a single overnight stay explains why. It's where all the proprietors of the other fine houses want to go: partly because of Lucy Madden's cooking and Johnny Madden's wines, but it's also because when the Maddens decided to have paying guests instead of just guests they didn't change anything that really mattered in the house.

Everyone wants authenticity. Hilton Park has patented it. The particular talents of its current host and hostess are most lavishly shown by Lucy's cooking, which, when it comes to table, is without fanfare or fuss and simply as what is grown, (the lambs are caracoling outside the windows) cooked and eaten in an Irish country house. The big windows look across acres upon acres of parkland, punctuated here and there by cascades of trees in hangers, by sheep and a small lake. Paths lead to the gardens; indoors all those things which seem so quaint – the light switches, the old radiators, the door handles and latches – are in full working order. There's nothing obsolete here, but there are no telephones in the bedrooms and there isn't a television anywhere to be seen.

'Nobody comes here looking for hotel service,' says Johnny Madden. The tables are illuminated only by candelabra and by the flames from the log fire gleaming against the panelling. The darkly mottled wallpaper takes on a lustre; its pattern seems to move as Johnny, considering his claret, explains that he and Lucy maintain as far as possible the traditions of the house; burgundy, for example, has never been brought to table at Hilton, not in the twentieth century. Sipping a particularly palatable white wine, I remind him that the dining-room was once used as a gambling den; the tradition was that the men would be locked in there to play cards (a very famous house changed hands here one night) until all the wine and in some cases all the money was gone.

This fine old custom could have brought Hilton Park to utter ruin, were it not for a rich father-in-law who, when the creditors arrived in pursuit of £52,000-worth of debts, arranged legacies and bequests in such a way that his daughter's marital home was secure. Originally known as Kilshanless, the house was built in the early eighteenth century and purchased by Samuel Madden for his third son in 1734. A new house incorporating much of the earlier one was then built, but this was almost completely gutted by a fire in 1803. Rebuilt over the next fifteen years, possibly to the design of James Jones, Hilton Park was changed again by the Victorian additions of John Madden. The Duncannon sandstone which now encases the exterior and the monumental Ionic *porte-cochère* are part of this 1870 upgrading by local architect William Hague.

The commission to create an Italianate atmosphere

Hilton Park. A lot of hard work, rewarded by a very good life. Lucy Madden (below) in the garden at Hilton.

involved digging out the basement, which became the new ground floor; this is now divided into an entrance hall and a staircase hall, both imposing but on the friendly side of magnificent. The 1870 ballroom, the dining-room and the inner staircase create a *piano nobile*, a suite of rooms which seems to float above the main entrance as if suspended over the parkland. As we take our coffee in the sitting-room and the soft gold of the brocades meld with the brass details of the fireplace and the facets of the chandeliers, there is a sense of being elsewhere, out of time. In a bedroom, the colours of the eighteenth-century French wallpaper are picked up in the hangings and carpets; long drifts of fine old lace frame the windows. Indoors are fine stucco in cornice and frieze with armorial windows; outside, the stable block with bell tower includes a unique colonnaded riding ring. In my room the bedspread is turned back, the lamps aglow, the rampart of pillows

Authenticity has been patented at Hilton Park. (images courtesy of paulgordon.org and the Madden family)

tamed into sleeping size above the soft pink hint of the electric blanket.

Breakfast is taken downstairs in a stone-flagged room, where Lucy arrives, almost apologetically, to offer stewed rhubarb in addition to the already attractive menu. It's from her garden and is deeply, sweetly red, cooked to a perfect consistency, which is all too rare with rhubarb, so there's a general scramble for this most delicate of seasonal delicacies. I ponder the enthusiasm with which both the Maddens admit that Hilton is a lot of hard work but a very good life. 'The heart of these houses is the family,' says Johnny. 'The problem for the future is going to be making sure families can continue living in them.'

John and Lucy Madden are semi-retired, and Fred and Joanna Madden are now proprietors and managers of Hilton Park.

Hilton Park,
Clones, County Monaghan
Tel: 047 56007

HILTON PARK 161

Hollywell

Carrick-on-Shannon

Even today there is a touch of the coaching-inn style to Hollywell, which stands in its own riverside gardens just beyond the big old bridge between the town and the Boyle road. Perhaps there was once a holy well just beyond the garden hedge, or perhaps it was just that the well was surrounded by holly bushes. The archaeologists, according to proprietor Tom Maher, prefer the possibility of a holy well, which would make this site a place of pilgrimage, but Tom says he has never heard any talk of this in the town. And it is a conversational town, with the river perhaps its great charm: on a sunny evening the broad lake-like sweep of the Shannon is benign, decked with boats and cruisers, with the townspeople strolling on its green banks.

The river is also the town's identity, not as geography but as its first native industry. Cara Droma Ruisc began as a ford across the Shannon linking crucial routes between Roscommon and Leitrim. The Annals of Lough Key mark the crossing in 1530, but it began its major development from the early seventeenth century. Later the Shannon Navigation Scheme of 1846 and the arrival of the Midland Great Western Railway in 1862 were the crucial events which settled its economic and cultural character.

Its attractions include the smallest church in Ireland. The Costello Mortuary Chapel was built in 1879 on much the same principle, although to a very different design, as the Taj Mahal, for here the merchant Edward Costello wished to commemorate his wife. Although it is consecrated as a Catholic chapel and mass has been celebrated here, it is now little more than a burial vault, built in cut limestone in Hiberno-Gothic style, the interior lined with Bath stone and the whole edifice standing on the corner of the main street. Around that corner is Hatley Manor, built in the 1830s for the prosperous St George family who named their Irish town house after their seat in England at Hatley St George. The manor is in splendid shape, thanks to the presence in Carrick-on-Shannon of the American MBNA, which took the house and its ten acres of gardens to accommodate the company's visiting executives and guests.

Main street is also the location of the Bush Hotel, founded in 1794 and built in its present form by Patrick Kelly of Longford, who was also the builder of the Costello Chapel. The Bush Hotel was the McDermott business, established in the town since the late eighteenth century and inherited by Tom Maher's mother. She returned to Carrick-on-Shannon in the 1960s to run the hotel until Tom, having trained at Shannon and worked all over Europe in the hotel industry, took over from her. With his wife Rosaleen from Belfast and their four children they kept it going for years, their enthusiasm softening the cost entailed in running a family hotel. When they sold

ABOVE: *The Shannon flows past the sitting-room. Rosaleen and the late Tom Maher (above right) in the kitchen at Hollywell.*
(images courtesy of James Connolly for the *Irish Examiner*)

the Bush the Mahers decided that there was a demand for a country-house type bed and breakfast accommodation: 'more discriminating clients who don't want just another hotel experience, but somewhere a little different, relaxing in itself and which wouldn't be so demanding on our energy'.

They were right, except that demand for a facility means demanding work, and Rosaleen's prowess in the kitchen (breakfasts are the main meal here) keeps guests returning and it takes a special kind of courage to open a country-house hotel in the middle of a town. While not really in the middle of the town but at its edge, the house has the atmosphere of tradition, of culture and of architectural dignity. Tom and Rosaleen can trace its several proprietors, from its first owner, Dr Munns, to that Captain Hanley who went off to the Crimean War and never came home, and to Eugene O'Neill Clarke, County Surveyor for Leitrim.

The lovely drawing-room is a Victorian addition to the house, which was first built in the 1790s. When the Mahers arrived they engaged architect Denis Kelly of Cork, grandson of that Patrick Kelly who had built the new Bush House in 1920. Now the old cornices are freshly painted, the old fireplaces laid, the dining-room gleaming with linen and table silver, and in my bedroom under sloping eaves bedside lamps draw out the scents of the flowers reflected in the lustre of the furniture. ♣

Tom and Rosaleen Maher retired and their son Ronan and his wife Grainne now run Hollywell; Tom Maher died in January 2012. MBNA reduced its workforce in Carrick-on-Shannon and Hatley Manor has been sold.

Hollywell,
Carrick-on-Shannon, County Leitrim
Tel: 071 9621124

HOLLYWELL

Hunters' Lodge

Lismore, County Waterford

The hedges on the roads leading to Lismore are crimson with haws. The gale of late September has loosened the leaves in this wooded part of west Waterford; the climbing hangers are awash, islanded in bronze lakes. In the paddock bordering the avenue leading to the home of Tom and Elsie Morgan the old hunter Edward lifts his head to the whiff of the season.

Edward is twenty-nine years old. The last time he wore a saddle the combined age of himself and his rider was 106. They led the field, clearing forty jumps on the way. His rider was Elsie Morgan, former Joint Master of the West Waterford Hunt, a role she shared with her husband Tom. Both are from Wales, meeting during the Second World War; within a few weeks of their marriage Elsie was on her way to Tom's regiment in Germany with a couple of hunters and a pack of hounds.

'We had three lovely seasons out there,' remembers Tom. 'It was lovely bank country, Schleswig-Holstein. Good grass, good winter ditches …' From the knocker on the front door to the gilded mask on Tom's slippers this is a house which gives every possible indication of a presiding commitment to the art of venery, of hunting, of The Chase. They acknowledge that the public image of the sport they love is not always uncritical. They are troubled, at times, by the ignorance of its opponents and indeed by the violence of its more extreme antagonists. Yet they speak with the confidence of lives full of respect for wild things and with an inherent understanding, something almost instinctive, of the relationships between the land, its fauna and its workers.

Elsie knows she's not going to change the attitude of those who see the hunt as a group of red-coated sadists. She knows and respects foxes. She knows how the species protects itself – the pregnant vixen, for example, has no scent. She remembers that when fox fur was fashionable 300,000 pelts were exported from Ireland in one year with no-one anxious about how the foxes were killed. All the hunts in the country together could not produce one-tenth of that figure.

It's been a long career. During the war Tom, a Captain in the Royal Artillery, had a colonel who was also a horseman. Taking the surrender of a German cavalry division fleeing from the advancing Russians in East Germany they picked out fifty of the best horses. With twenty-five gunners Tom set up a crash course in equitation in order to ride the animals back across the Elbe to the British zone. En route the orders changed; they were to make for the Dutch border 950 miles away. It took two months, but only two horses were lost on the journey, and the rest made up the regimental riding school Tom inaugurated once he got back to base.

Visiting friends in Ireland after the war, Tom and Elsie found 150 acres and a house near Lismore and

As well as a long career as Joint Master of the West Waterford Foxhounds Elsie Morgan and her husband Captain Tom Morgan were often abroad as hound-show judges. After her stellar reputation on the international show-jumping circuit they also achieved fame for the horses they produced, one of which was included in an Italian Olympic team, another winning the Grand Prix in Rome ridden by Captain Piero D'Inzeo. (image courtesy *The Irish Field*)

got their farm going. They joined the West Waterford hunt where Tom became secretary to the master. Those were the days when the hounds were kennelled at the marvellous stable yards in Dromana House, when the hunt balls were held at Ballynatray and when Isaac Bell lived at Lismore and wrote his *Foxiana* and *A Huntsman's Log Book*. Famous throughout the hunting world but crippled by arthritis, Bell saw Elsie working with the hounds and decided she had what is called 'the golden thread', the invisible cord of affinity linking hounds, fox and huntsman. He promised to breed a pack of hounds specially for the West Waterford, and the strong, largely white hounds with what Tom calls their 'tremendous cry and very good nose' became the mark of the hunt with which both the Morgans worked for thirty-one seasons in Elsie's case and thirty-four in Tom's. Hunting, farming and keeping the hounds became the Morgans' life for more than fifty years. In that time Tom became a course-builder of international repute working with Eddie Taylor at the RDS. Still, he thinks show-jumping is a bit too slow for his liking.

Hip replacement for Tom, her seventy-first birthday for Elsie, have brought their active hunting life to an end. These days they like to bring on three-year-olds which Tom Busteed of Monkstown County Cork trains and shows for them. As hunt followers they like to get up at five to see the winter dawn, to wait for the hounds to speak as the scent is found and then to hear the chorus as the cry swells through the pack. Waiting, Tom remembers his old roan: 'When the first hound would speak you'd feel the horse's heart beating through your knees ...'

Elsie Morgan died in 2009. Aged ninety-six, she attended the West Waterford opening meet at Camphire a week before her death. She had begun as a whipper-in at the age of twelve, represented Ireland twice in the Nations Cup teams and later bred top-flight show-jumpers.

HUNTERS' LODGE

Inch House

Thurles, County Tipperary

An ancient lineage, a spiritual nobility and an aristocrat of the turf: all these are enshrined at Inch House near Holy Cross in County Tipperary. The lineage is obvious enough in the history of the house, built in 1720 for John Ryan, a landed Catholic at a time when such a description was rare enough. John was upwardly mobile and in 1723 married Frances Mary Mathew (or Matthew), granddaughter of Lady Elizabeth Poyntz, whose first husband Thomas Butler had been heir to the earldom of Ormond; her son James became the first Duke of Ormond and, incidentally, the step-uncle of Frances Mary. Lady Elizabeth had a good eye for husbands, for through her second marriage to George Mathew her connections included both Father Theobald Mathew, the renowned temperance campaigner and, via other alliances among the Catholic families of Munster, Nano Nagle, foundress of the Presentation Order of nuns.

It wasn't until I queried a half-hidden photograph of a horse in full flight that I learned I had been walking that evening along tracks cantered over by Monksfield, twice winner of the Cheltenham Champion Hurdle, bred here by the Ryans before the estate was sold to John and Nora Egan. Now part of the impeccable farmyards behind the house is home to track and coursing greyhounds, continuing a tradition of sporting excellence. But these are things one has to find out for oneself. Even the floorboards have a tale to tell, while the rutted paths outside lead to a tiny, tottering riverside graveyard kept mown and trim by the local Tidy Towns committee.

Tall and austere in its setting of undulating fields, Inch is built in the tradition of the manor house. The wide hall gives on to a wide bifurcating oak staircase, which ends in a wide landing with its five wide guest bedrooms. Yet not a sound from below seems to reach these rooms; only in the morning does the busy family life reveal itself, and then by accident. Beguiled by the innocent clouds moving like shadows over the plain, I overhear from my padded window-seat the lively and various voices coming and going, making arrangements for later duties in far-off fields. There is something very comforting in this for the visitor, a sense of a continuum, of the countryside being husbanded as it has been for many centuries, in good heart because it is in good hands.

The Egans only intended to carry on farming, but crucial repairs drew them into a gradual process of restoration; this included the reglazing of windows, which are important at Inch, where dining-room and sitting-room are lit by panes of nineteenth-century diamond astragals and the turn of the stairs by a three-light spread of stained glass. Then, just as the children were growing up and away, a party of French sportsmen strayed on to the land for a last opportunistic pigeon shoot. Several generous en-suite bathrooms later, Nora

ABOVE: *Here and there are outbursts of opulent mirrors, while strong colours make the most of large spaces. In my own room they give way to gentle ecru and gold and add a vase of daffodils to the little writing table.* LEFT: *John and Nora Egan in the garden of Inch House.* (images courtesy of the *Irish Examiner*)

Egan makes the origins of her career in hospitality seem very rational: 'We needed to get rid of the pigeons, the men cancelled their air tickets, we put them up here and they returned to us for the next fifteen years.'

Formerly a nurse, she found she enjoyed this new way of life: 'I loved it. With eight children and a husband, I was doing plenty of cooking, and of course the children were given every kind of chore; they all had to help.' And help they did, so much so that third-level degrees in catering and hospitality have brought Máirín and her sister Sinéad back to work with Nora. Perhaps the signature of Inch House is friendly professionalism, aligned to the personal character of its host family and of the house itself, a style with drama.

In the blue-walled sitting-room I marvel at the dense plasterwork of the ceiling (restored with that in the hall by Michael Cleary of Templetuohy), which is continued into a small octagonal library with shelved niches in four of the walls. Although companionably furnished, the effect is ornate, with the roofs of the double doors sloped to muffle any noise. It's a kind of virtuoso house, originally a showpiece; outside, from the steps, the greening acres stretch away in a vista ending only in a low circle of hills.

Inch House Country House and Restaurant,
Thurles, County Tipperary
Tel: 0504 51348

INCH HOUSE 167

Inchiquin House

Corofin, County Clare

The longest part of the walk from Inchiquin House to the village of Corofin is the avenue. It begins as a rough drive, turns into a farm track and then – to the visitor's great relief – a pair of formal gate piers announces the smoother consistency of an avenue. There is no deception in this combination of rural features, for Inchiquin House was a farmhouse. Set in a little decline close to Lake Inchiquin and surrounded by 100 acres of woods and farmland, the house has an appealing rustic character.

Applied to a house which was built in the 1740s, the word 'authenticity' can have a cold ring to it, but not here. 'The people who built here knew about light,' says Ronan Harbison, whose business life in Dublin is interrupted by his attachment to Inchiquin House. He stands in the double-sided porch, added to protect the entrance front from the weather; with its armchairs and reading lamps the impression is immediately warm, even on one of the coldest of winter days. Beyond the arch for the original doorway the hall itself is narrow but again light shines in from the half-landing above. In the sitting-room the emphasis is on comfort trimmed with excellent upholstery, wide sash windows and a generous fireplace. The atmosphere is of traditional, tranquil but confidently presented hospitality, flavoured with family photographs, books and memorabilia.

The dining-room is more formal but again a kind of family-based exuberance sets the tone with the darker furniture (all the furniture restoration is the work of Nigel Barnes of Old Chairs Restoration) and a more dramatic paint scheme. With the bright inviting bedrooms and sparkling bathrooms, the work of Rory Kelly Interiors relied on a sense of the inner life of the building, uniting the contemporary with the best elements of the past. What in a grander house would be called the service wing has been transformed into a large, modern kitchen, floored with porcelain tiles. It used to have the dairy attached and ends in a wide French window leading out to a terrace area and the garden with a little paddock, complete with pony. This is to be the hub of the whole house which, when you think of it, is more or less what it must always have been.

Now that the impeccable and painstaking process of restoration has been completed by Tom Howard of Kilnaboy, Inchiquin House is once again going to earn its living. The Harbison plans for its future include the imminent introduction of a programme of weekend residential cookery courses centred in this kitchen, where the array of Dresden porridge plates keeps the old connections alive. The kitchen can also accommodate the demands of a wedding reception, with a marquee on the lawns close to the house, as well as those of corporate events and business meetings, and above all it will suit private rentals for family

ABOVE: *With the Burren outside the door, Inchiquin House has always been a family home.* BELOW: *Pat Meagher in the vegetable garden.*

gatherings or for holidays, for this was always a family house.

Inchiquin was originally the island of O'Quin and the area's history can be traced through the centuries until Colonel James MacNamara of the Royal Indian Medical Service bought the house in 1910. When James died in 1932 his wife Gertrude McDermott carried on the farm at Inchiquin House with the help of her nephew Desmond McSherry. In 1967 the house was inherited by Desmond's sister Sheelagh, wife of James Austin Harbison. Their sons are John, the former state pathologist, and Peter, archaeologist, art historian and author. It is with Peter's sons, Ronan, Maurice and John, that the management of Inchiquin House now rests. Like their parents and grandparents, these young men have been familiar with the house all through their childhood. As Peter Harbison strokes the fossils embedded in the

BELOW: *Inchiquin's décor relies on a sense of the inner life of the house.* RIGHT: *Dresden porridge plates in the kitchen, which is to be the hub of the whole house.* (images courtesy of the Harbison family)

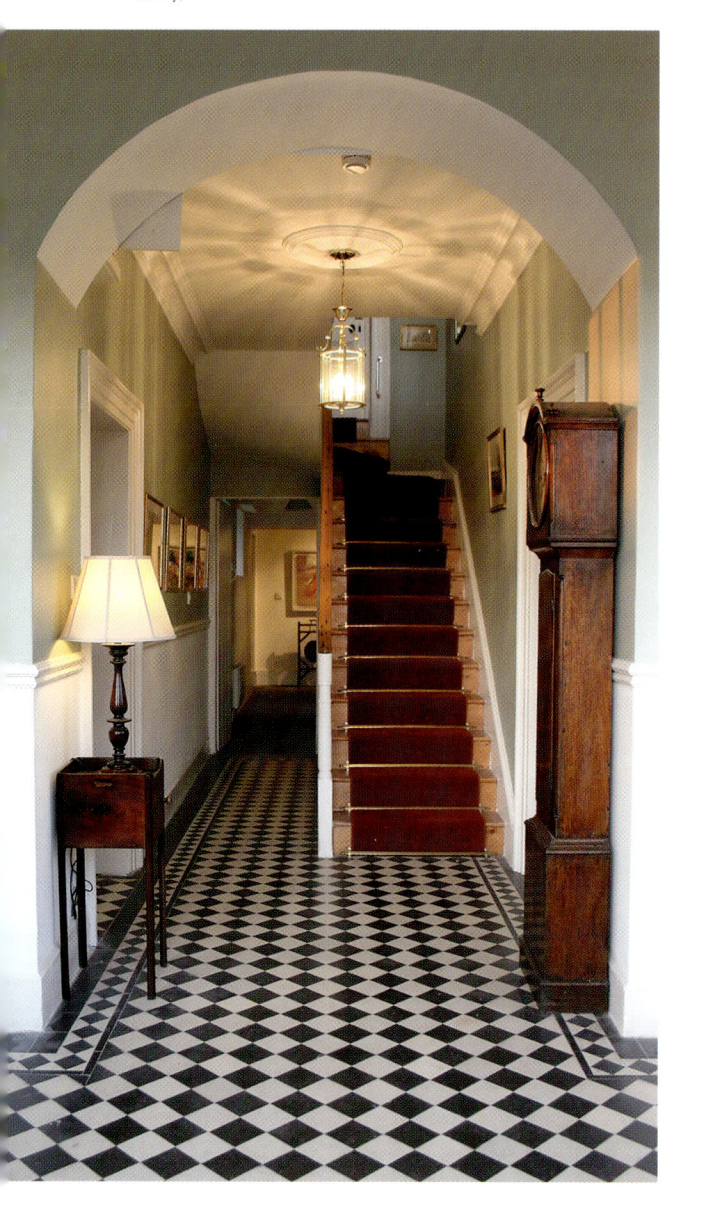

polished limestone of the dining-room fireplace, he recalls that this was where he first became fascinated by archaeology. From the padded window-seat of a bedroom he looks across to the woods of Clifden Hill and remembers what it was like to be a boy with all these summer acres to explore, the Burren outside the door. The hill, the woods, the lake are all still here; fishing visitors can have the services of Toddy O'Loughlin as ghillie. At the house Kathleen Cahill, wearing the green shirt with its Inchiquin House logo, is at hand as housekeeper, adviser and guide, and then she goes off to run her own farm.

Inchiquin House is now managed by John and Tracey Harbison; the cookery school continues and archaeological and botanical tours of the Burren can be arranged.

Inchiquin Country House,
Corofin, County Clare
Tel: 086 8231675

AT HOME IN IRELAND

Inis Beg

Baltimore, County Cork

Paul Keane talks of that Catholic coal merchant Morrough of Duhallow, whose marriage to a daughter of The MacCarthy created the name MacCarthy-Morrough. The family bought the island of Inis Beg in 1830, and the last of the line to live in this house died in 1996. As a building, Inis Beg began as a farmhouse, and the long ridge of the homestead is still obvious as a wing to the equally authentic country house built by Caverlys of Skibbereen in 1899. In-between, there was a period as a hunting lodge, when Inis Beg was only one of three MacCarthy-Morrough estates in County Cork and kept what was reputed to be the biggest beagle pack in Ireland. At that time the estate covered the whole island of 370 acres, but after the Land Commission took over in 1940 only 97 acres remained with the house.

A businessman whose publishing career was spent in constant international travel, Paul's Irish background has the pedigree of Irish parents, his childhood succession of holidays in Ireland and then his own family holidays in Glengarriff. With the

A stone-built slip leads to the water from the boathouse at the edge of the Ilen River.

support of his wife Georgiana, he always intended to get back to live permanently in Ireland, but there must have been times in the first few years since their arrival at Inis Beg in 1997 when both of them remembered ruefully the old adage about good intentions and the road to hell.

'It was daunting, especially through some of the coldest and wettest weather, but it was a great challenge, because what we had to do meant we could start completely afresh. Every single ceiling had to come down, the floor joists had to come up – but you could see the potential. And because we were very fortunate with the experts and the people who worked here with us, we've had great fun in the process.'

With a professional background in strategic planning and with Georgiana's passion for good food and good gardening, the Keanes aligned their determination to live at Inis Beg with their plans to transform its outbuildings into self-catering accommodation. The courtyard cottages, with their wide coach-house windows, have their own little gardens; the Lodge has both garden and paddock with views over the farmland, while the Forester's House hides within 10 acres of woods, with an open fire to complete the impression of rustic homeliness.

The original boathouse for Inis Beg sits at the very edge of the Ilen River, with a fine stone-built slip giving access to the water. On the other side are sloping fields, with thick glades hiding the farmhouses of Aughadown. Houses on the nearside bank are deep in the trees, their own boathouses the only evidence of their existence. With Tony Cohu as architect for the entire project, the family house at Inis Beg was restored without interfering with the characteristic integrity of what is essentially a conventional late-Victorian gentleman's residence. The old orchard was found, rescued and is fruiting again, along with new plantings of quince, plum, cherry, almond, pear and medlar. The woodland gardens have spring shows of daffodils, anemones and bluebells, but there are another 42 acres of woods and, although Paul Keane doesn't dwell on it, there must have been moments close to discouragement when the first years of work were all set back by winter storms. Yet the clearing and cutting were resumed, a woodland improvement scheme was approved by the Forest Service, the

OPPOSITE: *The family house keeps the integrity of a late Victorian gentleman's residence.* RIGHT: *Just a field when the Keanes arrived, the walled garden was first cleared of its wild vegetation by pigs and is now laid out in an overall scheme by Verney Naylor.* BELOW: *The entrance hall and staircase hall at Inis Beg.* (images courtesy of Paul Keane)

swampy patches used as bog or water gardens or, where intractable, as ponds named for the family's deceased dogs.

In the Inis Beg litany of special places, there's yet another: the walled garden. 'Just a field when we came,' remembers Georgiana. 'The walls and greenhouse had fallen down and the whole place was overgrown, so for two years we put in pigs, which ate all the vegetation.' 'And then,' adds Paul, 'we ate the pigs.' Self-sufficiency was the keynote and the garden is laid out in an overall design by Verney Naylor: raised beds packed with vegetables and herbs, soft fruit in high cages and with fine displays of flowers (including, for the Keanes delight in tradition, an auricula theatre, a shelved niche displaying these gorgeous little Alpine primulas or Bear's Ears). The glasshouse and frames lie by the pool building against the south wall. It's not just achievement here: it's enhancement. ♣

Inis Beg Estate,
Baltimore, County Cork
Tel: 028 21745

Kilcash Castle

County Tipperary

For years Kilcash Castle has been a gaunt but inviting finger against the skyline along the Carlow–Kilkenny route heading for Clonmel and Youghal. I must get in there someday, I used to tell myself. I must see what that poem was about, why the name seems to matter so much, why it has such a potent resonance. Inevitably, I never do call in. What brings me here in the end is a newly published book written by Phil Flood and her son John (*Kilcash 1190–1801*), which examines the history of a fortified house held for centuries by the Butlers of Ormond. It is known now simply through that poem encountered during schooldays.

The Floods went to a lot of trouble to unravel the mystique of the verses and also invited Eiléan Ní Chuilleanáin to make a translation in English which might update the versions of Thomas Kinsella, Michael Cavanagh and Frank O'Connor. The poem's original author is uncertain, yet its provenance hardly matters compared to the durability of its lines.

> *Cad a dheanfaimid feasta gan adhmad?*
> *Ta deireadh na gcoillte ar lár …*

Or, as Eiléan Ní Chuilleanáin has rendered it:

> What will we do now for timber?
> With the last of the woods laid low
> No word of Kilcash nor its household,
> Their bell is silenced now …

There is still some timber here, on the southern slopes of Slieve na mBan; the avenue of the poem is still the avenue, although now a roadway. Birds still sing here and, although 'the smooth wide lawn is all broken', there is still a lawn-like stretch of field before the castle's façade. To stand here is to reach a kind of medieval truth, a sense of the place as sentinel over the great valley which stretches between Slievenamon and the Comeragh Mountains, watered by the Suir and all its streams. To learn what was admirable about its most famous owners, the Butlers, and the system they represented, one has to examine the whole complicated, colourful and desperate story of the Butlers of Ormond.

By the dawn of the fourteenth century Kilcash was in the hands of a family named de Valle, whose most notorious member was Dame Alice Kyteler (born around 1262), widow of her third husband, Sir Richard de Valle. When tried for witchcraft, Alice put up such a defence that she was able to marry a fourth time before fleeing to England, where she died. All sides in the affair had complicated inter-matrimonial relationships with one another. When the Bishop of Ossory looked to the civil authorities to prosecute the dame, he found that the lord chancellor of Ireland was related to her first husband, so the bishop had to arraign one of her sons instead.

This brought Arnold la Poer, the Seneschal of Kilkenny, into the field on the son's behalf, la Poer

Kilcash Castle stands like a sentinel over the great valley stretching between Slieve na mBan and the Comeragh mountains. (image courtesy of Richard Cummins)

being related to Alice's fourth husband. He imprisoned the bishop for seventeen days, during which time the whole town of Kilkenny was placed under a papal interdict. The Seneschal was excommunicated and eventually died in a Dublin jail. Everyone suffered, except Alice. But the succession at Kilcash carries on from these de Valles until 1517, after which the estate was taken over by the Butlers of Ormond.

Phil Flood, a native of the townland and married to tillage farmer Tom Flood, took the opportunity of a university extern course to investigate Kilcash more thoroughly. Her son John, currently working for his Ph.D in Trinity College Dublin's Department of English, helped her with technical details and also encouraged the publication of her text. 'When I stand over here, I really feel that my roots extend from my toes down into the ground,' says Phil. Like a well-informed guardian angel she indicates the remains of the walled gardens; we see the little church with its ancient Romanesque doorway and its fascinating headstones and the mausoleum built between church and manor house.

By 1545 Kilcash was in the ownership of James Butler, the 9th Earl of Ormond, who married Katherine MacCarthy Reagh. But we are still generations away from the woman whose grave is now unmarked except by rank grass and weeds. Margaret Burke was born in 1673, daughter of the 7th Earl of Clanrickard and entitled Lady Iveagh by her first marriage to Bryan Magennis. Her second husband was Thomas Butler of Kilcash. Their benevolence is still remembered in these townlands, their only monuments the testament of the Floods and the poem which ends with the prayer that Kilcash will be restored and famous again. ♣

Phil and Tom Flood still farm at Kilcash; John Flood lectures in the English Department of the University of Groningen, the Netherlands. The OPW are continuing a programme of work on the protection of Kilcash Castle.

KILCASH CASTLE   175

Kilcolman Rectory

Enniskeane, County Cork

'I like to cook, I like to garden and I like to entertain,' and Sarah Gornall has found in Kilcolman Rectory near Enniskeane a place in which she can put all her likings to good use. The place itself is expressive of parts of Ireland which city-dwellers don't often find, because we don't often seek them. It's in a valley, the roads are deeply shaded with trees, its houses run their gardens beyond the boundaries of walls and fences, its fields are grassed or golden with corn, its streams slow-moving, thick with cress and banked with wildflowers. Those burns and rills run into the Bandon River, hidden from the main roads and thus from busy travellers, but its hidden distances seem to hint at vistas which on a sunny day in summer resonate like a landscape of the memory, or of the imagination, or of the heart.

It is in this landscape that Kilcolman Rectory was built as a clerical residence in 1855. When Sarah Gornall walked into it a year or so ago it had already been restored and redecorated to such a high standard that she felt nothing had to be done to it in decorative terms. It's Colefax and Fowler throughout, but what could be a signature prettiness is given life and immediacy by Sarah's own imprint. Although built as two storeys over basement, the kitchen area is hidden at the classically plain five-bay entrance front and the ground-floor symmetry is interrupted only by the arched doorway, picked out, like the window surrounds, in a buff finish. The grounds, obviously, were already mature, and the awareness grows that the croquet hoops on one lawn and the tennis court markings on another are there for use, with the rest of the equipment stored in the inner porch beyond the hall door.

The inherent awareness of what visitors are likely to want to do is indicated by the provision of French baskets for swimming towels and other gear in each of the three bedrooms, with robes and slippers in the built-in wardrobes and gumboots on the Lord Robert boot racks. With a fishery almost next door, there are ample appurtenances for fishing guests, and the stable yard behind the house, with its loft and tack room and loose boxes, is all ready for anyone wanting to bring rather than hire a mount. Sarah's Westmeath family background is very well known in racing and horse-breeding circles, but her own adult life has been spent mostly in Castletownshend. After school in England she trained as a cordon bleu cook and her working career included catering in corporate kitchens for City of London clients. 'It was like theatre, and the most wonderful training for one's life in terms of timing and discipline and just getting everything right.' After a business-like engagement with interior design, she trained as a gardener, until marriage and motherhood and a busy life in Castletownshend took up the years between then and now.

Here at Kilcolman Rectory, Sarah Gornall not only espouses perfection but somehow makes perfection look easy. (images courtesy of the *Irish Farmers' Journal*)

She's new to this business, but it seems to suit her. Her garden at one side of the house is a sweep of lawns and fine old trees, with groups of old roses forming miniature avenues to the boxed plots, with their cutting beds, their rows of coloured lettuces and courgettes, of sea kale and butternut squash. A long row of 'mummy' peas has been grown from the offspring of seeds found in, of all places, Tutankhamun's tomb. An uncle had been a friend of the explorer Lord Carnarvon, opener of the great reliquary; in that era gardening was a gentleman's pastime, and it is said that these seeds were discovered, dry and intact, in the tomb and then distributed among the explorer's friends. This likelihood is a much-debated horticultural controversy. What is incontrovertible, however, is that the peas grow larger, taller, paler and sweeter than more usual varieties, as anyone who stays here during pea-picking season will find.

Sarah Gornall has decided not to sacrifice the house to the en-suite doctrine of modern Irish accommodation and expects her guests to share the efficient and well-equipped bathrooms. She has also decided to support as much and as many local producers and shops as she possibly can, from Gubbeen to Glenilen (this dairy delivers its marvellous double cream and yogurts at 5.15 in the morning), while her eggs come from her own daughter at Sophieshens.com. She makes all her own breads, buns, muesli and granola. In a house which expresses a delicacy of style and thoughtfulness which endears it to its already enthusiastic visitors, Sarah Gornall is someone who not only espouses perfection but somehow makes perfection look easy.

Kilcolman Rectory,
Enniskeane, County Cork
Tel: 023 8822913

Kilmokea

Campile, County Wexford

At Passage East there's a sense of Ireland's outline spreading like a map from the point at which the road ends at the water's edge. On this summer's evening the topography is coloured as brightly as a fairytale. A green sweep of the Barrow estuary, the encompassing blue of the sea just beyond the lighthouse, the white sail of a yacht on the swell, the sky radiant even though the sun is now fading to the west. The ferry pants across the river to Ballyhack and the signpost to Campile and Kilmokea Gardens which are this journey's end. A detour to Arthurstown reveals a group of new houses puncturing the gentle sea-edge atmosphere, making it all the more important to cherish people like Mark and Emma Hewlett, the new custodians of Kilmokea House.

It's a bit difficult to do justice to this fine manor house, previously owned by Colonel David and Mrs Joan Price, creators of the seven-acre garden. Now the Hewletts are determined to maintain the loveliness achieved by the Prices while also putting their own stamp of individuality and interest on the house which they have opened to guests. I'm so beguiled by the bedroom view on to the carpet of lawn and so bewitched by the vista of flowering shrubs beneath the walls, the long stretches of cornfields in-between the distant trees and the meadows bordering the river, that I forget the high polish and freshness of the indoor arrangements.

Campile is thick with castles and their rootstock of ringforts and souterrains, Kilmokea is surrounded by a circular earthwork and at one side of the formal garden is a tiny graveyard with two stiles giving access from the road. Passing it to get from one part of the garden to another, I meet Mr Shalloe, patiently cutting the grass on the family grave and repainting the letters on the headstone. There will be a pattern at the graveyard in a week or two; it must be many centuries since some of these stones were set in place, yet as we talk in the sunlight it is obvious that this little cemetery is beloved and cared for, ancient though it may be.

Great Island at Campile was once called Hervey's Island as part of the barony of Strongbow's uncle and Seneschal Hervey de Montmorency. Kilmokea itself is described as a manor, with its status as a rectory for Whitechurch proclaimed by the inscription over the elegant front door of the date 1794 cut for Mr Hancock, the first rector to live here. The Prices took over in 1948 and now house and garden are inseparable. The Hewletts are so committed to this fusion that their major addition has been a conservatory, used as a breakfast-room for guests and as a tearoom for garden visitors.

Mark and Emma talk with enthusiasm of all that they still want to do at Kilmokea, but with the rider that it will be achieved gradually. Emma, from

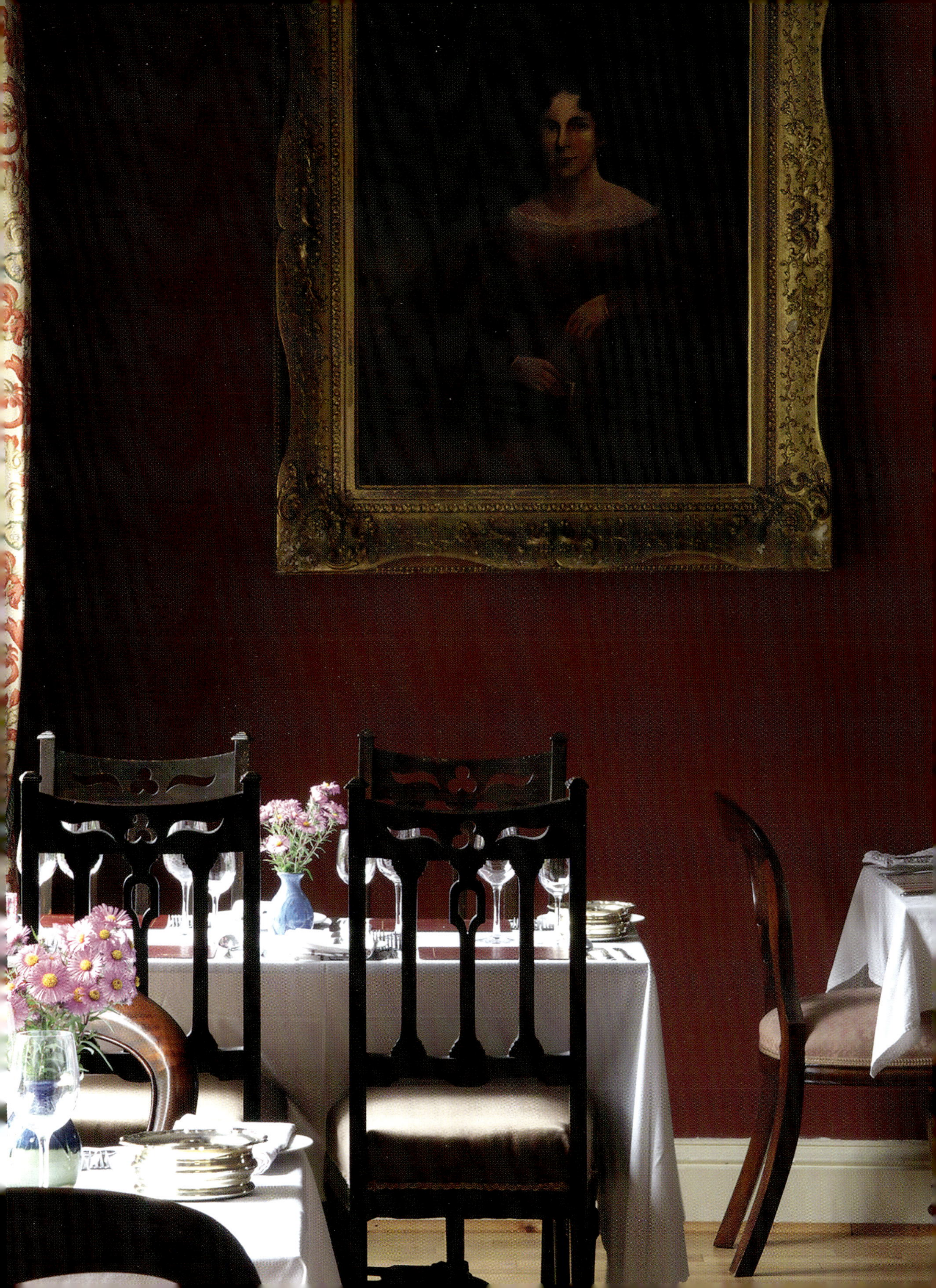

'We just walked into the garden, we didn't even step into the house, we just knew it was right.'

Rathmichael near Bray, met Sussex-born Mark in London; since they married ten years ago there was constant debate on the question of where they really wanted to live. They put Ireland to the test, staying at Hidden Ireland houses, which gave them the idea that they might eventually set up something of the same kind for themselves.

'Also, we had been coming to Wexford for the opera.' Emma, now one of the Wexford Festival Singers, remembers that 'Kilmokea was the second house we looked at here. We just walked into the garden, we didn't even step into the house, we just knew it was right.' They arrived on a brilliant August Bank Holiday with two dogs and the car packed with the bare essentials. And then it rained for the next five days and there was no hot water, or telephone, no Aga and only intermittent electricity. They reopened

AT HOME IN IRELAND

the garden, with Finola Reid cutting the tape in 1998, and immediately there was a telephone call, someone booking to stay. 'It was only when they left that I realised that the duvet on their bed didn't have a duvet-cover,' recalls Emma. 'We never mis-made a bed after that!'

Neither human beds nor flower-beds are mis-made at Kilmokea. The meticulous housekeeping is overseen by Molly Wall, who had also worked for the Prices, and the bountiful garden is in the care of Maurice O'Shea, who came to Kilmokea as a schoolboy in 1978. The future for Kilmokea looks assured: the present is relaxed, welcoming and so utterly comfortable that its unique quality and character unfold like a series of slow and marvellous surprises. ♣

Beguiling bedrooms with views of lawns, flowering shrubs and meadows bordering the river.

Molly Wall has now retired; a new indoor pool has been installed at Kilmokea, where the coach houses have been converted for self-catering accommodation.

Kilmokea Country Manor and Gardens,
Campile, County Wexford
Tel: 051 388109

Lisdonagh House

Headford, County Galway

Life for the Cookes of Lisdonagh House has been a matter of frequent relocation, from London to South Africa and now to this serene country house near Headford in County Galway. Lisdonagh is triumphantly the sum of all the parts, especially as three young children have been added to its attractions.

A home rather than a hotel, this is the place where John and Finola Cooke can perfect their interpretation of Irish hospitality. Finola, a solicitor from Midleton in County Cork, and John, an accountant from Castletown in County Westmeath, had worked together in England while always intending to return to Ireland. In 1995 a weekend tour of Galway brought them to Lisdonagh, with its 200 acres of land and 100 acres of lake. 'Our intention was just to live here, but we weren't quite ready for retirement. And we were determined also that we would restore the house in the best way possible, so we decided to make it a business, aiming for the *Blue Book* market and membership of the Irish Country Houses Association.'

John remembers that it wasn't quite what they had planned on doing, but the location was so lovely, the house had so much potential and there was all that land in which to enjoy his devotion to horse breeding and hunting (this is Magh Seola, or 'the plain of the hunting', according to Irish legend). Lisdonagh's history begins in 1727, when the St George family of Headford commissioned the building of a house here by the firm of Reddingtons. The landscape, however, is an ancient holding, with cairns and *crannógs* and even a visit by St Patrick, who is said to have converted the king of Connacht to Christianity in the parish of Donaghpatrick.

The St George estate was a successor to the Hacketts, who had arrived in Galway with the Norman de Burgos. Once this had been O Flaherty territory; for a few years from 1830 the householders were again O'Flahertys, among them Mary Anne Kelly, otherwise known as 'Eva of *The Nation*'. By 1910 Lisdonagh was owned by the Palmer family, of whom Valda, the last and the most eccentric, is still spoken of with awe and admiration in the neighbourhood. Valda was an indomitable character, hectically involved in family disputes and local arguments, threatening unexpected or unwelcome visitors with her shotgun, while living to the full the Irish country life of hunting, shooting (obviously) and fishing. Yet inside the house life was restricted to a single floor and a few rooms. In a way this may have protected its integrity. Certainly it protected the oval entrance hall, where a famous series of grisaille murals depicting Justice, Vanity, Strength and Liberty has survived long enough for John and Finola to bring it back to something approaching its original glory of foliage, urns and drapery. Depicted in imitation

A home rather than a hotel, Lisdonagh is a place where John and Finola Cooke can indulge and perfect their interpretation of Irish hospitality while offering a unique holiday experience. (images courtesy of the Cooke family)

bas-relief, the paintings are attributed to John Ryan and are believed to be the only remaining evidence of the work of this provincial artist.

Although this house is utterly modern in terms of comfort, service and cuisine, Finola and John Cooke have achieved a strong sense of period in the furniture and décor, using heritage colours for the paintwork and, in the dining-room, hand-painted silk for the curtains. Lisdonagh is a property which unfolds its beauties slowly, from the lakeshore walks to the paths behind the walled courtyards, from the phoenix-like carving from which the front-door lantern is suspended, to the depths of the cellar bar or the calm luxury of the sitting-room.

Galway architect Niall J. Kearns worked on adapting the stables and coach houses as neat, self-catering apartments and advised on the Palladian pavilion at one side of the house: its distinctive pyramidal roof and Venetian window make it a romantic retreat, a rival to the pretty gate lodge at the entrance to the lime avenue. 'This is a business,' says John, 'but it is one with a particular kind of style. We want to keep the homely atmosphere of the house while running an imaginative, high-quality dining-room here and incorporating hotel-standard services. To us it seems a great pity that Bord Fáilte hasn't yet found a way of classifying places of this kind. Houses like Lisdonagh are, or should be, a special category.'

I can only agree, as the Cookes at Lisdonagh maintain the best practice principles for this inspired way of making our fine old houses secure their future while offering a unique holiday experience to the public.

Lisdonagh House,
Cahirlistrane, near Headford, County Galway
Tel: 093 31163
E-mail: cooke@lisdonagh.com

Lismacue House

Bansha, County Tipperary

'We said we'd try anything once,' remembers Kate Nicholson as she speaks of the first time she took in guests at her home, Lismacue House at Bansha. That was to oblige a friend. When by 1990 she and her husband Jim had joined the selective listing of The Hidden Ireland organisation, their visitors came for all kinds of reasons. 'And it's very rewarding,' says Kate, noting that guests don't disturb the integrity of the house but instead complement it. 'A house like this deserves more than two people living in it, which is what we amount to when the three children are away.'

In fact there aren't many houses like Lismacue. The architect was William Robertson, whose task was to replace an earlier seventeenth-century house. Jim and Kate believe that this must have been the largest house in the district, as the records show payment of a hearth tax indicating at least five chimney stacks. There was a still earlier homestead, a fort which is remembered now only in the fort field but from which the name of the house survives, Lios Mhic Aodh.

Lismacue House was built in 1813 for William Baker and his wife Eliza Roberts of Britsfieldstown, County Cork (of the Roberts family of Robertscove and Carrigaline), who brought the then substantial fortune of £12,000 with her to the marriage. They had no children and were in their new house for only two years before William was assassinated while riding homewards from the assizes in Cashel. William Baker was a magistrate and had gone to plead for the lives of two convicted men; his killers seem to have believed that he had gone to condemn them and the murder may have been a reprisal. The Bakers survived at Lismacue; Kate's grandfather, Allen, was in the first graduate class (in 1904) of Ireland's new college of veterinary medicine. He used the stables of the house as a stud and looked after the South Irish Horse, based in Cahir, at the same time as he tended animals in the Glen of Aherlow, then used by the 3rd Brigade of the Tipperary IRA.

Embodying so much of the story of the district and of the county makes Lismacue and similar homes so historically valuable. It isn't just the domestic details, such as the paired donkeys photographed in 1900 drawing the cart they took so regularly to the railway station that they needed no driver. Alerted to their arrival, the station porters would catch them, the visitors would climb on and the party would return to the house. If not stopped, the donkeys would wheel around at the station and return passenger-less.

These links with the past are alive at Lismacue without being dominant. The wallpaper in the drawing-room is the original French watermarked material of 1813, but its delicate tracery of gold on a background of ivory is still wholly appropriate. Here also the pendant frieze catches the light from three large windows shuttered and panelled in pine under deep gilded pelmets; the mahogany doors

ABOVE: *It is the fact that they embody so much of the story of the district and of the county which makes Lismacue House and similar homes so historically valuable.* RIGHT: *The wallpaper in the drawing-room is the original French material of 1813.* (images courtesy of The Hidden Ireland)

show the three-arched design repeated throughout the house, which carries through the Gothic motif distinguishing much of the internal style.

The entrance is from the Gothic porch facing the valley of Sliabh na mBan and the long reaches of timbered pasture in-between. On the other side the Galtees rise in smooth green slopes, with the sound of the little Ara River making its way towards the Aherlow as a soothing background. Down in the courtyard the hens scratch between the cobbles while Kate, who took over the house on the death of her father, William, has reduced the resident stud business to more manageable proportions.

As a barrister practising in Dublin, Jim believes that at Lismacue there's an enviable quality of life; not one without its professional price perhaps, but the choice seems right when he listens to AA Roadwatch as he drives to Limerick Junction to catch the train which will have him in Dublin by 10 a.m. 'Life is about balance,' he says. 'You can't pass on a practice to anyone, but you can pass on a philosophy, and a house like this is a way of life.'

Lismacue House remains open to guests; the Nicholsons also maintain a private boarding stud farm on the property.

Lismacue House,
Bansha, Co. Tipperary
Tel: 062 54106

Lismore Castle Arts

Lismore, County Waterford

Leaning on a stone wall above the river Bride, I'm only halfway home. It's a bright warm day in early summer and all along the riverbank the fields are dense with grass and bordered thickly by distant groves of trees. A stranger stands beside me, captured as I am by the scene: two glossy mares, each with her foal, have trotted over to the shelving bank of the river to drink. The foals dither and skip about the running water but then follow the example of their mothers and lower their tentative muzzles to the stream. River, grass, sky and burnished animals: commonplace enough, yet it is a moment out of time, a moment time itself cannot erase.

In this case, on this day, it seems to glow with elements of perfection. At the Riding Gate entrance to Lismore Castle I discover that I can bring my dog Bobbie into the gardens so long as she's on the lead. This and the welcoming receptionist are the first indications that this is to be a day like very few others, a serendipity day when things – weather, place, people – just happen to go right.

Lismore Castle is the chief reason for this. I'm calling to see the exhibition in the castle gallery, a space created by architect Gareth O'Callaghan of Jack Coughlan Associates in an unused wing in this place of many wings and towers. For some years past the Devonshire family (another of their properties is Chatsworth House in England) have been introducing modern sculpture into the gardens, creating a kind of slow visual shock. They enhance these gorgeous acres and offer us more than roses to think about as we leave. The gallery too is designed to accommodate rather than to disrupt. It is utterly contemporary, yet its long austere space, with mullioned windows in which the drawn blinds reflect their own glazing bars, refuses to challenge the excitement of its contents. 'Titled/Untitled' is a kind of nominal pun on its display, as the gallery space is used for portraits from the Devonshire family collections – a distinctly titled series of dukes and lords and countesses – while the nearby yard buildings, deliberately ungentrified and completely unrestored, house items from the American Rubell family collections of modern art.

The contrasts are resolute. This is a collaboration between two famous collecting families (although the Devonshires have something of an edge, their accumulations beginning in the sixteenth century) using the resources in one case of a great English country house and its aristocratic traditions and in the other those of a unique American family whose collection is housed in a permanent museum in Miami, with a 30,000-volume research library to back it up. The Rubells chose the Chatsworth items and the Devonshires, in the persons of Lord and Lady Burlington (son and daughter-in-law of the current,

Lismore Castle Arts. Time seems to collide here: the world as it is today and the world as it was. (image courtesy of Lismore Castle Arts)

12th, Duke of Devonshire), selected their preferences from the Rubell collection.

With Bobbie tied under a shady tree between beds of peonies and lupins I go past the dozing borders to the stable yard. Here the modern installations of DVD sequences have been set against the old brick walls of the looseboxes. As I watch episodes ranging from prison cells to Monet's garden, I see also the mangers still set in the walls, the tiled floors, the halter-rings and the half-doors blue-painted to keep the flies away. Time seems to collide here, the world as it is today with the world, or part of the world, as it was, a meeting between Van Dyke and Simon Martin, Ezra Johnson and Joshua Reynolds, between the sumptuous silks of a Burlington family portrait by Jean-Baptiste van Loo in 1739 and the stained bunk beds of Pentonville jail.

Returning to the gallery, I exchange the high walls threaded with valerian and daisies for immaculate lawns, plots deep-set and pierced by spires of delphiniums, blue as a Harry Clarke window. At the steps by the Broghill Tower I find a russet acer floating above the outspread bronze wings of Bridget McCrum's Hunting Bird. As I drive away I think of the Gainsborough painting of Georgiana, Duchess of Devonshire, all foaming hair and hat in 1785, and of the DVD screening of a choir of young deaf singers, their voices innocent and poignant. Heading for Youghal through Tallow, we halt for lunch at the Bride View Bar and that scene of the mares and their foals at the riverbank. At Youghal the beach is immaculate, the people few and far between and the dog plunges along the tide in an ecstasy of sand and splashing. So much loveliness, I think, all in one day, all within a 30-mile radius of the city. Some days simply can't be bettered, and this is one of them. ♣

Lismore Castle Arts hosts a major international exhibition each year.

Lismore Castle Arts
Tel: 058 54061

Longueville House

Mallow, County Cork

National Dawn Chorus Day may be in May, but my dawn chorus begins in February, when a spectacularly territorial robin startles the entire neighbourhood with his claims on my garden and his denunciations of any other claimant, expressed at the very peak of his powers around four o'clock in the morning. This does not make one feel particularly fond of dawn, choruses, birds and especially not of robins, until the avenue at Longueville House opens its music book.

I should be grateful to my familiar robin on those cold morning watches. I can understand the longing of that emperor in the fairytale who caged a

Longueville House is an enterprise which already had a terrific national and international reputation. OPPOSITE: *The coach-yard and entrance to 3 acres of walled garden at Longueville.*

nightingale so he could always have its singing at his side. The imprisoned bird lost the will to sing until at last it was released again into the wild. The wild is all around at Longueville, and so are the birds. Their presence is so reliable and so life-enhancing that William and Aisling O'Callaghan have introduced a 'Dawn Chorus' gathering in May, beginning at – well, at dawn.

The couple took over from William's parents, Michael and Jane, at Longueville House in the late 1980s; they had the courage to take on an enterprise which already had a terrific national and international reputation. The young couple settled down to the task – which included raising their own children – and sustained the core of character permeating the

LONGUEVILLE HOUSE

Georgian house at the centre of its 500-acre estate, combining the light-hearted with the professional, the welcoming with the efficient.

Fields of cattle and calves, of sheep and lambs, a long vista of old oaks drawn up in regiments to mimic the Battle of Waterloo, a vineyard from which Michael O'Callaghan still produces wine, access to mountain trails and splendid river fishing, to ancient castles and old houses laden with history and with literary resonances from Spenser to Eoghan Rua O Suilleabhain or Elizabeth Bowen, a Turner conservatory in which to enjoy Longueville's deserved reputation for its cuisine, a 35-acre apple orchard from which William makes apple brandy, cider and apple juice, bees to pollinate the apple trees, a wart stone, a three-acre walled garden dating from 1829 and from which the soft fruit, berries, pears, plums and vegetables for the kitchen are cropped. The wild garlic is for pesto, the herbs for herbal teas and vinaigrettes, the oak and beech shavings go to smoke the salmon and cure the homegrown pork, while blackberries and even the brazenly golden gorse blossom are used to infuse liqueurs.

According to Aisling, this is using what they have:

'The key to any business is to keep hands-on; you have to be devoted to it.' OPPOSITE: *The cellar at Longueville House.* (images courtesy of Ireland's Blue Book)

'What God has given us, really. We have to keep competitive but without any reduction in the quality of our food or our service, and we have to chase the expectations of a changing clientele. But the key to any business is to keep hands-on – you have to be devoted to it.' Aisling and William have already introduced the hugely popular mushroom hunts which are held every October, with carefully guided groups walking the woodlands before returning to a picnic (children) and a sit-down lunch (adults) at the house. Now comes the Dawn Chorus event: wet woodland as a location carries its own message of macs and wellies. Birdsong indicates quiet children only, no dogs and no mobile phones. Patience and sensitivity to the surroundings are also prerequisites for this experience, guided by Michael Copley, who expects listeners to hear the first calls not only of the native birds but also of the migrant arrivals. 'Swallows sing as well, you know,' he says, adding that the cuckoo will be in full mating form and that it may be possible to hear the grasshopper warbler, or even to see the courting display of the snipe, whose call is only part of the act: the male falls from a high perch, vibrating his outer tail feathers as he descends, and then sings to celebrate his landing.

Although they also sing sweetly at sunset, dawn is when the birds most want to attest to their virility by announcing that they have survived and held their territory overnight. Some small birds are the sweetest singers, making up in volume and intensity what they lack in size. And as for my robin! Michael Copley says that, whatever we might think when he visits us in the garden, it is rarely the same one as last year, given that the life expectancy is only thirteen months. So I forgive his ghost as I remember too some lines from Leonora Speyer:

> *But a bird at dawn in a greening tree*
> *And the sound of its fluty filigree*
> *Is worth the night awake.*

Michael O'Callaghan died in March 2010.

Longueville House,
Mallow, County Cork
Tel: 022 47156

Lorum Old Rectory

County Carlow

The daily newspapers are arrayed on the breakfast table, the morning sunlight falls on the heaped strawberries on the buffet, there is honey in its comb, crab-apple jelly in a bowl, fresh country butter, bread still warm from the oven. From the kitchen the aroma announces Clonakilty black and white pudding being grilled to the accompaniment of a purée of local apples. Add to all this the lush pastures of Bagenalstown, a two-day-old foal in the paddock and a view across fields, rivers and woods to villages and towns such as Graiguenamanagh and Borris and Goresbridge; the total comes to Lorum Old Rectory.

Other guests have cycled here on a route organised by Don Smith and his friend Bill Passmore and they are cycling on again. Luggage is brought ahead, pick-ups and put-downs are arranged, and if there is a particularly long ride guests are brought halfway. They are guiltless as they sit down to the feast for what is commonly known as dinner at Lorum Old Rectory. I've done nothing to deserve all this. I've just driven through the landscape of long golden fields rimmed by margins of blazing poppies, along narrow roads bordered with hedges and here and there with garden walls spilling sweet peas over the stones. I've only halted for a few moments at medieval Gowran, the ford on the pass through the dangerous territory of Bealach Gabhrain. This is the place to revisit: granted by the heirs of Strongbow to the FitzWalter Butlers (later Earls of Ormond), this was the family's principal seat until they moved to Kilkenny in 1391.

Once the burial place of the 1st and 3rd Earls of Ormond, the monuments here include the niche tombs of the first Earl of Ormond and his lady, Eleanor de Bohun. But perhaps of greater interest is the memorial of 1646 to James Keally and both his wives, Ellen Nashe and Mary White, with the inscription to the effect that 'Both wives at once alive he could not have / Both to enjoy at once he made this grave'. There are more effigies and Butler tombs here from 1252 to the sixteenth century. There's a ruined Butler castle at Paulstown, which *The Shell Guide to Ireland* says is connected to Eamonn mac Risteard Butler, a famous warrior and literary patron for whom the manuscript Leabhar na Carraige, now in the British Museum and also known as the Book of the O Mulcronys, was written around 1450. And that's just Gowran and its neighbourhood.

Bobbie Smith, who runs Lorum Old Rectory, was born Bobbie Young, daughter of the Cork rugby player Tennant Young, who moved to Borris as manager of the Bank of Ireland. Built in 1864, the Old Rectory at Lorum had been bought as a place to which he could retire, but Bobbie's mother began to take in guests as part of the Fáilte Tuatha scheme;

OPPOSITE: *An inviting view into Lorum's dining-room.*

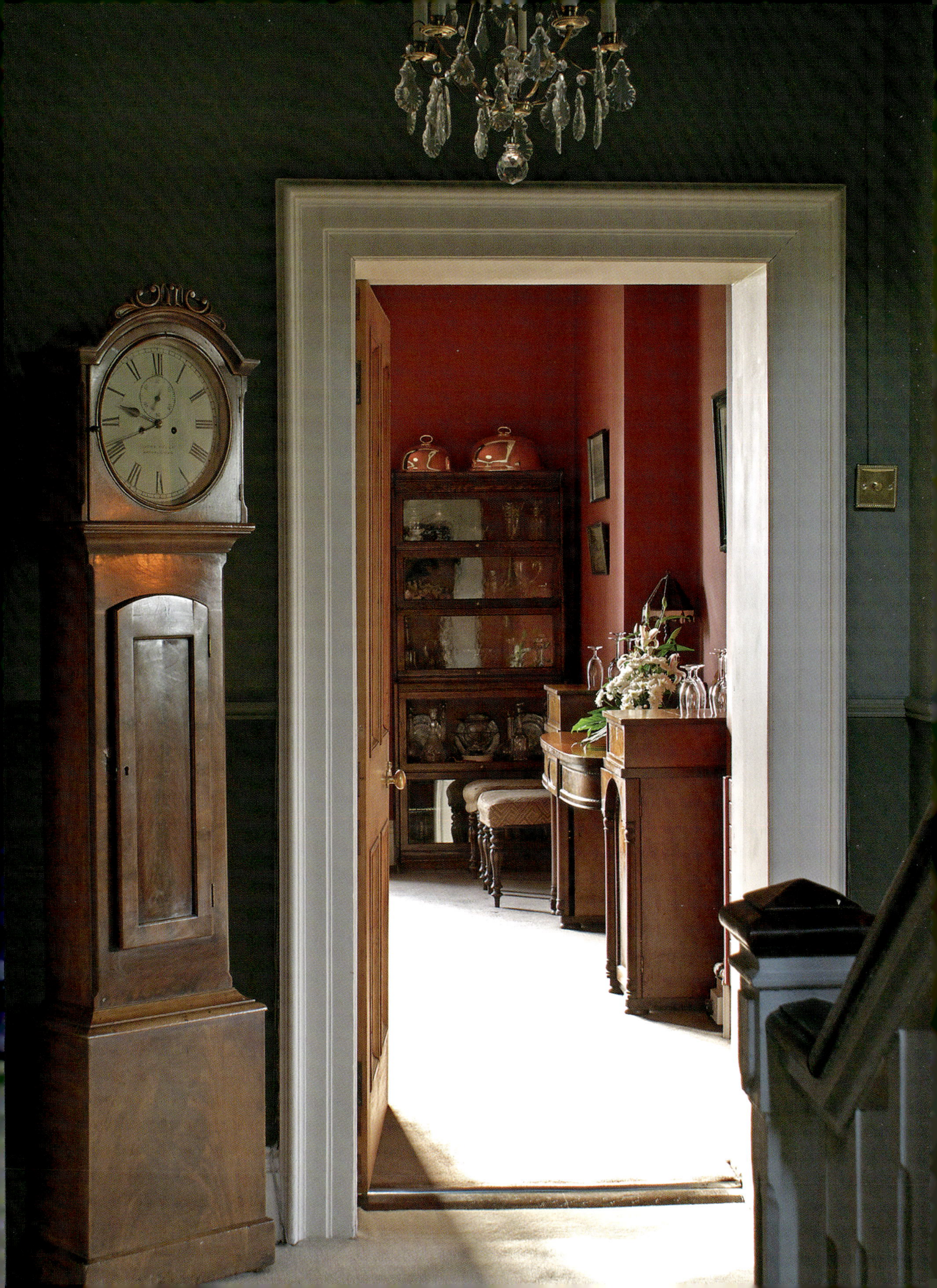

when Bobbie and her husband Don took over, they became founder members of The Hidden Ireland organisation. The stone house sits in eighteen acres, of which seven are farmed for Christmas trees; the rest graze Jacob sheep, the mare and her foal and the family ponies, with lawns, flowers and vegetables as well. Don was born in New Zealand, where he moved from accountancy to a career as a travel courier, landing now and again in Australia. There he met Bobbie, who had left Ireland to work her way around the country by cooking for Australian camping tours. She's now a Euro-toque chef, running the kitchen with Don's help. All in all, the cuisine at Lorum says

ABOVE: *The inner hall at Lorum. Add to all this the lush pastures of Bagnalstown, a view across fields, rivers and woods to villages and towns.* OPPOSITE: *Sixteenth-century panelling, lustrous old floorboards and all the glass and china of an old house shown to perfection.* (images courtesy of *The Hidden Ireland*)

a very great deal for Australian camp-fire cooking.

They've been working here together for fifteen years now, enjoying the teamwork but glad to escape now and again to their little bolthole. 'It's a little like living with the in-laws when you're at it all the time,' says Don. 'But if we didn't like this business we just wouldn't be doing it.' They're doing it well, too, from the magnificent bed made from the sixteenth-century panelling at Borris House to lustrous old floorboards and a dining-room which shows off all the glass and china of an old house to perfection. As I drag myself away, I console myself with Brandon Hill and St Fiachra's Abbey at Ullard and thirteenth-century Duiske, the largest of the Cistercian churches in Ireland. And at the lift of the road always the Barrow, shining between its steep and verdant banks. ♣

Don Smith died in 2002; Éamonn Barrett now runs the cycle tours based at Lorum Old Rectory.

Lorum Old Rectory,
Kilgreaney, Bagnalstown, County Carlow
Tel: 059 9775282

Loughcrew House

Oldcastle, County Meath

Despite the little Greek-revival gate lodge, I know that Loughcrew House as such doesn't really exist. I am visiting what has been retrieved from a series of fires and my head will rest tonight somewhere between an orangerie and a loosebox. But against the silver twilight looms a stark and thrilling relic of Grecian grandeur. How long has it been standing here, I wonder? How long have its great columns survived, for how long has its broken pediment withstood the winds of County Meath?

Well, since yesterday, actually, says Emily Naper, with all the pride of the successful restoration enthusiast. The specialist mason has just left. Slabs of the cut stone from which this facsimile has been created still litter the grassy verge of the ha-ha. Behind us, the house beams quietly where lamps glow through the ferns, the vines, the luxuriant creepers. Before us, the meadow merges invisibly into gardens too far away to be seen in this dusk but for which the temple portico completes a splendid design. This is the fantasy world of Loughcrew House, taking its cue from the whimsical history of the site and its houses which, in their turn, were overlooked as we are now by the magical prehistoric presences on the surrounding drumlin hills.

Although living at Loughcrew near Oldcastle for more than 400 years, the Napers are newcomers to this landscape – as are we all. Charles Naper takes me through the sheepfolds to the neolithic passage-tombs of the earliest people of Loughcrew. There are thirty, at least, of these chambered cairns and tumuli on the ridges. They are mysterious indicators of those first farming communities who honoured their dead and sent them to eternity with rituals we can no longer interpret.

Loughcrew itself was part of the Plunkett estates before Cromwell changed everything; a fortified tower house stood where the ruins of the medieval church can still be seen, but its stones were used to build the first Naper residence in 1673. This was the home of the sister of Sir William Petty, the cartographer and surveyor who founded Kenmare and amassed huge estates in Ireland. But the Plunketts came before Petty and his brother-in-law William Naper; now Emily Naper, of the Dashwood family of West Wycombe, is also, through one of those marital connections which unite so much of Ireland and Britain, a maternal granddaughter of the Plunketts of Dunsany Castle.

The little family church of the martyred St Oliver Plunkett, Archbishop of Armagh, ends a fine old avenue which cuts through the current recreation of a remarkable garden. When Charles and Emily Naper came back to Loughcrew in 1978, it was to consider the future of the house. This had suffered its third fire since 1888 (it had first been rebuilt in 1823 to a design by C.R. Cockerel) and had been more

ABOVE: *Alice and the caterpillar recreated in the gardens at Loughcrew House.* RIGHT: *Despite these shades of the ancient past, Loughcrew buoyantly embraces the future.* (images courtesy of Emily Naper)

or less abandoned. But they also took the trouble to look closely at what was left of the former gardens. This is a landscape out of time even though its references, carefully amassed and detailed, all exist within a horticultural chronology. The beautiful iron gates set into the high garden wall incorporate the original frame of the front door of Loughcrew House of 1673. Rebuilding the Georgian portico and the reconstruction of the seventeenth-century terrace and canal are part of an encompassing design stretching into the surrounding landscape.

Emily herself is an irrepressible personality: although she has immense respect for old crafts and customs, she knows how to enjoy what life throws in her path. Her creativity is a kind of communication in itself. Her workshops on gilding and decorative finishes, her guest lectures on watercolour painting, embroidery, pottery, sculpture and creative writing, are all held, so to speak, on campus. Loughcrew House is beautifully and imaginatively decorated with textiles, paint, stencils and murals, and in the workshops old Loughcrew meets and finds the new. The courtyard still reveals such ancient economies as the pierced steel of the ceiling of the bakery, overlain by a layer of sand and heating the drying-room immediately above it. The herring-bone cobbles still stud the stable yard, shaded by its massive cantilevered roof; the huge weighted bellows in the forge still hang from its corner shafts. The hay loft is now an arts centre, and the planked counters of the ironing-room are laden with materials for a gilding class. Loughcrew is all alive, buoyantly embracing the future.

Loughcrew House now offers self-catering rental as well as classes and studios.

Loughcrew House and Gardens, County Meath
Tel: 049 8541356

Mahaffy House

North Great George's Street, Dublin

Desiree Shortt was scanning the carpet for fragments of gesso which had fallen from a corner of her drawing-room ceiling when from outside we heard the clatter of horses' hooves. At the window of her house in North Great George's Street we watched the arrival of a score of dapper horse-drawn carriages. Something to do with Bloomsday, we decided, given that Joyce's house is only a few doors away at number 35. And so it was, with Senator David Norris, top-hatted and tail-coated, organising the cortège for the re-enactment of Paddy Dignam's funeral from the Hades chapter of *Ulysses*. Ron Massey, proprietor of the engraved glass hearse and the glossy pair of Belgian Blacks pulling it at a properly sedate pace, explained that this, he thought, was the eighth time he had buried Paddy Dignam.

On a sunny morning in June the scene appeared totally at one with the character of this street of tall Georgian town houses: the weathered red brick, the plaques on house after house, the balconies and exquisite fanlights and today the burnished horses and their ornamented harnesses. Yet when Desiree Shortt bought number 38 in 1975 for £8,000 there were twenty-seven people living in it. Its rooms were divided and its beauties on the verge of extinction. Friends of hers had bought across the road and she now says that for eight years she had been looking at number 38 and denying that it had any real claim on her attention. 'Then at four o'clock one morning I woke up with that awful knowledge one gets at four in the morning and said I'm going to buy that house, and I bought it the very next day.' Which was just as well because soon afterwards a riding accident left her almost paralysed. 'I lost my job, never saw my horse again, never saw my car again and at first was expected never to walk again. The house, which I had taken on more or less as an interest, suddenly became my only source of income.' She had always been good with her hands and took as quickly as she could a course in china restoration in London and moved as quickly as she could into the basement of number 38. Now she has the largest china restoration studio in Europe.

Built in 1785 by the stuccodore Charles Thorpe with four storeys over basement, twenty-two rooms and seven flights of stairs, Mahaffy House is named for the forty-year-long residence here of Sir John Pentland Mahaffy, provost of Trinity College from 1914 to 1919. The largest fanlight on the street spans the hall door and its two sidelights; there are two internal fanlights. Desiree Shortt insists that, so far as the house is concerned, she is not a purist. It took

OPPOSITE: *When Desirée Shortt bought Mahaffy House in 1975, its rooms were divided and its beauties were on the verge of extinction.*

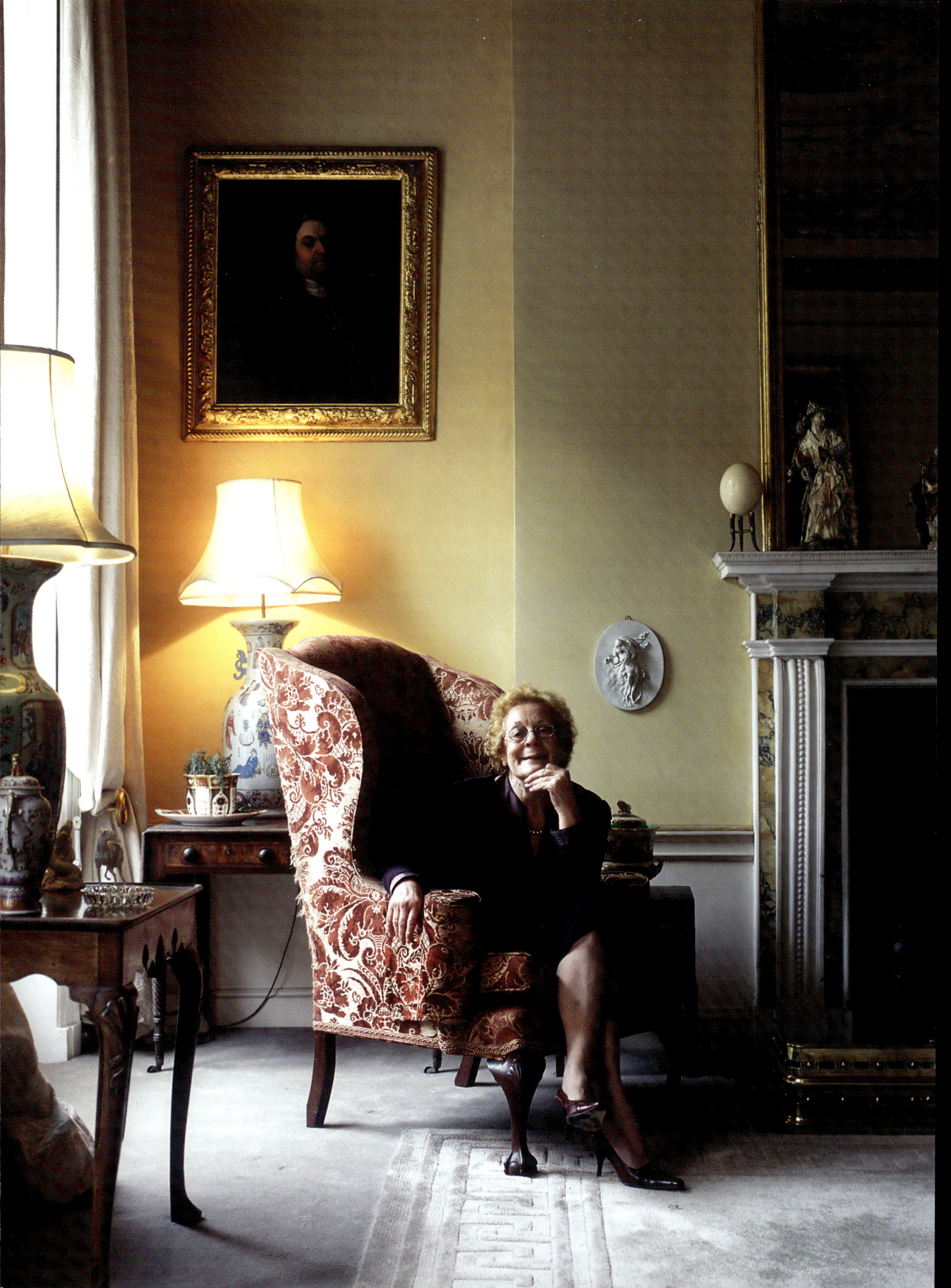

'seventeen years, three months and two days' – a term recited with the relish of a litany – to get final vacant possession, and she could only work on each room as its tenants left. That allowed her to gather items here and there – a nineteenth-century Italian gilt mirror was bought, she says, from a dealer who allowed her six months' credit, a beautifully carved door in the dining-room was rescued from a bonfire for £5, the luxurious wine-red damask hangings around her four-poster bed are dyed tablecloths.

The gas fires replacing the original chimneypieces have been removed room by room in the most expensive part of reaching carpet stage. In the drawing-room the chimneypiece cost more than the house, but here the ceiling is recognised as one of the most important Georgian town ceilings in Dublin. Seventy years of smoke and cooking fumes and the

ABOVE: *Dyed tablecloths provide the luxurious damask hangings in a bedroom.* ABOVE RIGHT: *Photographs of the earlier decoration of Mahaffy House have been found in the National Archives and recorded for future use.* OPPOSITE: *The ceiling in the drawing-room is one of the most important in Dublin.* (images courtesy of James Fennell)

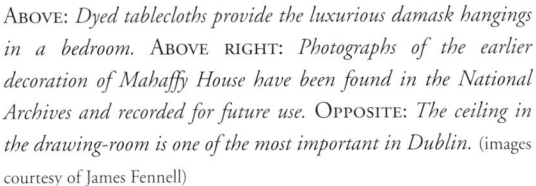

installation of electric lighting had damaged all this, but David Griffin, director of the National Archive, found photographs of the original decoration. The long shuttered windows are framed in carved pelmets and curtained in ivory damask: 'The colours really were my interpretation,' says Desiree. 'I have recorded the originals with the deed so that the next occupiers will have the option of restoring them again.'

Given her insistence that she's not a purist, Desiree Shortt has achieved a marvellous feat at number 38 North Great George's Street. Her own personality has flowered here, but her innate respect of the quality of the house and the intentions of its builder has brought back to life even the very meaning of the word restoration.

Renovation of the roof at number 38 by Sheehan and Barry of Dublin was grant-aided by the Irish Georgian

Society. The house was also used as a location for the 2004 film Laws of Attraction *and is available for conferences and private events.*

Mahaffy House,
38 North Great George's Street, Dublin 1
Tel: 01 872 2285

MAHAFFY HOUSE   201

Martinstown House

The Curragh, County Kildare

Here I am in Clogh. A chance visit, given that I have never before heard of Clogh, or of the mines that sustained its people for more than a century up to the late 1950s. Sheer curiosity has brought me to this well-kept midlands village, with a neatly thatched cottage or two and a Catholic church reached by an avenue of pollarded limes. Inside, the church has no altar at all, in the usual meaning of the word: just a raised slab of stone set in a planted garden.

Getting to Clogh allows a glimpse of the old mine works, a terrace of miners' cottages on the high road and then the little village itself. Martinstown House has set me up for all this. I am in a responsive mood after a businesslike morning, which began with eggs boiled fresh from the hen, an exchange of biscuits with two aged donkeys, a frisk through the hen coop for more booty, a conversation with fellow guests and a meandering inspection of the walled garden, one of the joys of Meryl Long's life at Martinstown.

In other words, getting away from Martinstown is difficult, even for travellers with the most pressing engagements. The languorous alluring landscape, with sheep like a blizzard on distant hills, sleek horses and their foals skidding to a halt at a fence and browsing cattle settling for the night under the trees: this is the territory of pastoral fantasy. It is the hinterland to which the motorway is the margin; we never move into it, except with some excuse. Now my excuse is Martinstown House and Meryl Long.

The house is a visual delight from beginning to end. It is simply an exercise in the mock-Gothic style, an ornamental cottage set in a lawn against a background of oaks, beeches, limes and chestnuts and an expanse of pasture. Horses and training and hunting and racing have all left their mark on the demesne. The immaculate stables, cobbled and drained with their mangers intact, may be empty now, but they form part of a purposely designed court of farm buildings, symmetrical as a chapel.

The house originated as a shooting lodge for the second Duke of Leinster, whose family seat was Carton. Emily Lennox was the first Duchess of Leinster (and mother of the ill-fated Lord Edward FitzGerald). Her sister Louisa married Tom Connolly and lived nearby at Castletown. As if there were not enough stately homes in the family (Leinster House in Dublin was another), Kilkea Castle, a dower house for the third Duke of Leinster and the seat of the 8th duke after the 1949 sale of Carton, is only down the road from Martinstown. Kildare was the centre of a particular kind of universe for the grandees of many centuries, and Martinstown House, secluded and discreet, was a playground.

It was designed by Decimus Burton, who was instructed by the duke to rebuild what had been the farmhouse home of a Miss Martin who was then, or later became, the duke's mistress. Throughout the house the Gothic detail is a constant pleasure. The pierced bargeboards, the porched stone-floored entrance hall, the fireplaces even in the bathrooms, the vaulting of the internal corridors, all express the freedom of a chosen style. Meryl Long's insistence on the continuance of the house as a family home means that the atmosphere is one of trusting fidelity to the designer's ideal. Rugs and deep armchairs, untroubled light from leaded windows and broadcast lamps – all the paraphernalia of a house which has

ABOVE: *All the paraphernalia of a house that has been lived in for centuries is here for discerning guests.*

been lived in for comfortable centuries are here for the discerning guest.

Martinstown House has had several owners, several tenants, many of them as colourful, for perhaps different reasons, as the dukes. Otto Scorzeny, the German paratroop commander who helped Mussolini escape from Allied captivity during the Second World War, was one of the more recent. Another was Major R. Turner, the official handicapper of the Turf Club.

MARTINSTOWN HOUSE

ABOVE: *A languorous alluring landscape is the territory of a pastoral fantasy.* RIGHT: *The Gothic detail is a constant pleasure throughout the house.* (images courtesy of The Hidden Ireland)

Meryl Long's late husband Tom, who bought the property in 1970, was master of the Kildare Hounds and, like Meryl, was devoted to terriers. Three of them follow us now as we turn back towards the house from which I must somehow detach myself. In the car I pass meadows gilded with buttercups. The roads are brimming with Queen Anne's Lace, and Lyric FM pours Carolan and Purcell into the air as I go on my way, rejoicing, towards Athy, and Castlecomer, and Clogh.

While Meryl Long remains involved, Martinstown House is now run by Edward and Roisín Booth.

Martinstown House,
The Curragh, County Kildare
Tel: 045 441269

Mobarnane House

Fethard, County Tipperary

The Craik-Whites at Mobarnane are preparing for what might be called a three-house party this Christmas. Their home near Fethard incorporates not one but three houses, the oldest recorded in 1544. Traces of such antiquity are few in what is an inviting Georgian building restored with flair, opened as guest accommodation and available for modern versions of old-fashioned house parties. 'That,' says Sandra Craik-White, 'is what these houses were built for, entertaining friends and relatives in days when travel was arduous and time-consuming.' Travel is still arduous and time-consuming, but the promise of fire-lit sitting-rooms, candle-lit dining-rooms and lamp-lit bedrooms can make any journey worthwhile. At Mobarnane that promise is generously fulfilled.

Sandra and her husband Richard made their own journey back to this mellow landscape between the Knockmealdowns and the Comeraghs. Although childhood friends in the area, career choices took them to England, where Sandra was a nurse and Richard a teacher. After their marriage they worked together at Richard's boarding-school and when their own two sons left home they decided that, as they were undaunted, foolish and still under fifty, it was time to begin something new. 'I wanted to cook, Sandra loves old houses and is an enthusiastic gardener, and we had always intended to come back to Tipperary some day. And by the time we wondered what had we begun, it was too late for us to turn back.'

The last renewal of Mobarnane had been the 1820s design by Thomas Tinsley, father of architect William Tinsley of Clonmel. It had been visited as a prospective home by Sandra's own father in 1946; he had turned it down as 'too far gone'. Richard calculates that during the reconstruction there was a potential for disaster every twenty minutes; there were, at one time, eight sub-sites of restoration activity, with Martin O'Reilly working not merely on the big recessed shutters with their meticulous little handles still intact but also on the vast beams of the stable-loft roof, while Tynan Construction repaired all the masonry.

Sandra remembers her own and her sister-in-law Gina Collins' interminable sewing for the cushions and curtains – many of the windows in the house have twelve-foot drops. The upholstery includes patterns of the pineapple symbol of hospitality, the furniture is uncrowded, the family portraits do not domineer from their apparently age-old positions along two wide staircases. The vast windows in which the sashes and glazing bars had to be replaced look over lawn and stream on one side and on the other the view reaches beyond the avenue to the purple Comeraghs.

Mobarnane is first mentioned in the Ormond deeds of 1544, as part of a grant of lands from the Ormond estates. By 1590 the tower house was recorded as the birthplace of the Revd Thomas Carron or Carew, an army chaplain; in 1654 it was described as 'a small castle wanting repair'. The old foundations of that castle, with some of its outer walls, can still be seen at Mobarnane, which Richard and Sandra believe is named for its location – a gap on boggy land. This was the site chosen for the three-storey farmhouse built on to the castle foundations in 1735. It was the home of Mathew Jacob, one of the jurors at the trial of Fr Nicholas Sheehy of Clogheen, who was convicted and executed for the alleged murder of a man called John Bridge in 1766. As a result it was said that the crows would never nest again at Mobarnane. Sandra gives the lie to both charge and curse: the crows have had a high old time in Mobarnane's chimneys and poor Fr Sheehy was the victim of a blatant conspiracy as the said John Bridge (so-called because he was a foundling infant rescued from a bridge) was subsequently discovered to be living in Canada.

No shadow of those troubled times now dims the serenity of Mobarnane. Their only trace is in the lower ceilings at the rear of the present house and the stone passages leading from kitchen to dairy, larders, laundries, stables and coach house. Or to the fine red-brick walls of the old orchard which now grows grass, surviving fruit trees and a flock of Rhode Island Reds so free range as to be an independent state. It's all available for family or friendly groups of six to eight people at a time. The house party is ideal for winter breaks and gatherings, perfect for companionable walks in the hills or trips to Cashel or Cahir. And while Mobarnane is built for and embraces the house party, its welcome extends to all who love the Irish countryside at its most hospitable best.

Mobarnane House,
Fethard, County Tipperary
Tel: 052 613 1962
www.mobarnanehouse.com

Built for entertaining friends and relatives in days when journeys were arduous and time-consuming, Mobarnane House can make any journey worthwhile. (images courtesy of The Hidden Ireland)

MOBARNANE HOUSE 207

Mount Rivers

Carrigaline, County Cork

'I was just very fond of it. That's the simple all of it, really.' Except that it wasn't. Lesley Roberts speaks of his home, Mount Rivers in Carrigaline, with an affection which disguises the many choices and terrors of taking it over at a time when it seemed as if there was nothing left for it to do but die.

In the kitchen, which they had to recreate from a jumble of pantries, corridors and rubble, Lesley, who prefers this version of his name, and his wife Dorothée and their two daughters present lunch at a long deal table; the walls bear framed evidence of Dorothée's talent as a painter of vibrant watercolours; the doors open onto the grassed terrace, from which ancient steps lead under a belfry to a walled orchard. Everywhere there are plants, pictures, books, indications of preferences and passions and signs of a house reclaimed and alive again.

'When I was at school in Bandon I was brought down here at weekends and allowed roam around the place, and of course I made my way to the attics, and I suppose I just got an appetite for what the house represented, both in terms of family and of buildings and history. I know that in the pecking order of Irish houses it's a minor subject, but I got interested. And I know that it's a very plain house now. But it has charm, don't you think?'

I do, but I wonder how much of this is due to the enthusiasm of Lesley and Dorothée themselves, and how much to the fact of having survived, despite the absence of its land and the effect on its proportions, on its intrinsic grace, of its location in a plantation of suburban housing. Survive it does, however, containing within itself its cherished history: in this kitchen a wall plate of Bath stone is inscribed by sculptor Ken Thompson to commemorate the date of the rebuilding of the kitchen. Outside the door are the flagstones from the Church of Ireland church in Carrigaline ('My parents were married on those stones,' says Lesley). There is a font from Mourne Abbey, stones from Bowen's Court, a frieze of dolphins and lyres from another Roberts home at Hoddersfield. In a bedroom the fireplace is lined with tiles from the Carrigaline Pottery's early days, when Lesley's grandfather Hodder Roberts farmed at Mount Rivers and established the pottery in 1927.

The house was built in the 1760s by James Morrison (of Morrison's Island in Cork). In 1786 it was taken by the Roberts family, which had been in the county since the early seventeenth century, settling at Bridgetown Abbey, Shanballymore and Britfieldstown in Roberts' Cove. Born in 1760, William Roberts bought out the lease of Mount Rivers and died here in 1826. He is buried, says Lesley with relish, in a cast-iron coffin at Tracton.

Reared in the French medieval town of Senlis, Dorothée studied art and architecture in Paris but

ABOVE: *Lesley Roberts in a house that remains busy, welcoming and graceful and which would still be recognisable to its earliest residents. The proportions are easy and any details removed or damaged are being replaced, as in the hall ceiling frieze, which is being copied from that at the old Roberts house at Britfieldstown.* (images courtesy of the Roberts family)

committed herself to painting and now exhibits both here and in France. When she arrived with Lesley at Mount Rivers in 1983 it had been virtually empty for nearly thirty years and they discovered that there wasn't one room even vaguely liveable-in. 'We had no choice, really,' she recalls now. 'We were full of hopes, and at that age you're more inclined to see things as they will be, not as they are.' Both agree now that this was all very fine at the time but that they wouldn't want to repeat the experience, yet there is also an acknowledgement that the hardship, the austerity, was an advantage in that it allowed a way to grow into the house.

Lesley likes the idea that houses can adapt to changed circumstances: 'I've seen so many places rotting away while the land is kept. So while we've been here it's been more a matter of repair than restoration, though in a way it has been transformed. And it's true that poverty has its virtues: most of the important things in the house are intact, it hasn't been interfered with in terms of improvements over the years.'

With prints and paintings taking up one of the lovely drawing-rooms, Mount Rivers would still be recognisable to its earliest residents. Bit by bit the few unfinished rooms are coming back – a chair rail here, a fireplace, a cornice, a banister. Amid children and work are hints of Lesley's addiction to collecting – headstones on the stairs, bags full of envelopes feeding his passion for postmarks: 'Ballyfeard, Ballinaclashet, Nohoval, Rochestown, Monkstown – all these places have lost post offices in the last twenty years. A postmark is a little relic of a place – and if you collect at all, there's an urge for completion, isn't there?'

Mount Rivers remains a private home for the Roberts family.

MOUNT RIVERS

Mount Vernon

New Quay, County Clare

Travelling westwards, take the road from Crusheen to Tubber and then from Tubber to New Quay. No – first get the folding landscape map of the Burren by Tim Robinson and on the tip of a centrefold you will find an area called the Flaggy Shore and a note showing Mount Vernon Lodge, 'Lady Gregory's summer home'. The road from Crusheen is vaulted by trees until the stepped escarpments emerge and the hazel woods descend to scrub. If you stop, you will find the rocks in bloom: scarlet cranesbill geraniums sprouting from the stone.

The field between Mount Vernon and the shore is thick with grasses silvering in the wind, with dog-daisies and poppies and with the deep blue of cornflower. Behind the house the lawns are shaded by cypress trees and walls supporting old roses, with wide terracotta bowls in which water lilies expand like botanical peacocks; the out-offices are white-painted and red-trimmed like the house itself. The thing about Mount Vernon is that, although there have indeed been different families in possession, they were all in love with the place. You sense it: the building embraces you.

The house was built late in the 1700s for Colonel William Persse of Roxborough, a soldier in the American War of Independence who became a friend of George Washington and who, on his return to Ireland, named his house after the home of America's first president. Authenticity is important to Mark Helmore and his wife Ally Raftery, even to keeping the ancient stile by the back gate. But they are not obsessive, so that while the original structure is largely unchanged, the house also represents all that has happened to it. The rooms suggest the accumulated history of its occupants: books bought long ago, baskets from someone's years in Africa, lamps from someone's time in Bahrain, furniture bequeathed, cabinets carved and painted, mirrors discovered and restored, a bed bought in China a marvel in itself and a divan gratefully received as a gift from a friendly antique dealer.

This might be called eclectic, but in fact it is calm; nothing is crowded except the bookshelves. My bedroom opens on to the terrace of the walled garden, the roses outside matched by the roses on the dresser, which also holds a rack of books but no television, radio, telephone or tea tray. That's a decision, not an oversight, for while Mark and Ally are offering accommodation (as part of the Hidden Ireland organisation) they are doing it their way. 'It's a place,' says Ally simply, 'where people just come to a halt.'

Even while active and engaged, Mark and Ally themselves embody that gift of coming down where

Mount Vernon. 'A place where people just come to a halt.'

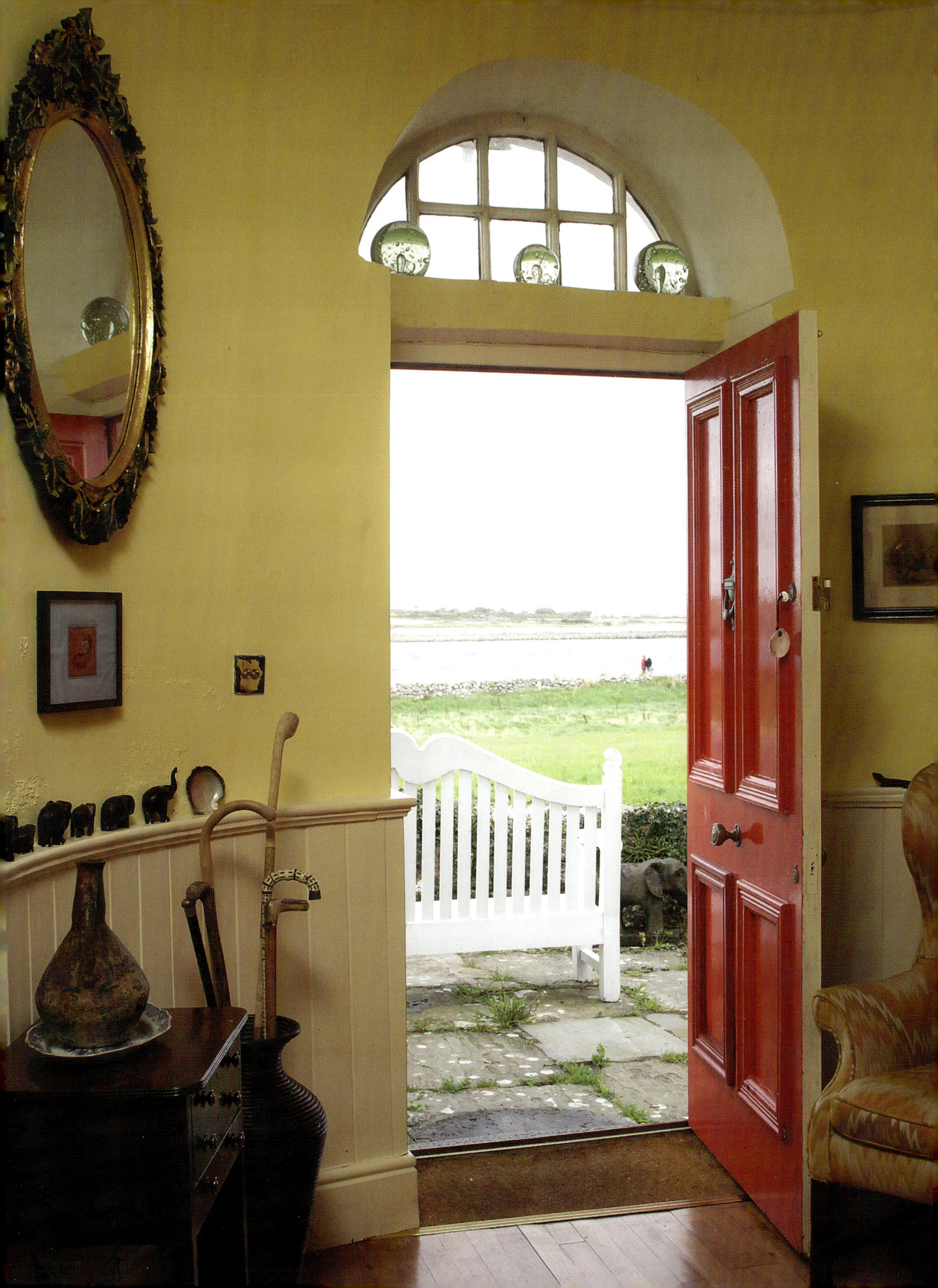

Mount Vernon has welcomed Lady Gregory's friends and those of her nephew Sir Hugh Lane, including W.B. Yeats, Seán O'Casey and George Bernard Shaw.

you want to be. Snug on its gentle, tree-sheltered slope, a narrow roadway separating it from the sea at the southern rim of Galway Bay, the house has been a holiday home for most of its long life. Lady Augusta Gregory was a descendant of William Persse and Roxborough was her girlhood home before she married and moved to Coole Park. By that time Mount Vernon was the dower house for Finavara House a few miles away, but in the late nineteenth century it was recovered by Lady Gregory's nephew, Sir Hugh Lane. After his death with the sinking of the *Lusitania*, she brought family and many of her friends here, including W.B. Yeats, his painter brother Jack, Seán O'Casey, George Russell, John Millington Synge and George Bernard Shaw.

They all worked here but they also had fun, not least when Augustus John came to visit and whiled away his time by building the three monumental brick fireplaces, the lemon-coloured one in the dining-room studded with ceramic tiles. It was Mark's mother, Mary Helmore, who made Mount Vernon into a permanent residence again when she moved here from London and restored the house internally; the group of decorators, led by Robert Hawes of this parish who came later to help Mark and Ally with

The rooms reflect the accumulated interests of the proprietors in a way which might be called eclectic but which in fact is calm. Augustus John whiled away the wet weather by building fireplaces at Mount Vernon. (images courtesy of Keewi Photography)

their refurbishments, remembered working on the house for Mrs Helmore.

As we talk, Ally remarks that so much that has been done at Mount Vernon has been done 'by hand'. That's true, and it informs the character of the house. After a dinner of freshly caught fish and homegrown vegetables, I walk to the strand. It's late but still lightsome and here, evoking all those Olympians of Lady Gregory's era, the sun is setting gloriously over Galway Bay: Mount Vernon's enduring masterpiece.

Mount Vernon,
Flaggy Shore, New Quay, County Clare
Tel: 065 7078126

Newbridge House

Donabate, County Dublin

Newbridge House and Demesne at Donabate in County Dublin is an example of a municipal adventure in the preservation of an historic property. As the responsibility of Fingal County Council it offers an object lesson in how a local authority tackles its heritage responsibilities. The first pleasure comes with the turn off the motorway at a hair-raising junction into what seems to be a quiet country lane. The house is visible from the avenue winding through the park, its mellow stone punctuated by distinct coigns and by the tripartite doorcase above a flight of railed steps. The roof, with its massive chimneys, is fronted with a parapet decorated with urns and eagles. This neat façade overlooks the 300-acre park,

Newbridge House continued as a home for a single family: everything here was used by the Cobbes and everything echoes them, including (right) the eighteenth-century kitchen. The house was built in 1737 for Dr Charles Cobbe, later Archbishop of Dublin.

the cobbled courtyards and beyond them not only the kitchen garden, now under restoration, but orchards and borders and a wildlife refuge established by the last proprietor.

Built in 1737, Newbridge was designed by George Semple (according to the handbook) or by Richard Castle (according to Mark Bence-Jones – although he adds the qualification 'probably') for Dr Charles Cobbe, Archbishop of Dublin from 1746 to 1765. Born in 1686, Cobbe came to Ireland as chaplain to his cousin, the Duke of Bolton, who had been appointed Lord-Lieutenant. He died at the Bishop's Palace in Dublin in 1765 but his descendants remained at Newbridge until 1985. While changes were made through the generations, they were organic alterations, growing from the need for more rooms or for more grandeur, especially after 1751 when Colonel Thomas Cobbe married Lady Elizabeth Beresford, daughter of the Earl of Tyrone.

The great distinction of Newbridge now, apart from its architectural attributes, lies in its continued existence as a home for one family. From the Cobbe coat of arms (a pelican and crown) to the heads of Abyssinian buffalo, from the altar table

NEWBRIDGE HOUSE 215

ABOVE: *The ceiling of the red drawing-room is attributed to Richard Williams, pupil of Robert West, one of the finest stuccadores in Ireland at the time.* OPPOSITE: *With no fewer than thirty children living in the house at one period, it's no wonder that the Museum of Curiosities is so educational.* (images courtesy of Shane Moloney)

from Malahide Castle to the steel and wicker baby carriage, everything here was used by the Cobbes and everything reflects them. The sunflower andirons at the hall fireplace, the chandelier with its fringe of swans, the mirrors and console tables, the cabinets and porcelain – all came here because they were wanted, used and appreciated. Recurring bowls of fresh flowers scent the air as Lady Betty smiles down from her place among the family portraits as if we were welcome, if somewhat unexpected, late-comers to one of her *soirées*. Extending the formal Georgian block into a bow-ended drawing-room or ballroom in which she and her husband entertained with gusto, the couple also brought to the house a substantial collection of pictures and furniture in what may have been the heyday for Newbridge. The red drawing-room, so-called because its expanse of crimson wallpaper was matched by the carpet and beautifully draped curtains, has an exquisite ceiling attributed to Richard Williams, a pupil of Robert West, one of the finest stuccodores in Ireland's architectural history.

This work is both intricate and light, and indeed nowhere in the house is there any decorative heaviness. Much of it – again thanks to Lady Betty – represents some of the best work of Irish craftsmen. The public rooms include the dining-room, the library (from which the fine collection of books was sold while the house was uninhabited for several years) and the inner hall, with its portraits of Swift's beloved Vanessa (Esther Van Homrigh) and of playwright Richard Brinsley Sheridan. Here also, suspended on its blue and crimson ribbon, is the Victoria Cross won by Lieutenant-Colonel Alexander Cobbe in Somaliland in 1902. An earlier Cobbe was Thomas, whose time with the East India Company won a huge fortune and a princess bride. The Indian princess, with whom he had ten children, returned to her homeland after his death but she left the children behind.

For some reason Newbridge was a house in which the children of various branches of the family were deposited. At one time it seems there were no fewer than thirty of them living here. No wonder its Museum of Curiosities is so educational, with its shells, seahorses and black-brain coral from the *Challenger* voyage of 1872 to an array of swords, shields and helmets, or volcanic ash, bricks from Babylon and bog butter from Donegal, the hair plait of an Indian dancing girl and a model of a bound female foot from China. With all this, with its eighteenth-century kitchen and the magnificent state coach built in London for Lord Chancellor John FitzGibbon in 1790, Newbridge House is a tribute to the vision of Fingal, to the management of the Dublin and Eastern Tourist Board and to the knowledge and affection of its voluntary guides.

Newbridge House and Farm,
County Dublin
Tel: 01 843 6534

Newman House

St Stephen's Green, Dublin

Newman House in Dublin is impressive, even in the elegant surroundings of St Stephen's Green. And it's not one house, but two, numbers 85 and 86. That Aidan O'Boyle, a contributor to Catherine Casey's masterwork on Dublin in *The Buildings of Ireland* series, is the guide this afternoon indicates the seriousness with which the care and interpretation of this premises is taken. He explains how Richard Castle's house of 1740 (number 85) was linked to its later neighbour and how the references to what else was going on in Irish architecture at the time can be discovered in the style of a salon, the setting of a door-frame or the coving of a ceiling.

Yet, even with such a guide, even with the sun gilding the brasses, the sconces, the chandeliers, picking out the mouldings and bringing inside the green shadows of the garden behind the house, it is impossible to forget that this is a building which housed three of the most famous misfits Ireland has ever sheltered, or repelled. It was the premises selected in 1854 for the Catholic University of Ireland, whose first rector was John Henry Newman, one of whose staff was Gerald Manley Hopkins and one of whose students was James Joyce. Not one of them was happy here.

Number 86 is the larger and less refined, although redeemed by what Catherine Casey's book describes as 'the sheer richness and vigour' of the plasterwork. This house was built in 1765 for Richard Chapel Whaley, father of the notorious rake and spendthrift Buck Whaley. Richard was notorious in his own right, commonly known as 'Burn-Chapel Whaley' for his priest-hunting activities. Aidan O'Boyle reminds me of the work of Robert West, stuccodore and builder of this house: 'Not all the plaster work in Dublin was done by the Italians!' he says, and West, who also designed Belvedere House in Westmeath, was one of the best of the Irish rococo stylists.

Restored to look as Newman might have known it, the somewhat institutional paintwork of number 86 would have been relieved by the magnificent carved over-doors by John Kelly, while those marvellous ceilings and panels must have brightened the spirits occasionally. They would have needed brightening: Newman believed that he had a welcome role to play in establishing a centre for Irish Catholic education. He had his ideas about the nature of a university, but perhaps the only one to materialise was the University Church at 87 St Stephen's Green, designed by J.H. Pollen, whom he appointed as Professor of Fine Art. Otherwise, for five years Newman struggled with the realisation that the university was basically a political strategy and that he was distrusted not only by the Irish hierarchy but by its superiors in Rome. The time came when he could struggle no longer and he left Ireland in 1858. More unhappiness lay ahead, lightened only by the success of his *Apologia pro Vita*

Not all the plasterwork in Dublin was done by the Italians and Newman House displays some of the finest work of Robert West, who was also responsible for Belvedere House in Westmeath and who is regarded as one of the best of the Irish rococo stylists. (images courtesy of University College Dublin)

Sua (1864) and the very belated award of a cardinal's hat before his death in Birmingham in 1890. It may not have been in Dublin that, as Lytton Strachey wrote of him in *Eminent Victorians,* Newman realised that 'he was a thoroughbred harnessed to a four-wheeled cab', but it was certainly here, climbing the cantilevered staircase of Portland stone to his rooms, that he tried to fight his solitary and fruitless battle against distrust and chicanery.

If Newman was a messiah of the Oxford Movement, then Gerald Manley Hopkins was one of his disciples, leaving his High Anglican background in 1866 and later being ordained as a Jesuit priest. In 1884 he was appointed Professor of Greek and Latin at the university in Dublin, but adrift from his supportive friends and colleagues, struggling with his workload and in poor mental and physical health, he wrote out of his despair such poems as 'Carrion Comfort' and 'No Worst, There is None'. He was, as he wrote, 'pitched past pitch of grief'. As we stand in the austere bedroom where he died of typhoid at Newman House in 1889, it is a little consolation to see that his window overlooks the Iveagh Gardens and, in his day, would have given the soft blue curves of the Dublin Mountains.

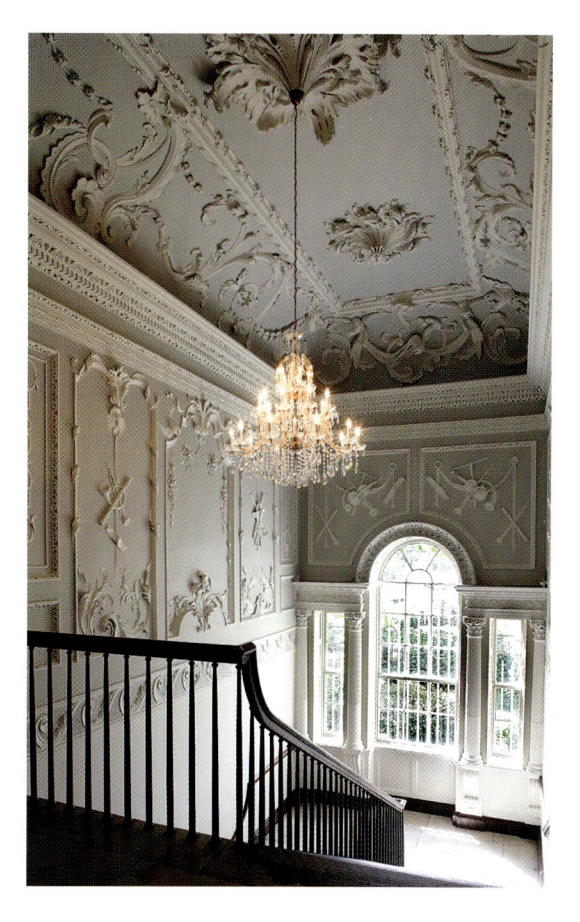

James Joyce would probably have given him a heart attack. It's diverting to find at the top of the house the lecture rooms Joyce (and Oliver St John Gogarty) would have known in his student days. So, even while accepting the crick in the neck for the sake of those exquisite ceilings, there is also the little susurration, the sense of immense presences who left their vivid and ardent mark not only within these walls but on the world.

Newman House,
85/86 St Stephen's Green, Dublin
Tel: 01 7167422

NEWMAN HOUSE

Newtown House

Kinsalebeg, County Waterford

Life has its own logic at Newtown House. Both Michael and Georgie Penruddock introduce me to the Harvesters' Lodging and I look through the beamed, wide-windowed room, with its views on one side over Youghal Bay and on the other over the potager-style kitchen garden, and find it all a welcoming mixture of traditional rustic and contemporary cosmopolitan. But I wonder why there should be a section called the harvesters' anything in Newtown House.

'It was a farmhouse,' explains Georgie simply. 'This was where the seasonal harvesters were put up. Lodged.' The explanation reveals both the authenticity of this farmer's house of 1888 and the success of the transformation she and her husband have achieved by honouring the character of both the house and the townland from which it takes its name. The range of attached outbuildings has been rescued from decay and recreated using the same footprint and the stone from the original farmyard. Tempted by double glazing when they had to replace the windows where the winds tore at the sashes, they listened to Myrtle Allen of Ballymaloe – 'a house has to breathe' – and so decided against the requirement for heavier glazing bars.

'We got all our information from our friends,' says Georgie. 'Really you could say that the house was refurbished by committee.' It's important to remember also that Michael and Georgie Penruddock were not coming to Newtown House without a little experience of other country houses. Although Newtown is on a slightly more modest scale, they have lived in style before now. It's impossible to doubt Michael's enthusiasm for the tied houses which defined his career. Having met and married Georgie while he was still training as a surveyor in rural practice, he worked first as a land agent at Madresfield, home of the Lygon family made famous by Evelyn Waugh's *Brideshead Revisited*. This was followed by twelve years at the Waddesden Estate in Buckinghamshire, where Michael was agent for Mrs James de Rothschild. After her death he and Georgie moved to Lismore Castle in County Waterford, where, during their fifteen-year tenure, 'hospitality was part of the job'.

'You don't plan a career like that,' says Georgie, who admits that she had talked herself into being a cook, learning by experience and absorbing all the influences inherent in this succession of homes, at least two of which remain central to the mythology of the English country house. Lismore, with its connection to Chatsworth through the Dukes of Devonshire, might belong to this tradition also, except that the family has always maintained its distinct Irish and local identity. 'In everything we did at Lismore we went to great lengths to involve Irish workers and manufacturers and artists,' remembers Georgie of the

While still a farmhouse, Newtown House is beautifully fresh and redolent of an easy-going individual sense of style.

relatively recent redecoration of the castle. And while it is obvious at Newtown House that Georgie herself is more than competent in the skills of upholstery, she gives full credit for the curtaining here, as at Lismore Castle, to Nora Foley of Castletownroche.

At Newtown, Michael and Georgie attribute their hall of polished stone slabs to Edward Byrne's salvage yard, a bedroom cornice to Roche Mouldings of Higginstown, the building work to Pat Ryan and his late father John and even the chestnut timbers of the Harvesters' flooring to the Hodder woods at Fountainstown. 'We were determined to keep the house looking like a farmhouse. It was already very nicely arranged and, especially, we didn't want to make it look smart.'

Well, it doesn't look 'smart' in the interior décor sense of the word, but it is beautifully fresh, redolent of an easy kind of style enlivened with extremely good and discriminating taste. Newtown House is set athwart the sea; the gardens end in a long beach walk,

NEWTOWN HOUSE

From Madresfield and Waddesden in the UK to Lismore Castle in County Waterford, hospitality has always been part of the job for Michael and Georgie Penruddock. (images courtesy of the *Irish Examiner*)

from which Georgie picks her sea spinach and where Michael directs guests to a wonderful display of bird life. The meeting of shore and lawn is marked by a leaning shard of ancient bog oak, found at Camphire on the Blackwater and pointed, like the gnomon or blade of a sundial, in the direction of the prevailing wind.

Very comfortable where they were at Lismore, the Penruddocks were anticipating eventual retirement when they saw Newtown. In 1995 it became their dream house, the first they have created for themselves. That's something else about the Penruddocks at Newtown House: a sense of wellbeing, and a feeling that the river has brought them here, from the towers of Lismore Castle above the Blackwater to its estuary at Youghal and to the little bay formed by the long sandbar on the Waterford shore.

Newtown House,
Kinsalebeg, County Waterford
Tel: 024 94304

Rathmullan House

Lough Swilly, County Donegal

The magic of a summer evening seems an unlikely recollection in the darkness of December, yet the beach below Rathmullan House in County Donegal breathes such a serenity that even the memory is independent of the seasons. Late at night, after a dinner of exceptional quality in a particularly attractive dining-room, the guests can wander across the lawns to the seashore. In July the light was a surprise: this far north the sky was still glowing close to midnight, the sea a transparent extension of the pale sands which run right up to the shadowing, dusky trees.

The sea is Lough Swilly, that dramatic inlet stretching deep into Donegal. Across the water the lights of Buncrana sparkle over their quivering reflections and it is strange to stand here on the almost deserted beach and to think of the abduction from nearby Fanad's Castle of the teenage Red Hugh O'Donnell. That act provoked the war of O'Donnell, Tyrone and Tyrconnell, whose defining battle was fought far to the south at Kinsale in Christmas 1601. The sand here is innocent and the innocent tide washes calmly up to its margins of tidewrack and flotsam. There is no hint of that old tragedy, nor of the later one when Wolfe Tone stepped ashore here as a prisoner from the French warship *Hoche*. Instead, it is as if events great and small have been happening here all through the centuries and our arrival now is just one more grain in the long stretch of sand.

That's the thing about Rathmullan House: it provides a sense of perspective. Its own history, for example, begins at a far cry from the graceful house above its sweep of lawns. As Mark Wheeler explains, it began in the 1780s as an upmarket bathing booth for the Batt family of Belfast. As bankers, however, the Batts were living beyond their means and so the family train journeys to Buncrana and the boat trips across Lough Swilly ceased. Passionate about this lovely corner of Donegal, Mark Wheeler says that, although anywhere else Rathmullan, with all its attributes, would be an important port, it was too dependent on the business from Belfast, despite a high time during the First World War when the entire British fleet was anchored here, a period only rivalled by the great oil crisis when Shell Oil kept all its tankers on the lake.

So what's keeping Rathmullan town going now? It's hard to credit, but the wholesale building of holiday homes in the area has taken away business instead of encouraging it, introducing a non-residential population bringing everything they need with them. The approach to Rathmullan House is an avenue through shoals of these houses, all of which, on an evening in July, appear to be empty. But they have nothing to do with the hotel itself, where the grounds open up beyond a final gateway like a delayed theatrical coup as the house is revealed

For all its timeless setting in a lovely corner of Donegal, Rathmullan is a young house and hearty with life for all those ready to recognise and enjoy its many pleasures. (images courtesy of Ireland's Blue Book)

in all its charm. When the Batts sold up, much of the furniture was bought for Glenveagh Castle, but Mark Wheeler's parents, Robin and Bob, who had established a successful fishing hotel at Milford, saw the potential of the house in its unique setting above the Swilly.

Now run by Mark and his wife Mary, his brother William and his sister Juliet, Rathmullan House has been extended to twenty-four bedrooms with a swimming-pool and steam room, and two all-weather tennis courts. There are delightful contrasts: there is a spitting log fire in the main sitting-room, where newspapers and magazines are added to the loaded bookshelves, but dinner is served under the tented glass of a flower-filled pavilion restaurant designed by Liam McCormick. It's hard to keep a level head when deciding between the tug of old books in such variety and the allure of a distinctive menu, and then there is the urge to sit in each of the three sitting-rooms at once, and the need to walk off the pleasures of dinner by a trip through the winding paths to the beach.

For all its timelessness and calm, Rathmullan is a young house, hearty with life and embracing all those who are ready to enjoy its many pleasures, indoors and out. And Mark reminds me that, now that his parents have retired, they live in the village itself, in a house which, once upon a time, used to be a hotel owned by the Batts of Belfast.

Rathmullan House,
Lough Swilly, County Donegal
Tel: 074 9158188
E-mail: rathhse@iol.ie

Rathsallagh Country House

Dunlavin, County Wicklow

Lardering is the sum of Kay O'Flynn's responsibilities at Rathsallagh House in County Wicklow, or so she would have us believe. Kay talks of chutneys and pickles and jams, her husband Joe of the price of calves, but both of them preside over one of the country's premier country houses, an establishment they founded, nurtured and brought to such splendid fruition that it's difficult to believe it could all have been achieved within one generation.

The O'Flynns – of the O'Flynn family butchers in Patrick Street in Cork – farmed for years at Kilbarry near Dublin Hill. Even there it was open house, as Joe and Kay enjoyed having company with whom, as Kay puts it, 'to break bread'. Kilbarry, when they began, was a rural neighbourhood; when they left it, the acres were surrounded by suburbia and industry. A Compulsory Purchase Order in favour of industrial development from the city council in 1978 forced the family to search for a farm unlikely to be threatened by urban expansion and they found it here, in the refurbished remains of a very early eighteenth-century house (1702 to 1704).

The home of the Moody family of horse breeders, the Rebellion of 1798 ruined the house and its owners, who rebuilt only the stables as a residence. They were fine stables, however, and grew into this long, many-windowed house cloaked with vines. Through the years, the outbuildings have been re-designated for different uses, with all the changes the work of Cork architect Dom O'Flynn and his daughter Jane. A modern new wing has arisen on the site of a hayshed; now managed by the O'Flynns' son Joe T, this professional enterprise retains the atmosphere of a family-run business.

When the O'Flynn family moved here they thought this area would never change. 'But farming changed instead,' remembers Joe. He realised that when there was more paperwork involved in registering a calf than in registering a child it was time to move out of farming, but the reality of agriculture is still one of the attractions of Rathsallagh. At the same time, those who have no interest in the life of the land needn't worry one bit about it here, although its goodness and immediacy bring vibrant ingredients to the celebrated kitchen run by John Kostuik. There are aromatic logs on the open fires, hunting scenes on the walls and, for all the sophistication of the conference centre, not to mention the long, green lovely spaces of the famous golf and country club, Rathsallagh behaves like an old-fashioned country house at its hospitable best.

'We had to decide what we could do in the changing world of agriculture,' says Kay, 'but when we examined our assets and I made a list I realised that, because I married when I was very young, I didn't really have any skills. I could scrub and clean

Built in 1704 and ruined during the 1798 Rebellion, the earlier owners of Rathsallagh House rebuilt only the stables of the house as their residence. However, they were fine stables. (images courtesy of Ireland's Blue Book)

and cook – that was it!' That's it; although Kay no longer scrubs or cleans, it's only in the last five years that, as she says, she took her head out of a saucepan. Or a wheelbarrow, for the garden with its box-edged paths, its cascades of climbers and its espaliered pears is largely her work as well. In the dining-room, of course, one never thinks to ask after the gardener who produced the artichokes, the salad leaves, the radish and raspberries, the thyme and lemon balm. Kay doesn't talk things up, but I suspect that while she has the help of Paddy Flood and of Joe himself, she's still in charge of the overall planning and maintenance.

While Rathsallagh offers a dedicated wedding-day service (ask for the imperturbable Catherine), the serenity and character of the house is paramount. Kay makes light of the course she set for Rathsallagh, from family farmhouse to a hotel of international renown. 'I started out thinking we'd do house parties. Then it began to evolve …' Walking in the garden later I look on a vista which by day is largely golf-course but now I notice the hens brought in from their open run, the sheep clustered in the fields, the coloured calves rejoining their mothers; beyond the oaks the sky deepens into a twilight of blues and ambers. At Rathsallagh, I think, Kay and Joe O'Flynn have left an indelible signature on the map of Ireland.

John Kostuik married Rathsallagh's head housekeeper, Patricia, and they now own and run their own inn in Canada – see www.auberge-appalaches.com. Paddy Flood has retired and was replaced by his son Derek; the calves in their turn have been replaced by sports horses and foals.

Rathsallagh House Golf and Country Club,
Dunlavin, County Wicklow
Tel: 045 403112

Roundwood House

Mountrath, County Laois

There seems to be little connection between Marrowbone Lane or Cole's Alley in Dublin and the pine-scented elegance of this tall country house in Mountrath, County Laois. Yet it was here at Roundwood, one of his Irish country estates, that the family of Quaker wool-merchant Anthony Sharp settled at some time around 1739, reclaiming lands and houses originally let to tenants as part of a property portfolio which included these Dublin premises and 'one twenty-fourth share of New West Jersey and New East Jersey' in America. Anthony's grandson, also Anthony, took over the family property at what was then called Killinure (and sometimes Friendstown, as the Sharp tenants were usually Quakers themselves).

According to Brian de Breffny's history of Roundwood House, this Anthony found the old mansion at Killinure too small and built something more appropriate to the family status and fortunes. Who designed or built Roundwood (so-called after the parish) is not known. It doesn't matter at all; this friendly house is a little like an architectural cousin, showing traces of different members of the family of Irish country houses yet having a distinct identity of its own, especially now that Rosemarie and Frank Kenning have incorporated parts of the out-offices of that pre-1741 mansion in their arrangement of the accommodation they provide.

In the sitting-room I lose myself in the winter satisfactions of a long, well-cushioned sofa drawn up to a typical wide-hearthed country-house fire, blazing with long sweet-smelling shards of local turf. Here the shutters are closed against the encroaching darkness outside, the air holds the sharp familiar tingle of the high Christmas tree in the hall and, when the door opens, a slight hint of roasting and basting emanates promisingly from the kitchen. At Roundwood the simplicity of the architecture, and its careful treatment by the proprietors, is given a kind of culinary authentication by Rosemarie's cooking skills, demonstrated usually by a five-course evening meal.

Roundwood House remained in the Sharp (and Flood Sharp) family with more than 1600 acres until mismanagement and mortgages introduced a cousin, William Hamilton, some time around 1835; the house was left with this branch of the family until it was sold to the Irish Land Commission in 1968. The Irish Georgian Society bought the house in 1970, along with 14 acres of garden, woodland, outbuildings and avenue. Here Brian Molloy conducted the renovations and repairs which have been so beneficial to the Kennans: 'We'd be terrified of overkill in terms of restoration,' says Frank. 'We don't mind things looking their age, so here it's an ageing beauty rather than anything pristine.'

Although there is some very attractive detail in the stonework and, indoors, in the shouldered window-frames and light, attractive plasterwork, especially in the study, this is not a house of marble floors and intricate cornicing. The main rooms are moderate in size, the pretty dining-room looking out on the sweep and the parkland beyond. The top floor, once given over to the nursery suites, with bedrooms opening

OPPOSITE: *Inside, the eye is delighted by the high space of the entrance hall and its curving second-floor gallery. Brian Molloy conducted the renovations and repairs without interference with the spaces and perspectives of the neo-classical building.* (images courtesy of Ken O'Mahony and Avril Kennan)

off a long, wide space, is now lined with books and outlived but unforgotten toys.

A business career in Ireland and England gave the Kennans an appetite for an enterprise which Frank, a helpless bibliophile, thought might be in the antiquarian line. But – 'As soon as we saw the house we knew that was it. It was in a reasonable state, we could live in it right away, and we were taking guests after three months.' As for the children's feelings about leaving their Dublin life, Frank replies simply: 'We didn't ask them. But for children there's nothing like a big house with woods and lots of places to explore.' More to the point, perhaps, was the discovery of how 'seriously good' local rural schools can be.

Rosemarie and Frank knew the house was going to have to earn its living if it was to be kept in good heart, but that living was to come from books. They still collect the books, but they keep them instead of selling them on. I wonder: is this the way the Kennans want to spend their lives? 'At this stage, yes,' says Frank, resoundingly. 'In another ten years we reckon we'll have met everyone in the world. And when I look around from the front door I realise that every tree I can see can't be cut down, because we own it. Now that's seriously privileged!'

Rosemarie and Frank have given place to their daughter Hannah and her husband Paddy, who still provide accommodation, five-course dinners and some music at Roundwood House.

Roundwood House,
Mountrath, County Laois
Tel: 0502 32120

Russborough House

Blessington, County Wicklow

'Don't touch the frame of the paintings,' warns our guide at Russborough – 'They're all alarmed!'

Life is continuing as normal in what Mark Bence-Jones describes as 'arguably the most beautiful house in Ireland'. This is a day of heavy cloud and rain, yet the granite of the pedimented entrance and pavilions seems to shine as if reflecting the Blessington lakes that lie beyond the fields. Visits are by guided tour and the elegance is soothing; it is only when we see in the music room the ripped panels in the wallpaper and the still-dangling electrical connections by which the stolen paintings were illuminated that we feel the shock of theft.

From the dining-room we hear the chimes of a clock that kept the hours for Louis XVI at Versailles. The house was built for no more aristocratic a citizen than Joseph Leeson, son of a wealthy Dublin brewer, but it was designed on the grand scale by the German Richard Cassells (or Castle) and completed between 1741 and 1748. In the music room, saloon and library the celebrated plasterwork is attributed to the Francini brothers. There are chimneypieces built like cathedrals; several are by Thomas Carter, whose work in the Tapestry Room depicts Aesop's fable of the dog with a bone and features a lovingly carved shaggy canine as the centrepiece.

The principal rooms at Russborough House have ceilings described by Mark Bence-Jones as of 'magnificent baroque plasterwork, some probably by the Francini brothers'. The great collection of paintings, porcelain, tapestries and furniture amassed by the Earls of Milltown was presented to the National Gallery of Ireland in 1902 after the death of the last earl.

Joseph Leeson became the 1st Earl of Milltown and, guided by experts abroad and at home, amassed a valuable collection of paintings, porcelain, tapestry and furniture, which was presented to the National Gallery of Ireland in 1902 after the death of the last Earl of Milltown. Russborough was bought by Captain Denis Daly in 1931 and twenty years later it was sold to Sir Alfred and Lady Clementine Beit. He was a diamond-mining millionaire, she a Mitford cousin of the more famous Mitford girls. An earlier Alfred went prospecting in South Africa, where he became a partner of Cecil Rhodes in the de Beers diamond mine. On his death his fortune was inherited by his brother Otto, father of Sir Alfred Beit of Russborough. Thus Russborough House became the home of the Beit collection.

In 1986 the Beits presented part of the collection, including the priceless *Lady Writing a Letter with Her Maid* by Vermeer, to the National Gallery, which in return lends pictures to Russborough. On a table made in the time of George II is a painting by Derek Hill of Sir Alfred and Lady Beit sitting in the drawing-room beneath a Goya now hanging in the National Gallery. It is in this room also, with its chimneypiece of grey Italian marble, that the walls bear the florid oval plaster mouldings made to frame four eighteenth-century marine paintings by Joseph Vernet which were sold from the house in the early 1920s; Sir Alfred Beit tracked them down to New York and restored them to the house in 1969.

In the Tapestry Room a fine four-poster bed and matching suite have the bed, quilt and canopy of hand-painted silk and the upholstered chairs all made by Wilsons of the Strand dating from 1794. The mahogany table in the dining-room bears a service

RUSSBOROUGH HOUSE 231

of Sèvres china; the porcelain dishes were once the delight of Madame du Barry, mistress of Louis XV of France. This must seem opulent, but that is not the effect at all. The touch has been light, and the only thing darkening the gilded front hall with its embossed ceiling is the heavily barred door, reinforced now to withstand even the assault of a four-wheel-drive jeep.

These Irish guides are proud of the house and seem to hate having to explain to foreigners the brutally ripped wall, the barred door. Like all good guides they keep the best till last. This is the staircase hall, where stucco garlands are suspended from the mouths of hunting dogs and horns and lances interweave with flags, cameos and lacings in a rococo cavalcade. But spare a few extra minutes to find, on the entrance front, the burial places of two mares who link their loving owners over the span of one hundred years. Here lies gallant Flying Rose, by Aeroplane, winner and dam of winners, owned by Mrs Denis Daly and buried here in 1952. Nearby lies Cruiskeen, whose 'heart and foot alike were sure' and whose epitaph, written by Barbara Lady Milltown in 1849, invites the visitor to

> *Mourn her loss nor blush to shed*
> *One human tear on this poor steed.*

This visit took place after the third theft of art from Russborough, following those of 1974 and 1986. The Irish Landmark Trust has now refurbished a wing at Russborough to introduce self-catering rental holidays from January 2012.

Russborough House,
Blessington, County Wicklow
Tel: 045 865 239
www.russboroughhouse.ie

OPPOSITE: *The façade of silver-grey granite is the longest in Ireland and is surrounded by the surviving elements of the Palladian landscape. Russborough was later the home of Sir Alfred and Lady Clementine Beit, who gave part of the Beit collection to the National Gallery in 1986.* ABOVE: *The state bed in the tapestry room.* LEFT: *In the saloon hangs The Judgement of Paris after Peter Paul Rubens. The painting was bought in Rome by the 1st Earl of Milltown, who commissioned its frame in Dublin in about 1750. Separated from its picture, the frame had been used as a mirror at Áras an Uachtaráin from the 1940s to 1997.* (images by Donal Murphy, courtesy of The Alfred Beit Foundation)

RUSSBOROUGH HOUSE

Salterbridge House

Cappoquin, County Waterford

It's easy to be lyrical about Salterbridge House. It's easy to accept that, when it comes to making an old property look fresh and absolutely designed for living, Susie Wingfield has the flair for the task. There is another ingredient, and both Susie and her husband Philip Wingfield have it in generous proportions, and that is a love for the house and its landscape.

Philip was brought up at Salterbridge, which stands on a small plateau on the hillside above the Blackwater. It was seen from the other bank of the river by his parents when they visited Ireland after the Second World War. At that stage it had been used by the Irish army for several years since 1940, requisitioned like other houses along the Blackwater in what may have been a defensive strategy against invasion via the south-east coast. The original builder of Salterbridge *circa* 1750 was Richard Musgrave – his family also built Tourin near Cappoquin – and it was when his daughter married Anthony Chearnley of Affane that the long tenure of the Chearnleys began at Salterbridge. At that time the house was at the centre of an estate of 18,000 acres; early in the nineteenth century it was substantially rebuilt and later again, probably about 1840, it was given what Philip calls 'the final flourish'.

Above its sloping fields and parkland and backed by farmyard and staff accommodation, Salterbridge is flanked by the acres which have been tamed into wide garden stretches of shrubbery, lawn and woodland. All this is heralded by a long avenue which is introduced by a little classical gate lodge, now restored by the Irish Landmark Trust for private rental. The estate was significantly reduced in the late nineteenth and early twentieth centuries and today the gardens cover about 7 acres, with Philip as the chief caretaker, as his father had been before him. 'Well, I keep it clean,' he says with typical modesty as he walks between the camellias and magnolias. 'I think it looks ok.'

'It looks wonderful!' says Susie, who explains the great cork oak, the impressive quartet of Irish yews and the surprise of Woodhenge, the circle of yew planks transformed by sculptor Jaomi Jobson. These are the exclamation points among the clusters of rhododendron and azalea, the aspens, field maples and scented outbreaks of witch-hazel and mahonia. Under these are spreading blankets of snowdrops, with small spears breaking through the soil in the promise of later swathes of daffodils and bluebells.

Entered from the porch, with its limestone Doric pillars, the hall is an immediately dramatic room, its oak panelling continuing the warm lining of woodwork to the Corinthian screen announcing the bifurcating staircase. There is some intense carving here but the decoration which Philip enjoys most is the simple lettering of the date, 1884. To one side of this large hallway is the dining-room, where the soft terracotta wallpaper catches the tint of a vein in the

ABOVE: *The courtyard of Salterbridge House is used for local gatherings.* ABOVE RIGHT: *The hall is the most immediately dramatic room, its oak panelling continuing to the Corinthian screen and the bifurcating staircase. Given its final flourish in about 1840, Salterbridge has a symmetry which is nowhere grandiose yet which expresses a Victorian solidity embellished only by the composure, inside and out, of detail and finish.* (images courtesy of the *Irish Examiner*)

mantelpiece and where the heavy curtains of blue velvet hang under a pair of rescued fringed pelmets. 'I didn't want this house to look new,' explains Susie, 'I just wanted it to be comfortable, not as if it had been attacked by all the decorators in Ireland.'

The calm stucco cornicing has its charms, as here with the fluted acanthus leaves at the corners of the ceiling: 'Well,' says Philip, 'that was a great device to hide any flaws.' The range of Wyatt windows enhances the interiors while adding distinction to the outward appearance. Different timber has been used throughout these main reception rooms, from oak in the hall to mahogany in the dining-room to maple in the drawing-room, all entered through deep-set double doors.

Salterbridge is a house established in its locality, with both Philip and Susie alert to the talents and activities gathered along the Blackwater valley. Planning her events for Mother's Day with tea in the whitewashed courtyard behind the kitchen, where the date of 1849 is carved on the keystone of the arched entrance, Susie is also arranging an exhibition of the work of Chris Yowell of Clashmore and of jeweller Sophie Bradshaw. Thinking again of his captivated parents walking up the avenue to lay claim to Salterbridge in 1947, Philip says that, well, 'they were optimistic and they were young'. It feels as if some benign bequest of that youth, and that optimism, still brightens the air at Salterbridge today.

Salterbridge House and Garden,
Cappoquin, County Waterford
Tel: 058 54952

Shankill Castle

Paulstown, County Kilkenny

Every time I mention the Copes at Shankill the response is a variant of the theme – 'oh, that's a Toler-Aylward house!' As usual I pretend a full and detailed knowledge of the Toler-Aylwards, waiting until I meet Elizabeth and Geoffrey Cope to reveal total ignorance of their fascinating house and its history.

It was, if not exactly a castle, at least the precursor of one, originating as a tower house and incorporating the building of 1713, when Peter Aylward's marriage to Elizabeth Butler brought him her family estates. Later enlargements give a charmingly uneven exterior, so that the more formal entrance front is belied by the irregularities of roofs and windows at the back, and further enhanced by the Victorian–Gothic conservatory perched above a stone arcade. The roadside church and embellished gate lodge are attributed to Daniel Robertson (of Dunleckney Manor, County Carlow).

'It's a small big house,' says the artist Elizabeth Cope as she leaves her studio to greet me. 'There are forty-something rooms in it, most of which we don't use. But it's our family home now, so we keep those main gates closed; people just drive up the avenue if we leave them open.' The trees here reach marvellous heights and lend their own optimism to Geoffrey Cope's recent planting of yew hedges, trained to provide a yew arch which might be mature in about twenty-five years from now. There are ancient limes soaring above the laurel lawns, and towering self-sown ash trees, and, as an example of how incidental woodland of this kind can be, a froth of fragile white blossom from a wild damson interrupting the evergreens. Geoffrey's policy is largely of non-interference, apart from essential maintenance, so that, in time, another generation 'will have a full canvas in which to plant again'.

The Copes love this place, but they won't sacrifice their lives to it, Geoffrey's gardening philosophy preferring things to look as if they've just dropped on to the soil. They restored the stream which runs through the whole estate, forming a canal and a little lake overlooked by the conservatory and also making a moat around this redesigned bed. Every garden worth the name has its unusual features and the Copes have been careful to preserve all that could be discovered of the original plans, so that the main lawn is open and serene, the sundial catches the sun and the rustic bridges link the glades and copses of the wood.

The Copes are hospitable people, and Elizabeth's work is vibrant and reverberating, although such a brisk description does it no justice at all. Still, although beguiled by tea and sandwiches in the Victorian drawing-room, I make for the walled gardens and the stable block designed, like the entrance, by Daniel Robertson. Various uses have

ABOVE: *The conservatory at Shankill looks down on the lake.*
BELOW: *These walks, some still looking like the original formal paths which would have had a gravel surface, are remnants of an earlier history as the 18th-century outlines emerge and then disappear among the greenery.* (images courtesy of Sybil Cope)

been found for the stables and Geoffrey is considering a few more, and at least one of the walled gardens is being kept trim and fruitful by the dedication of the annual visitor George Crumpler. The old orchard is a delight in spring, with its canopies of blossom underplanted with scarlet tulips, but this area is of special interest because of the surviving evidence of practice – or fashion – from long ago, as with the pear trees cordoned to assume a goblet shape against the rosy brick-lined walls. A suckler herd makes good use of the other enclosed areas, which, as Geoffrey says, 'are there for posterity, even if we can't get around to doing something with them ourselves'.

In a way, of course, Geoffrey and Elizabeth and their family are themselves posterity; quite close to the house the estate includes the ancient church and burial site which give it its name, Sean Cill. Before the Butlers, before the famous Toler-Aylward sisters Maria, Nicky and Jill, this was a pre-Reformation parish church; perhaps even older than that again, as Geoffrey thinks the site was a pre-Christian burial mound. A visit to Shankill Castle is more than a trip around a garden; it's a trip around history.

Shankill is now a venue for events such as summer fairs, country markets, weddings and exhibitions; the family produces its own apple juice and fruit preserves for sale, the farm is managed by Reuben Cope and the gardens are open to the public.

Shankill Castle and Gardens,
Paulstown, County Kilkenny
Tel: 059 972 6145

Shelburne Lodge

Kenmare, County Kerry

It's very understandable that in the publicity material for Shelburne Lodge in Kenmare Maura Foley should be named as Maura O'Connell Foley. In one way or another, her own family have been prominent in the hospitality affairs of this town for many years, and it retains a presence apart from the establishment Maura runs with her husband Tom.

Acknowledging the personality and influence of her mother Agnes and the foundation of the former family business at The Purple Heather in Henry Street, Maura's career includes a cordon bleu course in London, working with Declan Ryan of the late lamented Arbutus Lodge in Cork, with Colin Daly at The Park in Blackrock, County Dublin, and with Sonya Stevenson, Master Chef of Great Britain, at The Horn of Plenty.

In 1985 she opened The Lime Tree restaurant in Kenmare, bought from Ernest Weeland, formerly of the town's famous Park Hotel. As Maura traces this and other events and engagements through the years, we settle at last on the opening of Shelburne Lodge in 1996. Except that Packie's Restaurant on Henry Street crept in there somewhere, along with five helpful children ('any mother can multi-task,' insists Maura), before it was decided to sell The Lime Tree in order to buy the Lodge. There Maura and Tom, by then retired from teaching, could run what they thought of as a small guest house.

'It's been tremenduous,' Maura says as she offers tea and cake in her sitting-room. 'Tom has a taste for running the business side of things and is a historian who loves entertaining people and, although it took a while to build up a customer base, now we get a very great number of repeat visitors.' The work to be done when they took over was supervised by 'two great builders', Jerry Mahony and the late Johnny Rice, and involved local labour as much as possible. Maura has kept her colour palette soft and glowing so her furniture and pictures have a chance to shine for themselves. High sash windows, wide mirrors arranged to revive old wardrobes, limed furniture which was already in the house when the Foleys arrived, are all given an effective place.

What one gets here is authenticity and a sense not just of taste but of scale. Things fit and seem right. The doors have old brass fingerplates. Much of the furniture is mahogany but there's nothing dark or overbearing about it. There are panelled headboards in some rooms, interesting items such as the flat lantern-like sconces, the fireplaces, the salvage tiles in the inner hall, the doors to the dining-room bought for £5 each at an auction where no one else thought they were worth anything. It's all about eye, really, when it comes to restoration, furniture and fittings and Tom and Maura Foley, singly and together, have the eye. They also know a good artist when they

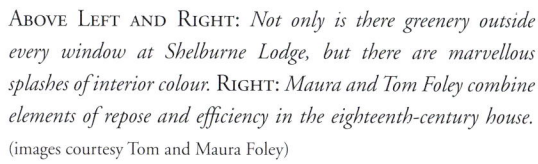

ABOVE LEFT AND RIGHT: *Not only is there greenery outside every window at Shelburne Lodge, but there are marvellous splashes of interior colour.* RIGHT: *Maura and Tom Foley combine elements of repose and efficiency in the eighteenth-century house.* (images courtesy Tom and Maura Foley)

see one and not only is there greenery outside every window at Shelburne Lodge but there are marvellous splashes of interior colour, with streaks of gold shining from an expanse by Maurice Henderson or contrasts in style and content from such painters as Tim Goulding or Pauline Bewick.

Continuing the achievement of repose with efficiency, the garden stretches from a patio to a grass tennis court, with the old orchards coming back to life and the coach house reclaimed to make an attractive two-bedroom suite. Visitors are especially appreciative of the fact that Shelburne Lodge is within easy walking distance of the centre of the town: 'They're so tired of driving by the time they get here,' says Maura, 'that all they want to do is leave the car behind. And also we try to plan out scenic and interesting routes for them which won't be too exhausting.'

That's Tom's speciality, but history is also part of the house. The mid-eighteenth-century lodge was the Kenmare home of the Petty-Fitzmaurice family, springing from doctor, surveyor, cartographer and statistician William Petty, who founded the town in 1670. William Petty Fitzmaurice was the Lord Shelburne who, despite a prominent political career (and a short-lived term as prime minister in 1782–3), found time to organise the planning of the town in 1775. Exploring that connection alone brings fascinating encounters, while the terrain at all points of the compass from Kenmare offers some of Ireland's finest scenery and its most absorbing legends. ♣

Shelburne Lodge Country House,
Cork Road, Kenmare, County Kerry
Tel: 06466 41013

Sion Hill House

Ferrybank, County Waterford

Through the dark, the light of Hook Head flashes its brief warning. There is a ship in the living-room, stacked high and white with only a meadow intervening between the window and the docks. From the garden itself the scents of viburnum and narcissi, heady and tender in the night air, float like a promise that this is real, this little Eden of Sion Hill House in Waterford city in its oasis of primroses and magnolia while the world whirls on below.

George and Antoinette Kavanagh have made this distinguished old house their business. Built *circa* 1800 it sits in its garden at Ferrybank, softening the industrialised and highly developed contours of the hillside above the main road to Rosslare. The scale is modest but elegant, the house with its stone steps and pillared portico flanked by two short terraces ending in little steeply roofed pavilions; it fits into the fall of the land so that the outbuildings behind are backed by fields, trees and the boundary with County Kilkenny. Around its immediate exterior primroses burst among the paving of the terraces and old shrub roses twine along the railing of the lawns. A pool area has been created beneath the dining-room window where tree ferns shade the elderly goldfish. Some of the four acres here are in woodland, and an old coachman's cottage awaits restoration, its roof thatched with roses. Trees cluster above swathes of daffodils, where 9,000 bulbs were planted and ancient apple trees rival the 147-year-old camellia. Once eight gardeners were employed to manage this estate; a quarter-mile of box hedging had to be clipped each summer and, although the Kavanaghs have no intention of reproducing that little feature, they are anxious to identify the more unusual plants found at Sion Hill and to reintroduce examples of the daffodils bred by Waterford's Lionel Richardson. In all this they are assisted by the memory and knowledge of Michael Hannon, the retired gardener who maintained his connection with Sion Hill House for over sixty years.

It has to be admitted though that there are few pleasures in modern life to rival that of sitting at a pretty breakfast table eating a well-cooked and generous meal and listening to all these plans, knowing that one has to do nothing at all about them. Or so I think, until George Kavanagh suggests I should retrieve my Wellington boots because he has a tree to plant and perhaps I might like to help? We agree quickly that he will do the digging and we set off down the hill followed by the family's intrepid cat. Near the remains of the old tulip tree, blown down in the Christmas storms of 1997, he presents a new tulip tree. We won't see it flourishing perhaps – these trees take time – but I like to think of it sitting there on the sunny hillside.

The preliminary report on garden proposals for Sion Hill by James Howley of Dublin gives some of the history of the house, which was built for the Pope

Built circa 1800, Sion Hill House is a delight. The avenue entrance is massed with rhododendrons and azaleas and opens out to reveal the south-facing lawns as it reaches the front door. Modern Waterford sits on its edges but George and Antoinette Kavanagh are making this a very special place. (images courtesy Deirdre Kavanagh)

family of merchants and shipowners of Waterford. 'Sion,' says Howley, 'may be an Anglicisation of the Irish *sidhean* meaning fairy mount', and he could be right, given that on some maps the property is shown as Mount Sion. The Popes prospered during the eighteenth and nineteenth centuries as among the civic dignitaries of the city, acting also as agents for Lloyds and building several houses along this Ferrybank area. The ferry, which was the only means of crossing the unbridged river until 1790, was sited immediately outside the garden wall of Sion Hill and this immediacy to Waterford city is an entrancing aspect of a visit here.

When I open the shutters of my bedroom window in the morning, rigging and roofs and steeples crowd the vista like a quotation from Wordsworth:

> Ships, towers, domes, theatres and temples lie
> Open unto the fields and to the sky
> All bright and glittering in the smokeless air …

A bed draped crisply in white, softly toned wallpaper and curtaining, settings of china in the bedroom and dining-room and a wide-ranging breakfast including home-grown honey combine to show that the Kavanaghs understand the kind of thing that will make Sion Hill House a very special place; things which include the lovely fanlight of the hall, the curve of the stairs, the decorated arch openings and even the holes in the risers of the steps outside the door which were cut to ventilate the wine cellar underneath.

Sion Hill House,
Ferrybank, Waterford
Tel: 051 851558

SION HILL HOUSE

Springfield Castle

Dromcollogher, County Limerick

'It's quite a simple house, really,' says Betty Sykes as she shows me around Springfield Castle. 'But it has passages …' These passages suggest hidden depths, linking the residence visually and atmospherically to the fine tower house in the courtyard, which is what remains of the first home on this lovely site of Gort na Tiobrad.

Getting to Springfield in Dromcollogher (or Dromcolliher according to some road signs) in County Limerick at this time of year has a tranquil magic captured in the approach to the castle: the gateway is a mixture of what might be called Maori antique and Celtic Revival, striking a note which later echoes throughout the house in door-cases, window-frames and fireplaces. Ttowehe avenue leads straight on for three-quarters of a mile, lined with beeches, limes and chestnuts. Either this, or the unused back avenue, which is a mile long, is said to be the longest tree-lined avenue in Europe, but Betty Sykes and her husband Jonathan have never actually

OPPOSITE: *The poet Daithi O Bruadair who lived here for years with the FitzGeralds, wrote in 1666 that Springfield was 'the home of choirs and music ... Cosy, hospitable, vassal-crowded, festive', but then lying in darkness after the death of its cavalier, Eamon FitzGerald.* RIGHT AND BELOW: *Where Betty Sykes has found usable original materials she has matched and trimmed from coverlets and curtains to silk-lined canopies.*

measured either one. The Sykes are farmers and much of their 200 acres is given over to red deer, but the avenue borders the areas grazed by a herd of fallow deer, shy and graceful and not at all as bold as the assertive brilliance of the peacock sunning himself near the door.

Explaining as she leads me from room to room, Betty Sykes, who was brought up in this house, reveals her talent for the appropriate, her instinct for the right thing in the right place. Springfield Castle is a rebuilding of the old house, which was burned down in 1921 in a conflagration which also took its panelling, its plasterwork, its Romneys and Gainsboroughs and Lelys. But Betty doesn't mourn that loss; instead she works on the house produced by her ancestor Robert Deane Morgan, who succeeded to the title of Lord Muskerry in 1929. While the drawing-room with its two walls of windows has a traditional grace and comfort, its silk curtains hang under restored pelmets; where she has found usable original fabrics, she has matched the materials, trimming another set of curtains with braiding left by her grandmother. A sauna completes a bathroom in which window-seats are cushioned for comfort, a deep old bathtub has been restored to its plinth and matched with a modern reproduction loo, a wide bed in a sunny room is spread with a coverlet under a matching canopy whose interior is lined with pleated silk.

Here as elsewhere in the house things seem to marry happily, including Betty's successful search for fabric designed by the legendary American Elsie de Wolfe. As Jonathan wields a long-handled duster to banish a spider from an archway, Betty's descriptions join her childhood memories – the suspended clothes-rack which lived in the kitchen was known as 'a winter hedge' – to power-showers, efficient heating and all modern amenities in a house which still holds on to its old larders, with shelves and safes and iron coat hooks. It is this wedding of the old and the contemporary which makes Springfield so popular with the guests who now rent it, usually on a self-catering basis, by the week or the month.

There are the walks through the parkland, the

SPRINGFIELD CASTLE 243

courtyard with its thatched summer house and attic playrooms, its battlemented tower, the ship's bell from the *HMS Ajax* and the monkey pillar commemorating Tomás an Apa, the infant survivor of an ancient battle. And then there is the avenue, down which I follow Betty to her home in the restored kennelman's house, where she talks of the history of the house dating from a castle built here after a FitzGerald marriage in 1280. Although the long tenure of the FitzGeralds ended in 1703, their era endures through the work of the great Irish poet Daithi O Bruadair, who lived here with the FitzGeralds for years. For him, writing in 1666, this was 'the home of choirs and music. Cosy, hospitable, vassal-crowded, festive'.

The FitzGeralds were followed by the Fitzmaurice family and in 1775 Anne Fitzmaurice eloped with Sir Robert Deane of Dromore in County Cork. Later elevated to the peerage as Lord Muskerry, he renewed Springfield's earlier prestige. It was rebuilt later by Robert Deane Morgan, an engineer whose journeys brought him to Australia and New Zealand. Succeeded by the late Hastings Fitzmaurice Deane, the Limerick

Here as elsewhere in the house things seem to marry happily, from the muslin drapery of a four-poster or the successful search for fabric designed by the legendary American Elsie de Wolfe to the stripped beech-wood floors and their rugs and carpeting. (images courtesy Jonathan and Betty Sykes)

radiologist and father of Betty Sykes, Robert Deane Morgan seems to have epitomised, like the FitzGeralds before him, Betty and Jonathan after him and, with variations, the Munster rugby team, the motto carved in the Maori-style entrance gate: 'Nothing is difficult to the strong and the faithful'.

Springfield Castle,
Dromcollogher, County Limerick
Tel: 063 83162

Stable Diet

Yoletown, County Wexford

Nothing could be easier. All I have to do is keep an eye out for the thatched farmhouse and I'll be at Katherine Carroll's home. What no one has warned me is that thatched houses are two-a-penny in this parcel of County Wexford. A recent consultation document for the Heritage Council lists twenty-one groups, interests and organisations which have something to do with thatch and thatching. There are problems, but down here in Wexford they seem to have been ignored or surmounted: in the village even the supermarket is thatched. With grassy spines splitting the boreens and trees bent like set-squares away from the prevailing winds, there is no hurry on anyone and it is with easy friendliness that I am directed to Katherine Carroll, her aunt Christina Keating, and the business established at the Keating farmstead.

'It started by accident,' explains Katherine, who came to help on the farm when Christina was widowed. She built a pine-log cabin in the old orchard and reared her two sons there; in the meantime she had been asked to make a few carrot cakes for the wholefood shop in Wexford where she bought the organic flour she still uses. One thing led to another and in 1996 she began her business, working from her little bakery in the garden. A state-of-the-art purpose-built complex of kitchen, bakery and cold store followed, now employing fourteen people as Katherine's label, Stable Diet, appears throughout Ireland, marketed by business partner Vincent Power.

As we talk of barbecue sauce, of the lemon syrup cake (there was so much juice left over after using the zest in the carrot cake) and herb oils and dressings, of tomato chutney, apple chutney, apricot preserve, the Wexford fruit cake, the flapjacks, the marmalade, I realise that the delightful drawing by Brian Dennington used for her labelling is a faithful reproduction of this home-place. Stable Diet Kitchen could be called a cottage industry, especially as Katherine and her staff still use as little engineering as possible, the only machinery being the choppers now needed to deal with the fruit and vegetables, and the mixers required for the batches of cakes, biscuits and muffins.

'We can't claim to be organic, but everything we use is a basic raw ingredient, from local free-range eggs to the best-quality imported oranges, lemons and oils. My policy has always been based on the need to be aware of what we eat, and we use no enhancers or additives here, and I think everyone who works here takes pride in what we produce.' Some of those products have now won a gold medal, a silver and two bronzes at the Great Taste Awards, run by Fortnum and Mason in London.

Making our way through the garden to the farmhouse, Katherine stoops to collect the coal-black lamb from its pen. Nearly feeding time and the lamb,

The thatched, mud-walled farmhouse is the origin of the Stable Diet brand. A consultation document for the Heritage Council lists twenty-one groups, interests and organisations which are concerned in one way or another with thatch and thatching.
(images courtesy Katherine Carroll and Maureen Roe)

found abandoned in February and so small that Katherine thought at first it was a dead blackbird, settles in her arms with a proprietorial air much resented by the old sheepdog who walks with us. The straw thatch of the 200-year-old dwelling is pierced by two chimney stacks and pitched steeply to let the rain slide off so the thatch won't rot too quickly. This is a mud-walled house, fitted with every amenity conceivable at the time of its origin, including several staircases and many cupboards, rooms which run the length of the house and others which open up from unexpected doorways, unchanged sash windows under sloping eaves, a loft over the kitchen once used to store grain and making the ceiling sag until supported by a massive beam from a ship – or rather, we suspect, from a shipwreck, for these coasts were notorious and in this amiable house we see former cabin doors still marked with barnacles.

The gateways with their round capped piers are unique to this district; a small old dovecote which was home to a family of kittens last year, cowhouse and byre and stables built of rubble and brick with ashlar coigns, are all trim and functional. We stand to look southwards as Katherine remembers her home farm near the buried city at Bannow, landing place of the Normans in 1169. Katherine's retired horse, whose usual escort is a sheep, stares at us from the sunny field shared with the foundling pony and the foundling pony's unexpected foal. Later, at the Lobster Pot in Carne, we talk of Tacumshane and its windmill and Rostoonstown and its wrecks, and Faythe and Ballyhiho and Yoletown and all the places which are getting on just grand in the sunny south-east. ♣

Stable Diet Kitchen,
Yoletown, County Wexford
Tel: 053 9131287

Strokestown Park

Strokestown, County Roscommon

On this sunny morning, with glossy cattle and horses browsing in meadows hedged with woodbine and dog rose, with trees in long abundant ridges on the low skyline, famine is not to the forefront of my mind. Strokestown Park gardens in Roscommon are in radiant summer bloom, but I wander instead into the series of quiet rooms laden with disaster. Within minutes I am gripped by a lucid reduction of eighteenth- and nineteenth-century Irish history.

This adjacent Famine Museum reveals that Strokestown was once a model of good husbandry. Absenteeism only became a feature of land management after the Act of Union in 1801, when political power and opportunity were centred solely in London. The story of the Famine itself is told in localised detail: it is the story of this countryside. This compelling archive views the Famine from the perspective of this one town and this one house. The context assists understanding: what happened here happened all over Ireland and, while chilling in its particulars, the story is so well presented that the concluding emphasis on recovery and self-assertion is a kind of absolution.

After that, you can enjoy everything else Strokestown House has to offer, including its participation in the Great Gardens of Ireland Restoration Project. Within the house the question is why, given that its owners were so recently departed, no one had wanted the family memorabilia which lies in layers throughout the rooms. The story of the Mahons and the Packenham Mahons of Strokestown is complicated enough to explain what may have been a preference to leave it all behind: 'old, unhappy far-off things, and battles long ago'.

Perhaps it began badly, with the building of the first Strokestown House in 1696 by Nicholas Mahon on lands that originally belonged to the O Conors of Roscommon. Its remodelling by Richard Cassells (or Castle) towards the middle of the eighteenth century provided the two-storey wings and the arched Georgian-Gothic entrance which still dominates the wide main street of the town; all in keeping with the status of Thomas Mahon, MP for Roscommon, in Grattan's parliament. His son Maurice gained a peerage by supporting the Act of Union and, as Baron Hartland, added an Ionic portico to the front as well as spending generously on the drawing-room, hall and library.

While the house now is rich with evidence of its owners – much of the exquisite furniture was either left behind or bought back – the estate was heavily in debt when it was inherited by Major Denis Mahon in 1845. His reaction to the impact of the Famine on his income and his tenants was to encourage emigration to Canada. The long journey on often unseaworthy emigrant ships festering with disease resulted in a terrible death toll. Mahon was shot dead in Strokestown

The wealth of objects and memorabilia within the house provokes the question as to why no-one seems to have wanted all the evidence of generations of family life left behind at Strokestown, from toys to nightgowns, button-hooks to baby-carriages and photographs and newspaper cuttings. (images courtesy Strokestown Park)

in 1847; the subsequent trial and execution of the perpetrators blackened his reputation even further. It was not until his grandson, Captain Henry Standford Packenham, went back to Strokestown in 1893 that the house began to recover from this blight.

Henry's daughter Olive married Edward King Harman of Rockingham in Boyle in 1914. She was pregnant when he was killed at Ypres later that year. The baby was a girl and, as the palatial Boyle estate was entailed in the male line, Olive returned to Strokestown with her infant daughter. In 1921 she married Major Stuart Hales and lived in England for the duration of his military career. It is her early life which is on view: the copy books, the childhood photographs and letters, the little desks canted to prevent use of the left hand in writing, the old rocking-horse, the doll's house with its miniature bentwood chairs and its china tea service. Olive lived on at Strokestown until her death in 1981. In old age she had ordered that all her ball-gowns should be burned after her death and they were, yet here in a bedroom is draped a nightgown trimmed with hand-made lace. On a desk there lies open a newspaper account of her first wedding.

Not long after Olive and her husband returned to Strokestown in the mid-1950s, Westward Garage was opened close to the demesne's gateway. Proprietor Jim Callery began a relationship with the family which led to such mutual goodwill that, when Westward needed to buy a few acres for expansion, its directors were encouraged, instead, to buy the entire demesne. It was while examining boxes of documents in the estate offices that Callery realised the importance of the material he uncovered. Rather than selling on the surplus land, it was decided instead to undertake one of the most significant private restoration projects in Ireland and, with the inaugural curator Luke Dodd, to open it to an appreciative public.

Strokestown Park House,
Strokestown, County Roscommon
Tel: 071 9633013

Temple House

Ballymote, County Sligo

Guns and blackberries: these are the traditional staples of country life in the autumn, and at Temple House in County Sligo they are so commonplace that there is no doubt, from the moment of entering under the *porte cochère*, that this is a grand old-style house. It is Serena, one of the Perceval daughters, who greets me with the rifle as I drive on to the sweep. The gun is replaced on its rack and, as Serena goes off to check arrangements for that night's traditional music session in nearby Ballymote, her mother Deb arrives to show me to my room; this light-filled space is called 'the half-acre' for a very good reason.

I am nervous about meeting Deb Perceval. Guests to Temple House are told, before they make their booking, that the house has a strict no-aerosol ban. Perfumes, hair-spray, even deodorant are all to be left tucked up in one's baggage (substitutes are provided in every room). When a friend kissed me goodbye

ABOVE: *The soaring proportions of the inner hall display the status of a house built to endure.*

earlier this morning she said, 'You smell nice', and I shrieked in alarm. I'm not supposed to smell anything. So I know that Deb is going to run her in-built sensory Geiger counter over me the minute we meet. 'Am I all right?' I ask as we mount the stairs. She reassures me.

Essentially this is to protect Deb's husband Sandy who as an active farmer, has had a bad experience with sheep dip. He is not unique in the farming community: others have had a similar reaction to the organo-phosphates used in that mixture, but Sandy's is a life-threatening chronic chemical sensitivity. As Deb later shows me around the walled gardens, the source of the marvellous vegetables all used for the table, we talk about organo-phosphates and I am reminded of how very commonplace these chemicals are (fly killers, air fresheners, the treatment for head lice, even hand cream). On a recent visit with my cat to the vet I was warned against using a flea collar. 'Organo-phosphates,' said the vet briskly, as if I would know exactly what the problem was. I didn't; Sandy and Deb Perceval do. Precautions have been widely advised and an association of victims has been established, although without much success, admits Deb, as most members were too ill to attend.

But Sandy is a genial and knowledgeable host in a house which has been in his family for many generations. An enthralling family history compiled by Serena, a folklore archivist, runs from the twelfth-century castle of the Knights Templar from which the house takes its name and whose ruins stand between the lake and the terraced lawns. Temple House itself was built in 1864, replacing the house of 1665. It was made to last and for considerable display, hence the soaring proportions of the inner hall. Sandy Perceval admits to having closed off one wing of the ninety-room residence entirely, but 'We moved in quite happily,' says Deb, 'We had no idea what we were taking on.'

ABOVE AND RIGHT: *The entrance hall indicates the sporting as well as the architectural history of Temple House, rescued from the lists of Encumbered Estates by a Perceval who had become immensely wealthy as a merchant in Hong Kong.* OPPOSITE: *The ruins of the twelfth-century castle of the Knights Templar stand in the park between the lake and the terraced lawns.* (images courtesy of the Perceval Family)

Reared in a south of England town, she found herself tackling problems she had never heard of in her life. But when some friends asked if they could come to shoot, or fish, for a fee and the Percevals said yes – lo and behold! – the house had another future. With pike in the lake and snipe on the bog, a livelihood to buttress the hard work of farming was obvious and the Percevals took to it with such determination and success that they became founder members of the Hidden Ireland organisation.

I think of all this as I eat my blackberries and cream at breakfast, the prelude to porridge served with thick dark sugar followed by toasted brown bread. At dinner the night before I had felt a mild

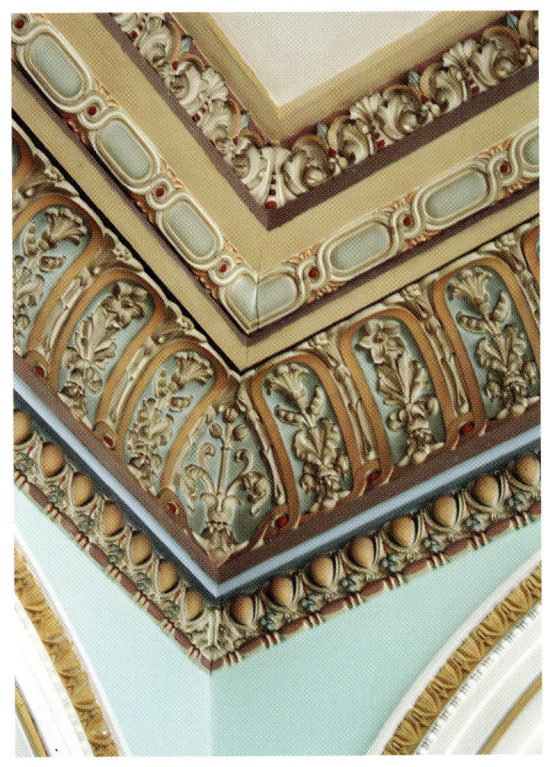

AT HOME IN IRELAND

discomfort under the portrait of Jane Perceval, Sandy's ancestress, who had died in 1847 of typhus caught through her labours on behalf of distressed tenants during the Famine. According to Serena's history, that line of endeavour and commitment runs through the Perceval generations, from Geoval de Perceval, who arrived in England in 1066 as William the Conquerer's cup bearer, to Alexander of China, who retrieved the demesne from the Encumbered Estates lists resulting from expenses of Famine relief, electioneering and inheritance taxes. It was Alexander, immensely rich from his time in Hong Kong, who had the house redesigned by Johnstone and Jeanes. Two generations later Alec Perceval and his wife Yvonne restored the farm and built up a large dairy herd, and then came Sandy and Deb and the beginning of another era. ♣

Sandy and Deb Perceval have now been succeeded by their son Roderick and his wife Helena, who manage Temple House and its rental courtyard cottages.

Temple House,
Ballymote, County Sligo
Tel: 071 9183329

The Glebe House

Ballinadee, County Cork

Here's another lovely part of the country absolutely unknown to me though it is only fifteen miles from Cork city: Ballinadee and Kilmacsimon Quay and The Glebe House where from the front door the square tower of the church for which the house was once the rectory can be seen in a gesture of intentional sympathy. Ballinadee is at a narrow inlet on the estuary of the Bandon River where the trees bordering the road have been allowed flourish and bend now with the weight of their bright leaves. Gaps in the ditches allow views of hilly fields or of the full flowing river with its hundreds of swans. At Kilmacsimon the river is turbulent, getting up steam perhaps for the wider reaches of its delta-like approach to the sea.

The community which has made this district its own has lived with its tides and vagaries for centuries. As close as a hundred years ago there was a mill, a linen industry, a brickyard and a slate quarry all thriving here. Bandon was then a garrison town with a need for many things which were brought up the river from Kilmacsimon. whose history goes back beyond the days when Kinsale was a bigger port than Cork.

'That's the kind of thing our visitors love to discover', says Gill Bracken, who runs the Glebe House with her partner Caroline Forde. Filling the days is not a problem to those who decide to stay longer than an overnight at Ballinadee. 'We give them the chance to relax, it's as if they re-discover the sounds, the scents, of their childhood. If they weren't born in the countryside then here they remember their visits; the river bank, the birdlife, the bluebells and gorse, the dawn chorus which here can be pretty deafening. They love going to the pub – people there talk to them as if they were long-lost cousins and they get a sense of belonging for a while. And we see them reading in the drawing-room by the fire, or on a sunny day sitting with a book beneath the trees in the garden – the kind of thing we'd love to do ourselves if we had the time!'

Glebe lands were the acres allotted to the upkeep of the parson and his family and the Glebe House is a small Georgian rectory, probably dating in its original form from 1690, but now a much-restored building still showing the simple characteristics of perfect proportions, beautifully – spaced windows with inner arches and high ceilings distinguishing its structure. A rampant wisteria drips its pale blossoms over the door, at the other side of which a Zeperine Drouhin rose is already laden with breaking buds.

Beneath them heathers form a mat of colour and beyond this new plantings of camellias, lavender and lilac lead on to the herb and vegetable garden. This produces fresh herbs and unusual salad greens for the kitchen. The caged fruit garden grows black, red and white currants, raspberries and strawberries

'If people want houses of this kind to survive then they have to have the support of a public willing to use them.' A bedroom, sitting-room and (below right) tea in the garden at Ballinadee. (images courtesy Gill Good)

and loganberries and great clumps of rhubarb. 'The core business is the guest business,' says Gill. 'It's something I always wanted to do, even though in this case it crept up on me while I wasn't looking. Glebe had been a guesthouse when I arrived here with my family. One day while I was away the builders took a booking – we decided to honour it, never believing that the people would turn up. But they did – and I've kept going from there!'

Gill says, but without regret, that she feels that the house has to support its own life. 'I feel, too, that if people want houses of this kind to survive then they have to have the support of a public willing to use them.' Gill and Caroline use the Glebe to the hilt. The old coach-house has been cleverly transformed into two self-catering cottages. Pastel-painted, these have stove fires and central heating and doors opening on to garden and patio areas for their private use. Self-catering is all very well, but then you miss out on Gill's version of Glebe House cooking. 'The standard has risen so much in Irish guesthouses now, we're all trying to do something different. And so many people make breakfast a hearty meal which sustains them until dinner-time so we provide waffles, duck-eggs, French toast, scrambled eggs with rosemary shortbread, kippers, soda and rye breads, and our own speciality, date bake with crisp smoky bacon. It's a kind of flapjack, one of our most talked-about items.'

Gill's enjoyment of the work involved in running a guesthouse of this quality has a lot to do with the creative opportunities it offers to herself and Caroline, both of whom have both brought this lovely house into a new inviting future.

Glebe Country House, Ballinadee, near Bandon, County Cork
Tel: 021 4778294

The Glen House

Kilbrittain, County Cork

When you take the road off the Bandon by-pass to Kilbrittain, the route to The Glen winds in ever-deepening curves through what is, in fact, a glen. Before the wide sandy acres of Harbour View and Courtmacsherry Bay come into sight there's the well-kept village of Kilbrittain itself, where the short route to the Scotts turns uphill. But this sunny breezy day is one for the scenic route, which winds on again, this time with a coastal tang and views opening gorgeously to the sea before a causeway offers a bluebell-rich avenue to the Victorian gables glimpsed earlier from far away.

The Glen continues the Scott family residence in these parts which began in 1724; their time in Ireland began in Dublin around 1666. As I sit seduced by tea with scones topped with home-made loganberry jam and cream, Diana Scott etches genealogical architecture as a way of identifying some at least of the fascination of these parts. Kilbrittain Castle, for example, is a couple of miles away, its location the more stunning as the building has been romantically Georgian-ised and perhaps Victorian-ised during the last few centuries. But there was once a grim rationale to this defensive site and the castle was to be fought for, seized, beseiged, captured and alienated from its MacCarthy lords.

The MacCarthys themselves, of course, were only blow-ins, supplanting the De Courcys (who had themselves replaced the earliest builders here, the O Cowhigs) after trapping and killing leaders of the De Courcy clan on Inchydoney strand in 1295. Two hundred years later the property was once more in De Courcey hands, and despite a few skips back to the MacCarthys it stayed with them until 1510. Then, according to a story retold by James N. Healy in *The Castles of County Cork,* it was retaken by the MacCarthys as payment of a debt secured by the loan of a white ferret. There they stayed for 130 years, years coloured by uprisings and local disputes but not so tumultuous that the castle itself could not be refashioned in 1596.

Their day ended in 1642 with the Confederate Wars, when Lord Kinalmeaky took Kilbrittain; he also took a collection of manuscripts found there and sent it home to his father, Richard Boyle, Earl of Cork, then living in Lismore. This, accumulated and copied to celebrate the marriage in 1500 of Donal MacCarthy Reagh and Caitlin, daughter of the Earl of Desmond, became known to scholarship and to history as the Book of Lismore.

Even if it were winter, I suspect, The Glen would still evoke this atmosphere of easy linkage with the past. It's as though comfort were something that came with the house and grew with it; the narrow, working shutters, the squabs in the window-seats, the small white-painted fireplaces in the bedrooms, the

The Scott family residence in these parts dates from 1724: now providing pet-friendly accommodation for guests, the house gleams with an unforced awareness of visual style inside and out.

fresh contemporary yet cottage-style wallpapers and upholstery, the breakfast-room with the light from the windows, still with their old original glass, falling on garden flowers and antique table-linen bought from Granny's Bottom Drawer in Kinsale.

Altering the interior of the house to provide a roomy attic for their own family life allows five attractive guest bedrooms, several with views of the sea, all full of green garden light and two linked by a bathroom to provide accommodation for parents with children. But this is not a matter of room space; the house is unmistakably a family home, and its tastefulness, enhanced by some fine new work by the artist Carol Hodder, has an inherited quality to it. It's no real surprise to learn that the painter Patrick Scott was born here and is Guy's uncle; the place suggests

THE GLEN HOUSE

an unforced, perhaps inherent, awareness of visual style. It's in the garden too and, as Guy outlines plans for greater gardening activity, I wonder, viewing the old espaliered pear trees in the walled garden with its beds of potatoes and sea-kale and spinach, or as I catch jewelled glimpses of the sea between tall stands of pine across the lawn, I wonder if they shouldn't just leave well enough alone. Knowing when to stop is a rare, but valuable, gift; knowing where to stop is easier. ♣

Glen Country House,
Kilbrittain, County Cork.
(a dog-friendly house)
Tel: 023 49862

It's as though comfort is something that came with the house and grew with it, offering a fresh contemporary tone matched with cottage-style wallpapers and upholstery, along with antique table-linen. (images the Irish Examiner)

The Grain Store

Ballymaloe, County Cork

A family wedding reminded Rory Allen that he needed to raise the roof of the grain store. Now the wedding is over, the roof is on and the management of this new venue created from an old farmyard barn at Ballymaloe has been entrusted to the capable hands of Events Coordinator Rebecca Cronin. Co-ordinating events had been far from Rory Allen's mind when the germ of this venture took root. Many people discriminating enough to appreciate the pleasures of a visit to Ballymaloe forget that this famous country house hotel is based on a large working farm. Some of its most enchanting accommodation is in conversions of discarded buildings, of which this is one of the largest.

'I'm a farmer,' says Rory, who has just hopped down from his tractor. 'I'm a musician for fun, but basically I'm a farmer. And here we had this old building in the middle of the farm-yard. It used to be a grain store: the grain was grown on the farm and stored here heaped up in the middle of the floor. There was a hammer mill and mixer inside that door' – he points to the elegant entrance – 'and that's where the rations for the pigs were mixed by Moss Murray. I remember how he used to whistle "The Bard of Armagh" while he was working.'

In those days the farm had over a thousand pigs and gradually it became obvious that swine and paying guests were not compatible. There are still pigs at Ballymaloe but they are free-range and fewer. The

From fortification to barn and now to concert and banqueting venue, the thick Grain Store walls and the depth of its window-sills reveal the age of the building and its various functions through the centuries. (images courtesy Rory Allen)

store became a kind of junk-yard and its galvanised roof began to leak. Rory had to fix the leak and put up 'a lovely slate roof that cost a lot of money' and then let things rest for six years or so when the only occupants of the store were birds building their nests.

Then came the wedding. For all its sophistication, Ballymaloe does not have large function spaces, but the bride could see the potential of the old grain store and Rory worked with architectural draughtswoman Gilly Fereira and with builder Eugene Rice of Aghada in a collaboration which has resulted in this large, high-ceilinged, soft-toned space which boasts a perfect concert acoustic. There can't be many venues in Ireland which still have the original gun-slits in the walls, a feature explained here by the fact that the store was once a fortified building. These are now glazed, but the new windows set in an arched succession of openings have the same deep reveals so that this pleasantly contemporary building shows by the thickness of its walls and the width of its sills just how old it really is.

'The wall on the south side we reckon was built in the 1700s and the front as it is now would have been about a hundred years later than that. I decided to leave the stonework at the entrance because that is the original wall, and as I remember it the store also had a kind of loft, so we decided that we would put in a gallery – what could be nicer than a gallery?' The double height of the grain store has clerestory windows under the coved ceiling; that allows for a balcony seating area, bracketed only by the delightful curve of wrought-iron railing designed by Rory Allen and fabricated by the staff in Eugene Rice's workshop. The walls have a rough interior finish, a mix of lime and white sand which was blown on wet with a pneumatic gun rather than plastering with a trowel. In a colour scheme of blonde, grey and soft green the floor of bamboo wood offers a welcoming expanse to users such as a mother and toddlers group, crafts guilds, yoga classes and, hanging under slender racks of exhibition lighting, an art display. But what about a stage? Rory takes a remote control from his pocket and lo! the big carpet at one end seems to rise as if about to take flight and under it, silently, appears the hidden hydraulic platform. Honestly, the Grain Store has everything.

Yet it wasn't for yoga and toddlers that the grain store was converted. Rory intends to have the premises used as much as possible by as many groups as possible but his inclination is towards music and the arts. Classical music is a joy to hear in this venue, and Rebecca Cronin is busily promoting such bargains as early dinner and concert ticket for €60 a head. 'How can you make this pay?' I ask. 'It's a brilliant deal', responds Rory, 'but this is a new dimension for Ballymaloe: I'd like to have the place as renowned for its music as for its hospitality in the future.'

The Grain Store,
Ballymaloe House, Shanagarry, County Cork
Tel: 021 4651511

The Old Convent

Clogheen, County Tipperary

The road between Mitchelstown and Clogheen was blocked by a herd of cows making its slow way from one field to another. As the two last animals swayed through the gateway the farmer placed a hand on each rump, letting it rest there as they passed. I know he may have been simply measuring the ratio of flesh to bone, but it looked like affection to me, and I went on my way, rejoicing. It was a good omen for a day in the country, I thought, and I was right, for my destination was the Old Convent in Clogheen itself – and anyone who thinks that that isn't in the country doesn't know Clogheen. Or the Old Convent if it comes to that.

At the Old Convent Dermot and Christine Gannon have staked their future on the success of what they call a gourmet hideaway. This is a young couple who have built their reputation at Gannon's Above The Bell – that is, above The Bell pub in Cahir. When expansion suggested new challenges, they wondered, if they were going to remain in the catering industry for the rest of their lives, what was the part of it most likely to make them happy.

By finding what was most likely to make them happy, Christine and Dermot found what is likely to make lots of other people happy too. The Old Convent was built in 1885 for the Mercy Sisters managing the local workhouse and teaching in the schools. Standing tall on the road from Clogheen to the mountain gap of the Vee, the premises was then a guesthouse and later a healing centre. By then the Gannons were pondering a bed and breakfast option but one to which they might like to go themselves. 'Comfortable, chilled out, in a great location and not costing the earth.'

The cost of the earth is often determined by the quality of the experience. In this case Dermot and Christine have designed an environment in which doing nothing at all is an acceptable option, despite opportunities for doing just about anything. There's no daily exclusion time at which house guests are expected to be gone; the papers arrive, the fires are alight, the lamps glowing, the sofas and armchairs waiting to sag under your weight as you settle to your book or magazine or board game or cards or easy conversations. No lunch, but dinner, the eight-course tasting menu, is in the offing. Even breakfast, sometimes as stern as a roll-call in other establishments, is a gentle wake-up around, oh, ten or so? Maybe eleven?

Christine likes to think of her guests having a little lie-in. 'That's what they come for, to be at ease.' The thing is, these breakfasts are worth getting up for: porridge only if someone asks for it, as Dermot has an aversion to its borstal connotations. But when it does come it's from an organic producer, like the Ballybrado eggs, or bacon, or the pork used at dinner. The smoked salmon is from Graham Roberts in Connemara.

Niamh Myles prepares the tables in the long dining-room at The Old Convent where the Gannons (opposite) have designed an environment in which it is totally acceptable to do nothing at all.
(images Joleen Cronin photographer)

Christine, from Colorado, and Dermot, from Connemara, met in America, where Christine was preparing for law school and Dermot was working as an executive chef. His first job was summertime employment at Renvyle House Hotel and then a more formal engagement at Rosleague Manor, where he came under the influence of the Foyle family of Clifden.

With Christine ready to enrol at University College Cork, Dermot himself ready to try whatever might come his way and Paddy Foyle still their mentor and guide, they decided to come back to Ireland. So here they are, in their polished marble hall with paintings of saints just to remind us of the convent which, with the exception of its serenity, is gastronomically contradicted by what the Gannons are achieving here. The little niches once filled with statues are filled with flowers, the bedrooms all have small sitting areas with couches and tables and mirrors. As for dinner – well, the menu changes every day according to what the local producers and suppliers have on offer, depending too on the seasons and on inspiration. 'We knew it was a gamble,' says Christine, 'but one thing we've learned – you can't be everything to everybody. So we're just us, this house, this experience – and people seem to like it.'

The Old Convent,
Clogheen, County Tipperary
Tel: 05274 65565

262 AT HOME IN IRELAND

The Quay House

Clifden, County Galway

'She got lost in south Connemara,' explains Paddy Foyle as his wife, Julia, meets us in the hall of the Quay House in Clifden. We are all pilgrims, the message seems to be; we are all capable of getting lost in south Connemara, a landscape designed from the time of creation for that very purpose. Ceantar na nOileán is a magical, unsuspected grouping of islands linked by causeways and bridges, with unspoiled pearl-white beaches lurking beneath every turn of the road. But the road obeys the biblical injunction to go forth and multiply, and none of these winding offspring leads anywhere but to the sea. And Screeb: if you're trying to be somewhere at anything approaching a given time, well, just don't miss the turn for Screeb.

The terrain here is cratered with small lakes and floored with expanses of heath. The panoramas of the west of Ireland open out here and close again at Cashel's wooded creeks. But ruinous planning decisions are defacing this part of our country; I realise that those who are paid expensive salaries to be vigilant on our behalf simply, on this evidence, couldn't care less.

Clifden on a sunny July afternoon is thronged and thriving, colourful and, as always, welcoming. At the very edge of the harbour is the tall, primrose-painted Quay House and, as I collapse in exhaustion on my bed's white counterpane, I admit that there is something, after all, to be said for a television in the bedroom with a remote control and for a host who insists on sending the tray of tea up the three flights of stairs rather than let you plug in the bedroom kettle yourself. The tray comes: china, a silver teapot, little biscuits. It is set on the small table by the window and there I revive myself slowly as people meander along the harbour walk and the shark-fishing boat chugs into its mooring and the world seems a pleasant, but distant, place.

The Quay House was built in 1820 by John D'Arcy, JP, the most notable subsequent owner being Thomas Martin, MP, of Ballynahinch, son of Richard (Humanity Dick) Martin. For a while a monastery and then a convent, it was run as a hotel by the Pye family until 1912. Later the Burkes of Galway lived here for forty years until Paddy and Julia Foyle bought it in 1992. Their arrival brought back the hotel tradition, for Paddy's family are hoteliers throughout the west, and he himself was born in the old Railway Hotel in Clifden (now the Clifden Bay Hotel) and worked with his sister Anne on the restoration of Rosleague Manor, which is a bit further up the road near Letterfrack.

When the Foyles arrived at the Quay House all the buildings on the harbour were derelict, including the old grain store, which is now under restoration. These buildings are tall, and the three storeys of the Quay House compose an elegant yet characteristic

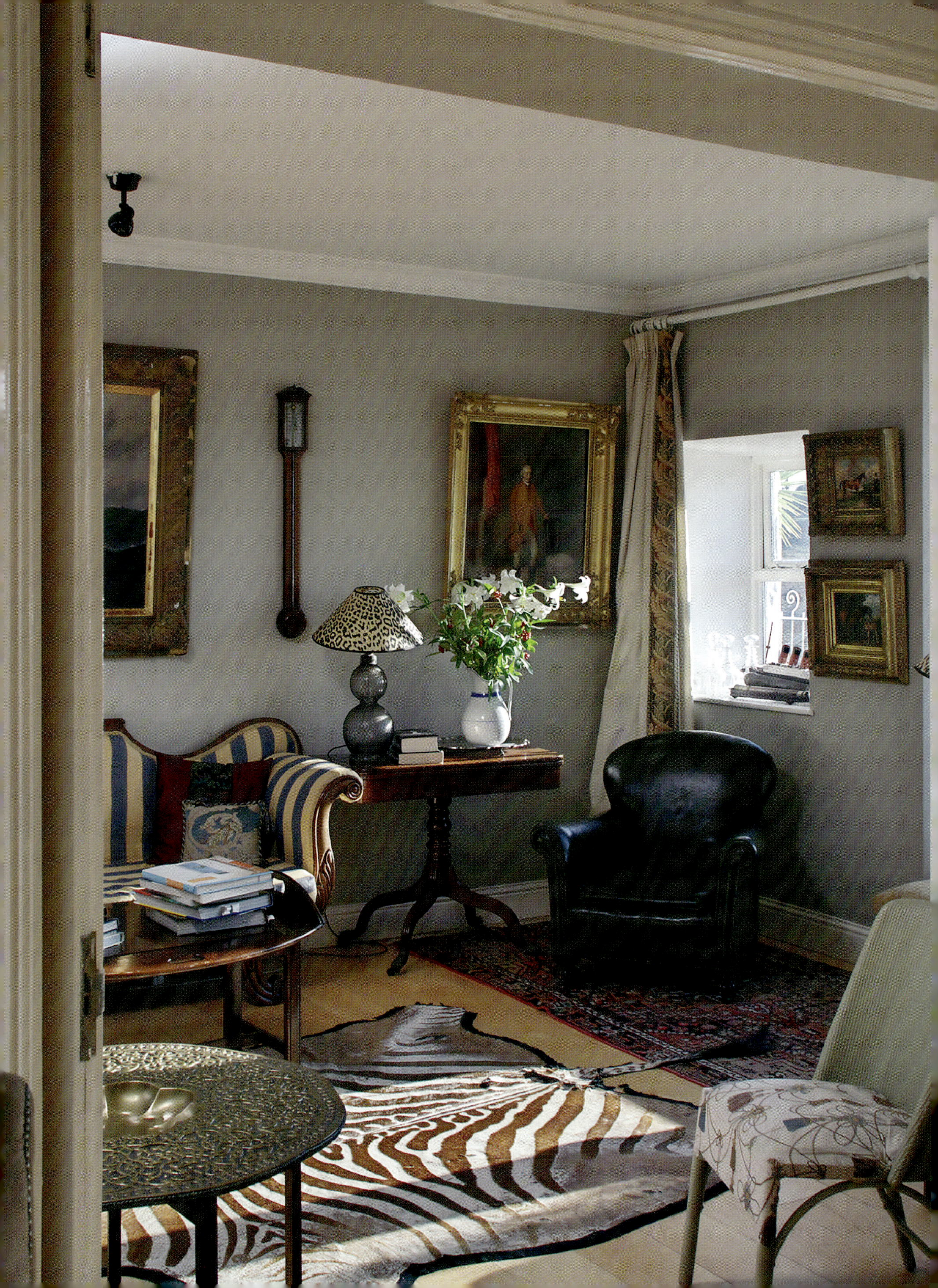

OPPOSITE: *The drawing-room at The Quay House has the decorative extra of very dead, very wild animals, giving a touch of the exotic to this house in Connemara.* ABOVE: *Paddy and Julia Foyle have a very sure touch for the integrity of what they offer at the Quay House.*

façade. A garden has been cut out of the cliff at the side, with stone terracing flowing with flowers and shrubs, and the dining-room has been continued into a conservatory where, in this heat, the roof is curtained like a tent. The drawing-room is a country-house drawing-room, double-spaced with lots of easy furniture and the decorative extra of very dead, very wild animals. 'I'm a hypocrite,' admits Paddy. 'I'm totally against all blood sports – well, except for deep-sea fishing – but I've always been fascinated by the big cats and when working as an antiques dealer in London I got a lot of them fairly cheaply. And in a place like Connemara, you know, they give a touch of the exotic. A little incongruous, but I love it.'

Paddy and Julia are not afraid of the incongruous. They are totally in command of this enterprise, having

THE QUAY HOUSE

ABOVE: *The house stands at the very edge of the harbour in Clifden.* TOP RIGHT: *The conservatory.* RIGHT: *Tusks stand guard in the hall.* (images courtesy of Keewi Photography)

a very sure touch for the style of what they offer. My room is like a Hansel and Gretel room, white-painted iron beds with immaculate white counterpanes, lots of pillows, walls of deep matt blue and small thoughtful things like a luminous clock by the bedside and a refreshed tea-and-coffee tray at night. And a big, gleaming, warm, well-appointed bathroom. The Quay House is a distinctive, memorable creation influenced by the best traditions of Irish hospitality. Living in Clifden with their four children and completely committed to the town, Paddy and Julia Foyle revel in their way of life: 'Our ambition is to make people remember this place and to go away happy. We're determined to give the best we can possibly give.'

The Quay House,
Clifden, County Galway
Tel: 095 21369

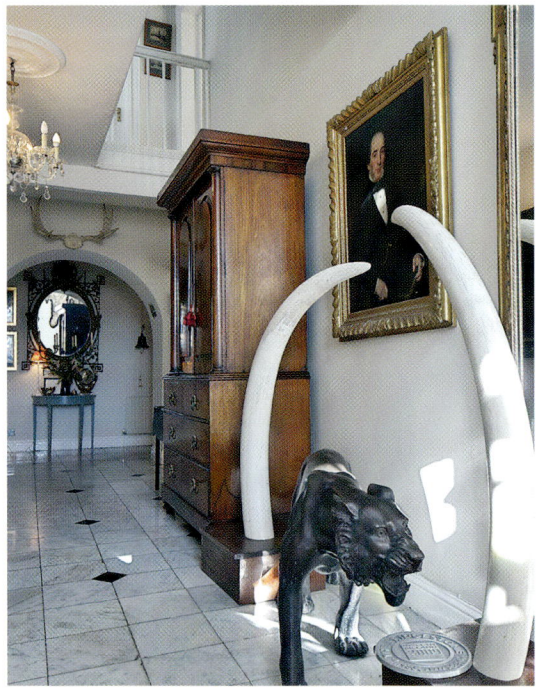

The Sprigging School

Rathbarry, County Cork

The white cottage is set against a background thick with trees. From the chimney a coil of smoke twists high into the branches before it fades into the blue January sky. A fairytale of west Cork, I think, but in fact this is a sturdy, time-worn, beloved little house, a place of industry and enterprise once crucial to the domestic economy of this region of Rathbarry and Castlefreke. And leaning against the whitewashed stone wall inside the Sprigging School is the framed Italian testament won by the Traditional Lace-Makers of Ireland, represented by my guide Veronica Stuart. It comes from the Biennale Internazionale del Merletto, the celebration of threads and lacemaking run by Tuscany's central cultural region of Sansepolcro; Sansepolcro is the homeplace of the Renaissance painter Piero della Francesca, and this linking of artistry across so many centuries, the certificate inset with the golden medallion as an emblem of Pegasus, the winged horse, signals the triumphant renewal of Irish lacemaking.

Not all of it stems from this little house at the edge of the woods. Here the fire in the small hearth is lit almost daily by Breda Hodnett of the post office nearby; its flame is encouraged by the wheel-bellows in the wall of the chimney breast, its fuel is stacked in small traditional piles and stored in black scuttles. The walls are alive with memorabilia, including a few examples of the kind of work women in the locality learned to do here from 1825. That was when the then Lady Carbery of Castle Freke established the Sprigging School as a way of training women to profit from the worldwide renewal of lacemaking, a revival which was greatly helped in Ireland by Catholic Emancipation a few years later and the need for lace to trim the vestments and altar linen of Catholic clergy. Sprigging itself is not lace, but a technique of decorative open cut-work embroidery in the shape of sprigs, or leafed sprays, on fine Irish linen, the scalloped edges finished with buttonhole stitch.

This building, so carefully restored by the village's Tidy Towns committee as a millennium project for 2000, was reached initially by a set of steps set into the bank of the stream, which led to stepping-stones from which the steps on the opposite bank could be reached. Both sets of steps are still there, mossy but firm in their damp, ferny bedding; I can't help thinking of those women with their long heavy skirts walking barefoot down the steps and into the rushing water. But waiting at the bridge is Veronica Stuart of Carrigaline, whose love of embroidery and lacemaking led to the development of the West Cork Lace Trail.

'I always wanted to do research of this kind,' she says. 'And while I did take on the job for the West Cork Leader Co-Op Society and set up the local courses in lacemaking, I had an awful lot of help!'

Many Irish families survived the Great Famine through sale of the lace made by women trained in such little establishments as this Sprigging School. (images Veronica Stuart)

The Lace Trail moves from Kinsale, to Cape Clear, Bantry, Bandon, Clonakilty, Rosscarbery, Macroom, Glengarriff and Ballingeary. Many samples of this work were acclaimed at international exhibitions; it was bought by royalty, princesses were married in it. It was worn by the princes of the church. Which in its own way is a bit of a problem for Veronica, who wants to be able to provide samples for current displays: 'It was local communities who ordered vestments as an ordination gift for a priest from the parish. But priests liked to be buried in their vestments, so we lost a lot of lace in that way.'

The school was only one part of a movement that spread throughout Ireland in the nineteenth century, again helped greatly by convents intent on giving girls and women a means of earning their living, relieving them from the age-old drudgery of carding and spinning wool. Many Irish households survived the Famine through the lace produced by the womenfolk, and lacemaking could be said to have had an architectural impact as well: the necessity for utter cleanliness drove livestock out of the kitchen and installed ceilings under the bare thatch; the need for bright light also widened cabin windows and encouraged the whitewashing of interior walls.

The Sprigging School at Rathbarry was once a two-roomed house where the teacher slept on the kitchen settle-bed. Now the stone-flagged floor, the wide sash windows with their deep reveals, the benches set close to the door all speak of a simple rural economy of life and of tradition. It came to a slow, sad end with the introduction of machine-made imitation lace after about 1840 and the few attempts at revival eventually foundered during the First World War. It would be easy, now, to suppose that as a cottage industry lacemaking is gone forever, if it weren't for Veronica Stuart and people of that ilk.

Tourin House

Cappoquin, County Waterford

'*Higher up is Tourin, the seat of Sir Richard Musgrave, Bart, to whose spirited and persevering exertions we are indebted for the opening of the navigation of this beautiful river . . . The hills tower aloft, and houses, rolling up their smoke, announce a town.*

The town is Cappoquin, the river is the Blackwater, which glides brimful to the edge of the gardens at Tourin; the hills may not exactly tower (J.R. O'Flanagan's prose of 1844 had its little exaggerations), but they mount gently above this farmland to form the long high rim of the Knockmealdowns. If one follows the river southwards to Youghal, other fine

BELOW: *Tourin is on the site of the old fortified tower house built like many others along the banks of the Blackwater River.*

The staircase hall, with its oak stairs stretching from the arched ground floor to the upper galleries, is the glory of the Italianate building designed by the Dublin architect Abraham Denny.
(images Kristin Jameson and the *Irish Examiner*)

houses can be glimpsed on the shore at either side: a great gateway here, the high sparkle of a row of windows through the trees, the quay at Villierstown, the bend off the road to Dromana. Kristin Jameson of Tourin explains that many of these houses began as fortifications along the river from the coast to its inland source. 'They were defences against the Vikings,' she says, 'and our mother came from Norway!' Right enough, her home at Tourin, shared with her sisters Andrea and Tara, remains the site of the tower house which was forfeited by the Roches in reprisal for the rebellion of 1641.

The Blackwater was a highway and bore the freight of Irish history, but as it sweeps past Tourin its presence is benign. The house overlooks a tillage farm which supplies apples for cider and rapeseed for oil and which trains that splendid dog, the Irish red setter. Well, actually, there's more than one kind of dog here. While one of the sisters concentrates on pedigree working dogs, another has a failing for waifs and strays; the best way of describing the canine component of Tourin is that there are house dogs, yard dogs and kennel dogs. And perhaps a studio dog. And certainly a study dog. And retirees.

Tourin House is an Italianate creamy-yellow

building whose garden front is broken by a three-light bay window, its roof distinguished by a deep-cut bracket cornice with a string-course trim between the two storeys. Built in 1840 to replace the Georgian house attached to the tower, and attributed to the Dublin architect Abraham Denny, it was given an additional wing in the late nineteenth century. Although both its drawing-rooms – one revealing the tapestry upholstery worked by the late Didi Jameson – and its dining-room are impressive in a friendly way, the glory of the house is the inner hall. Lit from the glazed roof lantern overhead, an oak staircase spreads its imperial wings from the arched ground floor to the upper galleries, with arches matching the fenestration below. Danish stucco panels decorate the upper wall, while delicate plaster tracery heightens the lower pillars.

The Jameson sisters work the house, farm, kennels, orchard and heaven knows what else. Their father was Shane Jameson, their mother Didi, who, with her husband, was responsible for much of the present shape of the garden. Shane's mother was Joan Jameson (née Musgrave), the painter, who studied and worked with Mainie Jellett and Nora McGuinness, and these artistic affiliations are one of the surprises of Tourin which keep it alive and fascinating. Both Kristin and Andrea are painters, Kristin having studied in Italy for many years while Andrea's work has been exhibited in London, Dublin and Canada.

'Our parents were dedicated to three things,' explains Tara. 'The house, the farm and us. We worked here like everyone else, and that's what we do still.' Kristin has recently planted 70 acres of hardwood trees nearer the river, where the view is interrupted by the old tower house. One path leads to the kitchen garden (all three sisters speak of the work of Michael O'Gorman and Michael O'Sullivan), where the walls still support pear and apple trees gnarled like a Dürer etching, an old rose from Italy flaunting itself amid the more dutiful clumps of delphiniums or – a new development which is Tara's pride – the groupings of bearded irises of many colours and habits which she is propagating.

Returning, we pass the bleaching green which gives the house its name and where linen shipped over from Affane and Tallow was washed and dried.

Kristin and Tara describe how the garden was redesigned by their grandfather Richard Musgrave with Richard Beamish of Ashbourne House in Cork. We pass the big old shed used by their father, once squash champion of Ireland, and stand under the pines and eucalyptus planted by their mother. 'We loved growing up here,' remembers Tara. 'It's always been a very happy place.' ♠

Tourin House and Gardens,
Cappoquin, County Waterford
Tel: 058 54405
'The Irish Red Setter' *by Raymond O'Dwyer (Cork University Press)* €59

Ulusker House

Adrigole, County Cork

There is a nurturing quality to Lorna and David Ramshaw's hospitality at Ulusker House – also known as Mossie's – in Adrigole, which tempts me to begin their story with a bolster. Stout and creamy-yellow, it lay on the inviting creamy-yellow couch drawn up before the fire in the lounge. This bolster declared itself slowly as Billy the bulldog, whose seamed old face said 'do not disturb' so plainly that, well, I did not disturb him. But he is of a sedentary disposition and I was able to sit beside him, pondering as we got acquainted Lorna's affectionate suggestion that his was a face only a mother could love.

In the absence of his mother, we fell to wondering

It wasn't easy for the Ramshaws to leave their lovely seventeenth-century house in England, but here they are, making it easy for us to relish what they have to offer. And inviting our dogs as well, by special permission of Billy.

272   AT HOME IN IRELAND

Inside the gates the garden is full of surprises, with cultivated lawns, arbours twined with roses and sweet pea, borders rich with phlox and astilbe, hollyhocks, delphiniums, lupins and hardy geraniums in profusion.

why God had made bulldogs, with their collapsed muzzle, undershot jaw, projecting teeth and negligible nostrils. The answer of course is that God wouldn't dream of it; man made the bulldog to suit the supposed needs of mankind. But God did give the bulldog a soul, and Billy is still a model of stoutheartedness, loyalty and courage.

Both Lorna and David had to be stout of heart at times during their restoration of Ulusker House, which stands with its back to the hills above the village of Adrigole looking out over wide swathes of Bantry Bay. The land is all gorse and heather, harvested in small unadulterated Irish fields. The scents of woodbine, of hay, of sea and heather seep into the clean air. Inside the gates the garden is full of surprises, with lawns, arbours, borders, trees and shrubs, with mounds of hydrangeas massed in shades of blue which Lorna loves and which, she says, were 'one of the reasons we settled here'.

Living in Bath, David ran a company specialising in restoration and salvage while Lorna, having trained as a dance-drama teacher, also had experience in catering and was managing a clothing company. They were frequent visitors to Ireland, where their holidays reminded them of the life they remembered from childhood. 'And in the UK we had often been in lovely old houses where you could go and stay and eat and be spoilt,' says Laura, 'and we felt that we could do that kind of thing here.'

The house began as an eighteenth-century summer retreat for Bantry House, after which it was sold as a presbytery for the Catholic church at Massmount nearby. Perhaps seventy-five years after

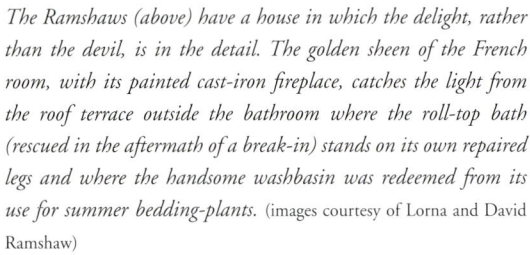

The Ramshaws (above) have a house in which the delight, rather than the devil, is in the detail. The golden sheen of the French room, with its painted cast-iron fireplace, catches the light from the roof terrace outside the bathroom where the roll-top bath (rescued in the aftermath of a break-in) stands on its own repaired legs and where the handsome washbasin was redeemed from its use for summer bedding-plants. (images courtesy of Lorna and David Ramshaw)

that came the Powers, important landowners in the area of whom Maurice, a son of the family, was the last representative. A gentle and popular man, known for his skill on the 'squeezebox' – and as a barber – it seemed to the Ramshaws that he should be remembered at Ulusker House, and so it remains 'Mossie's'.

On the ground floor a balustraded porch leads into a hall which divides on one side into a lounge and on the other into a dining-room, the walls half-lined with lincrusta in a copy of Victorian décor, the wide windows of a conservatory showing the bay glinting in the distance. The painted tables hold roses in the china cups which are Lorna's passion; on the dresser is a Wedgewood service which is in daily use. Because the Ramshaws are selective rather than opportunistic salvage hunters, the house, redesigned by architect Donal Hoare of Skibbereen, reflects their taste, their inspiration and their skills. The salvage stock the couple had accumulated underpinned their decision to settle at Ulusker, providing solid items like the pitch-pine flooring from a convent in Dublin, as well as the branched German candelabra in the garden, the amber spirals of Italian glass in the conservatory, the art deco finger plates for the doors and the brass peacock door handles.

In the twin room the iron beds were recovered from the undergrowth in the garden. The Italian room matches its trimmed dado with the embellished panelling of its walls, while the seductive Russian room is the result of David's last salvage before leaving England. There had been water damage in a bedroom in the Russian Embassy in London and David had to remove everything, damaged or not. With the Ramshaws' shared genius for transformation, their Russian room is now distinguished by curtains, cushions and quilted coverlet of hand-painted silk on a bed specially made in Harrods. The room faces the sea and its calm yet luxurious beauty is enhanced by a deep-framed oval setting of parchment roses, made by Lorna's gifted hands. ♣

Ulusker House remains open under new management. Billy died in 2008.

Ulusker House,
Trafrask, Adrigole, County Cork
Tel: 027 60606

Woodstock House

Inistioge, County Kilkenny

There is a generation – and it is my own – to which Woodstock means only one thing: a rock weekend of limitless potential. It is with a determination to banish all thoughts of that American Woodstock that I take to the hill above the village of Inistioge towards the ruined house and revived gardens of Kilkenny's Woodstock.

I'm glad to leave Inistioge behind: Bobbie has disgraced me there. The glistening Nore laps the village green and ducks, drakes and ducklings plus a clutch of swans speckled with coots and water hens had gathered near the water's edge. It is a day

The trees and shrubs of the arboretum send blissful shade across the grass where a family party has spread its picnic rugs beneath the walls and small children tumble and chase, their calls light echoes of voices which must have been calling here a hundred and more years ago.

OPPOSITE: *The feeling is that Woodstock is set on a plateau. The wilder areas falling towards the Nore mask the incline of the hill and the drama of this location is best seen – perhaps in the autumn when the woods are gloriously coloured – from the far side of the river.*

of drenching heat; the green, the trees, the river and the riverside restaurant bring people to sit or lie out in the sun and I keep Bobbie on the lead until we are safely past anything that might attract her romping attention. We walk, she swims and then we turn back towards the village.

I have forgotten the basking wildfowl, but Bobbie has not. She races ahead and scatters the flocks, plunging into the river after them, oblivious to my calls, to the shouted abuse of old men shaking their walking sticks, to the screams of the girls perfecting their tan. Delirious with water and the chase she rollicks in the mêlée. I try to disappear up a laneway as if she has nothing to do with me at all and she leaps on to the bank, shaking off water in wide-ranging sprays. I smuggle her into the boot of the car, half-afraid we'll both be burned at the stake in Inistioge.

At Woodstock, however, all is calm, although the house and its remarkable library were burned in 1922. For nearly sixty years after that the fine gardens were neglected until an International Scout Jamboree in 1978 encouraged a clean-up by the Forestry Department. It is too hot to walk all through the estate but I follow a recommended route towards a waterfall and an ornamental cottage. The wilder areas falling towards the Nore mask the incline of the hill and the drama of this location is best seen — perhaps in the autumn when the woods are gloriously coloured — from the far side of the river.

Built to a design by Francis Bindon in 1745, Woodstock had formal gardens which can still be traced. The pleasure grounds were famous in their day, especially during the era of Colonel William Tighe and his wife Lady Louisa, born Louisa Lennox, a daughter of the Duke of Richmond. It was Louisa who installed the terraced borders and who, in a fruitful horticultural partnership with her gardeners

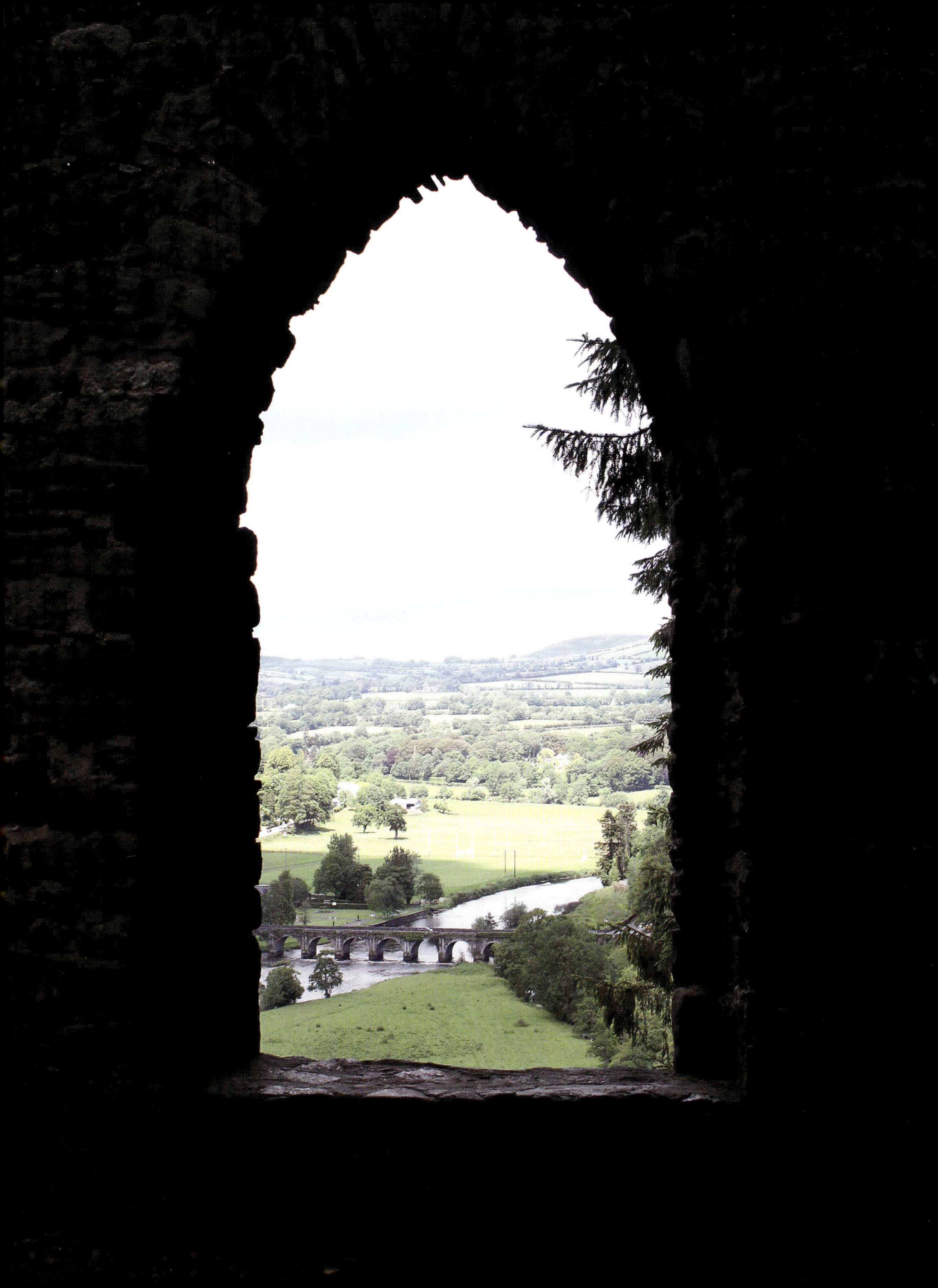

These walks and avenues were aligned with the different faces of the house and the restoration programme follows the garden patterns and designs such as the circular conservatory built by Richard Turner – there is even a surviving garden seat of his drawing.
(images courtesy of Carmel M. Cleary and Kilkenny County Council)

laid out in terraces and the atmosphere now is of airy spaciousness. The trees and shrubs of the arboretum send blissful shade across the grass. The house was never a great building, despite Lady Louisa's work at transforming what was a relatively small mansion into a ducal seat.

She may also have been anxious to pare the skin of scandal from Woodstock, for it was here, in the 1770s, that Lady Sarah Ponsonby lived with her cousins, Sir William and Lady Betty Fownes. Woodstock was built for Sir William Fownes and it was by the marriage of his daughter and heiress to William Tighe that it passed to the Tighes of Wicklow. The most renowned of the Tighes was Mary, a poet known as 'Psyche' who died here in 1810; her portrait by Romney is in the National Gallery in Dublin.

Mary was not the mischief-maker at Woodstock. That credit goes to poor Sarah Ponsonby, whose intense friendship with Eleanor Butler of Borris was so disapproved of by both families that Eleanor was kept locked up at her sister's home near Carlow. She escaped to join Sarah at Woodstock until the two women got away together and settled in Wales, where they were celebrated as the Ladies of Llangollen – although I admit I do not know why. Now a heritage museum in the village high street shows you what to look for and what Woodstock looked like, once upon a time.

Charles MacDonald and Pierce Butler, created the sunken parterres of the winter garden, and the great rockery, and the avenue of forty-five pairs of silver firs, and the Monkey Puzzle Walk, this the longest, and most impressive, in Europe.

The restoration programme managed by Kilkenny County Council is following the outlines of the garden patterns and designs such as the circular conservatory built by Richard Turner. Low box hedging marks off the beds and the herbaceous border is set against the turreted stonework of the walled garden. Lawns are

Woodstock Estate is managed by Kilkenny County Council.

Woodstock Gardens and Arboretum,
Inistioge, County Kilkenny
Tel: 056 7794373
www.woodstock.ie

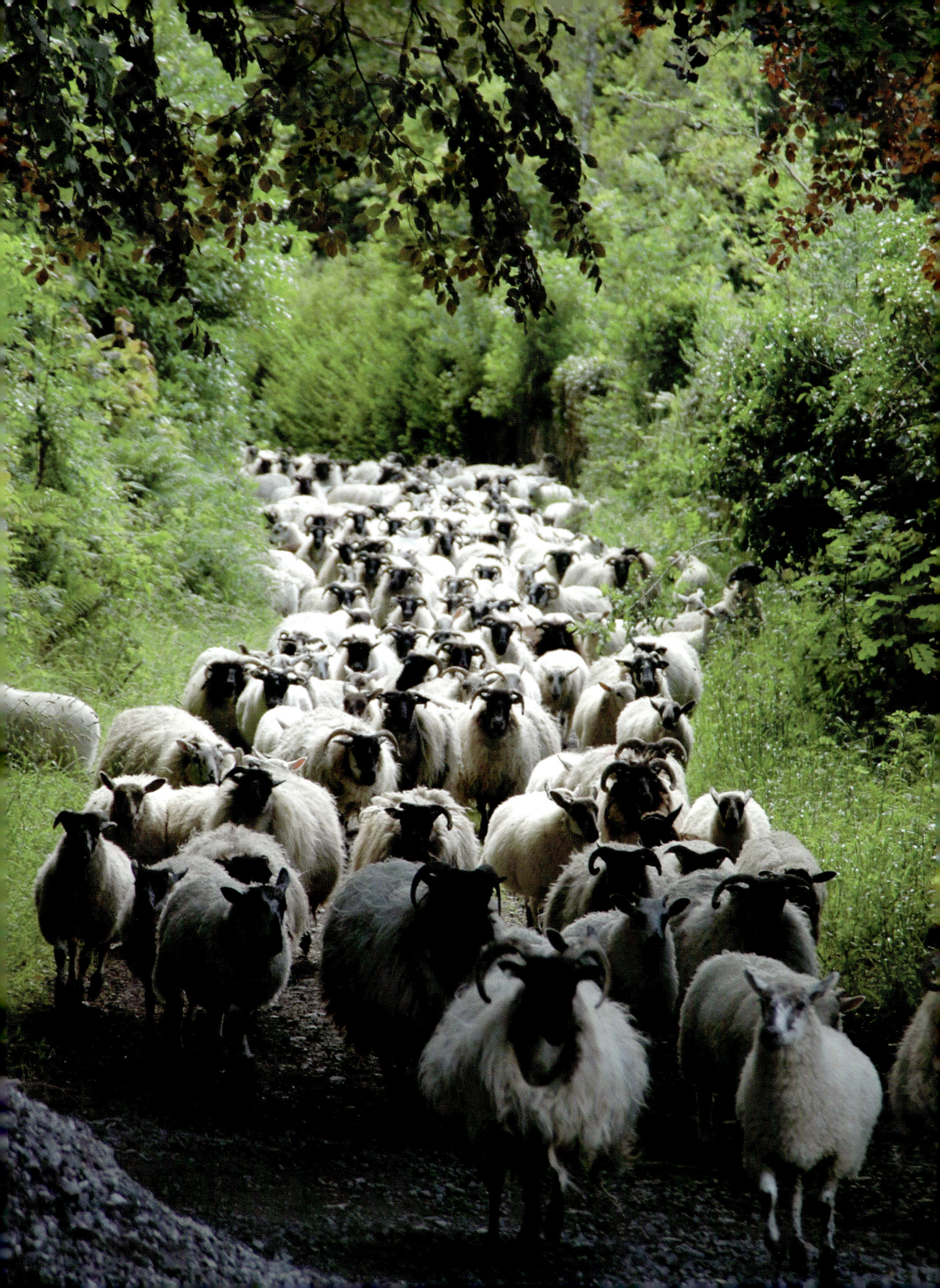

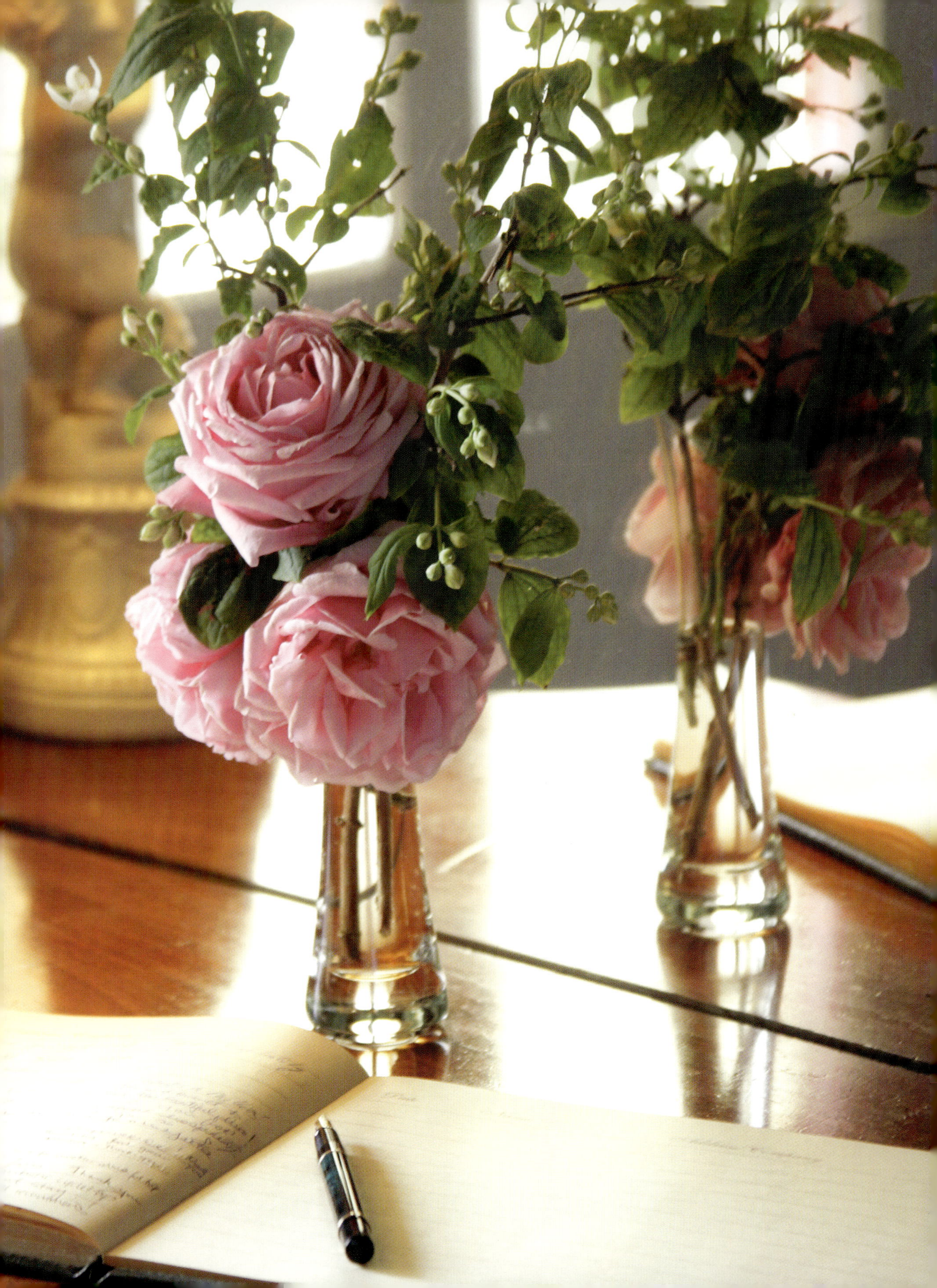

Eating for Ireland

Country house hospitality in Ireland has developed a fine reputation for its farmers, cooks and kitchens. They offer a glimpse of more than a tradition and of an increasing willingness to grow and to provide food of high quality presented with skill as well as the personal touch of individual proprietors.

Even where bed and breakfast means that breakfast is the only meal available, it is always something to be enjoyed to the full.

The following are typical of Irish country house cooking drawn from a variety of premises during the past fifteen years.

Annesbrook House

The courgette and rosemary soup, the garden peas and creamed spinach and crumbling potatoes dug minutes before being simply boiled to accompany the salmon, the crisp salad and the piercing sweetness of the raspberries served with folds of cream and ice-cream are all of the land on which this house was built, all grown behind the walls stretching beyond the coachyard and spinneys.

Ballaghtobin

Breakfast consists of a variety of fruits including fresh strawberries, melon, nectarines and blueberries, of cheeses, of muffins and croissants and five varieties of bread, of juices and yoghurts and baked ham and cherry tomatoes and a choice of cooked dishes. This colourful array reminds me that Catherine has studied with china restorer Desirée Shortt in Dublin – and I notice, without much surprise, that even the ketchup on this graceful table comes in a silver stand.

Ballinkeele Country House

John dishes up the pancakes, muesli, cereals, stewed plums, rashers, sausages and eggs and the brown bread and toast which constitute breakfast at Ballinkeele. Dinner consisted of carrot and parsnip soup, fresh wild salmon with hollandaise sauce, stuffed peppers, fresh vegetables and potatoes, salad, cheese and pudding and, of course, a choice of wines. There was also quiche with a tomato sauce, boeuf bourguignon and boiled rice, steamed vegetables from the garden, Irish cheeses with fruit, home-made praline ice-cream with fresh blackcurrant and apple compote or a rum savarine.

Barberstown Castle

There was a table d'hôte menu for dinner, which began with spiced pumpkin soup or a game and foie gras pie with orange and turnip sauce or a tempura of red mullet, minted pea purée, vine tomatoes with a balsamic vinegar reduction. A raspberry sorbet clears the way for main courses which included braised venison, a fillet of sea bass with prawns Wonton and curly kale, roast mallard duck, a chargrilled fillet of Irish beef with wild mushrooms, all with organic vegetables and potatoes and followed by a choice of desserts of which no more need be said other than that the vanilla crème brûlee is recommended.

Derrynane House

The Ireland of today has an appetite, and the house has one of the best tea-rooms I have ever found at a heritage site. They serve a variety of dishes, from a Chicken Kiev in a light pastry to seafood chowder or spinach and lentil pie (and, I have to admit, a stunning fruit and cream sponge).

Dunbrody House

My dinner consisted of a parcel of smoked salmon with crème fraîche topped with a scallop and forest mushroom spring roll, followed by the roast loin of bacon on a bed of braised cabbage leaves with a potato cake. Then came the raspberry torte.

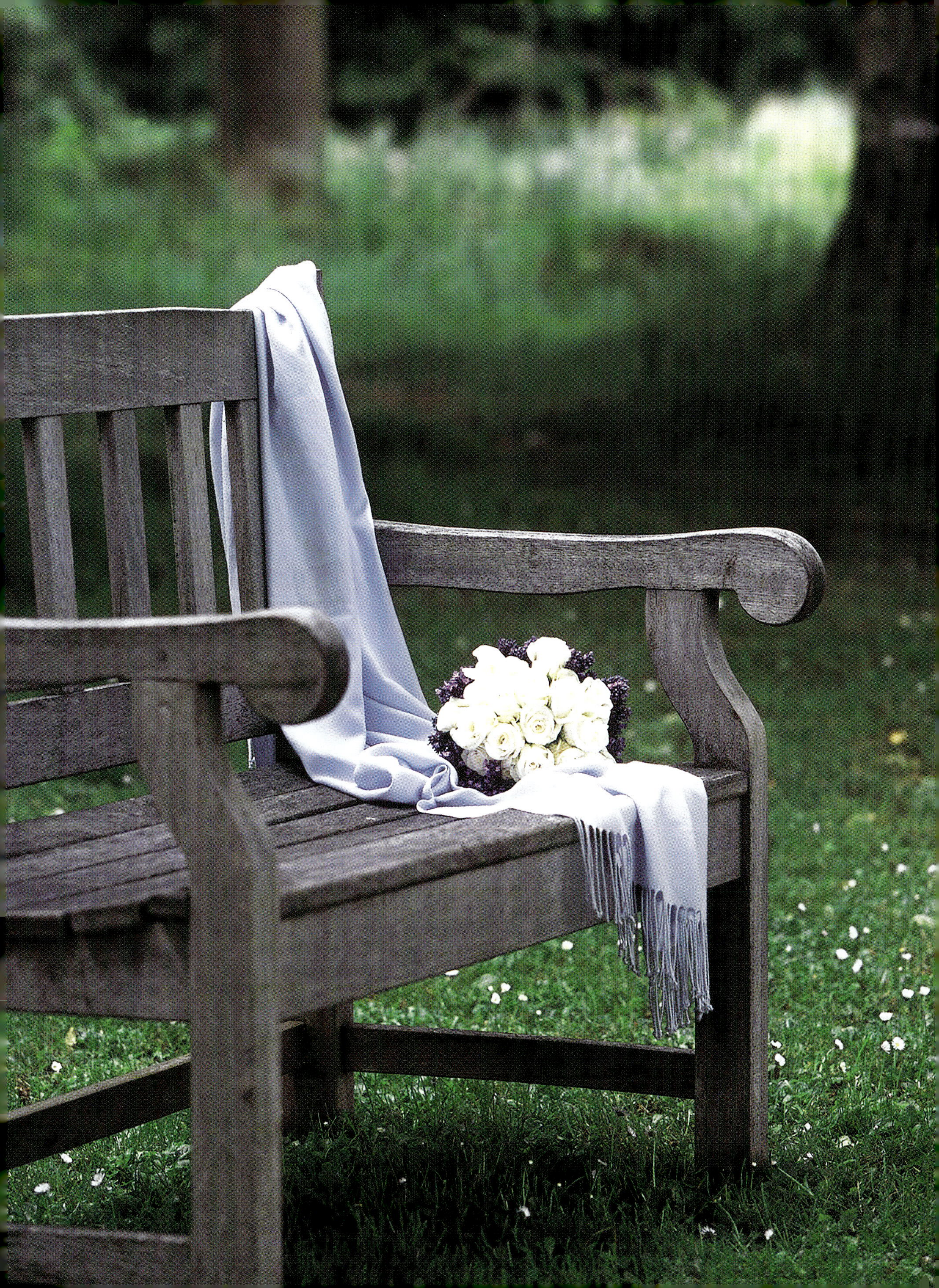

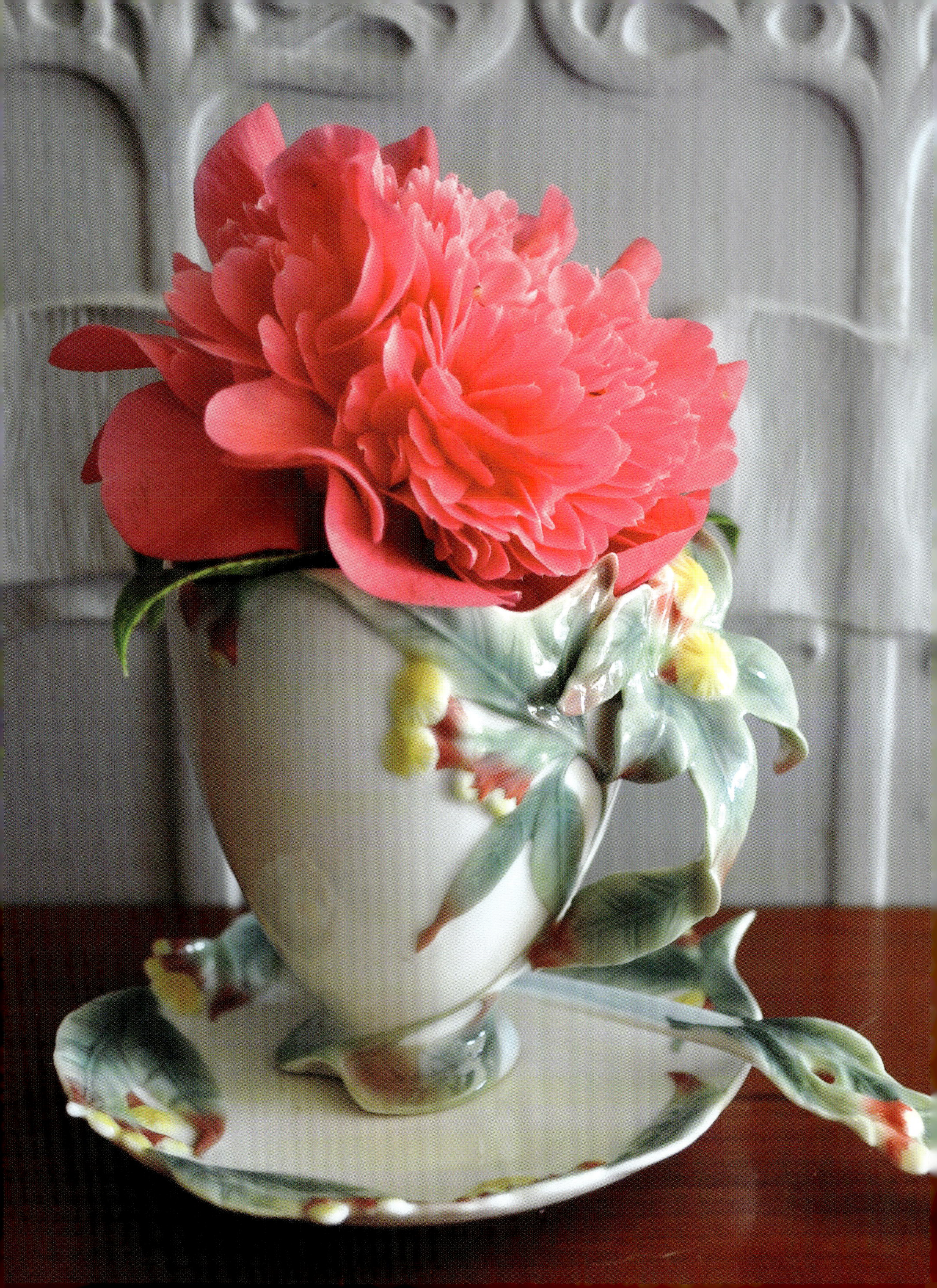

Foxmount Farm

The breakfast menu is generous, with fresh orange or apple juices, grapefruit or stewed fruit and yoghurt, home-made muesli and other cereals, porridge with cream, an Irish breakfast with a variety of egg dishes, a cheese plate, and Margaret's own bread, scones and jams.

Glenlohane

For breakfast there is fresh fruit juice, porridge with glazed brown sugar and cream, eggs and bacon and mushrooms, soda bread and toast, marmalade and bramble jelly. Our informal supper the night before was eaten off trays in front of the fire crackling with logs – a smoked salmon and tartare terrine, chicken and vegetable pie and chocolate mousse in its little lidded china pot.

Glin Castle

A crusted cheese soufflé boasts of the hens in the orchard; a lovage soup (like the spinach at lunch) tells of Tom Wall's kitchen garden sea-kale, asparagus, celeriac, bee-hives, vines and more. Tender beef from a local supplier is served with a creamy horseradish sauce from the herb beds; leeks, spring cabbage, carrots, a foaming roast potato are served to fill the gap before a dessert of garden raspberries, wines from a discerning but sensibly-priced wine list – this is a dinner built on Bob's credo of country house food in the Irish country house.

Griesemount

It's a talkative, unending lunch: a soup, we think, and then just bread and cheese, but this somehow gets the added value of smoked salmon, and there's a pâté, and a tingling salad and fresh rolls, and fruit for the cheese, and on it goes and on I sit listening to the story of how Carolyn and Robert, back from Africa, found the house in 1983.

Lorum Old Rectory

Smoked duck salad, tomato and basil soup, raspberry and rum sorbet, rack of lamb with fresh mint jelly, boiled new potatoes and home-grown sugar peas, a cheeseboard bearing Lavittstown (down the road), Gubbeen, Cashel Blue and Boileau cheeses with a bunch of dusky black grapes are all followed by a chocolate mousse, which ends what is commonly known as dinner at Lorum Old Rectory.

The Glebe House Ballinadee

So many people make breakfast a hearty meal which sustains them until dinner-time so Glebe House provides waffles, duck-eggs, French toast, scrambled eggs with rosemary shortbread, kippers, soda and rye breads, and their own speciality, date bake (a kind of flapjack, one of their most talked-about items) with crisp smoky bacon.

The Old Convent, Clogheen

A signature breakfast dish is the fruit martini, layers of yogurt and fruit in a cocktail glass; then there are five different kinds of bread made in the kitchen, French toast, Eggs Benedict, fresh juices, plum jam from the local farm and, if you can't hold off until dinner-time's cheese platter, the new 'Select' cheese from Baylough, a producer literally across the road from the Old Convent.

The Quay House

The full dinner menu offered a stunning lettuce and lime soup, a warm salad with goat's cheese and quail's eggs, a rack of Connemara lamb with couscous and rosemary cream, medallions of monkfish with king prawns in a Thai coconut sauce or a breast of Barbary duck.

Rathsallagh Country House

Breakfast consists of a buffet of cereals, kedgeree, grills, ham on the bone, wild Irish mushrooms, fresh breads and home-made jams. The dinner menu offers brown trout with wilted spinach, brill with devils on horseback on a saffron sauce, quail, oysters, gravadlax, guinea fowl, beef, duck, salmon. The dessert included lemon tart with red berry ice-cream, passion fruit mousse, vanilla crème brûlee, dark chocolate pavé with Kirsch and black pepper ice-cream.

Ulusker House

The breakfast menu for residents is generous and imaginative (French toast made with cream and served with bacon and maple syrup; lemon scrambled eggs with kippers; baked free-range eggs with ham served with 'soldiers'), while dinner also depends on fresh local produce: turbot, prawns and scallops from Castletownbere, garden asparagus and spinach, Slaney Valley lamb, Irish beef.

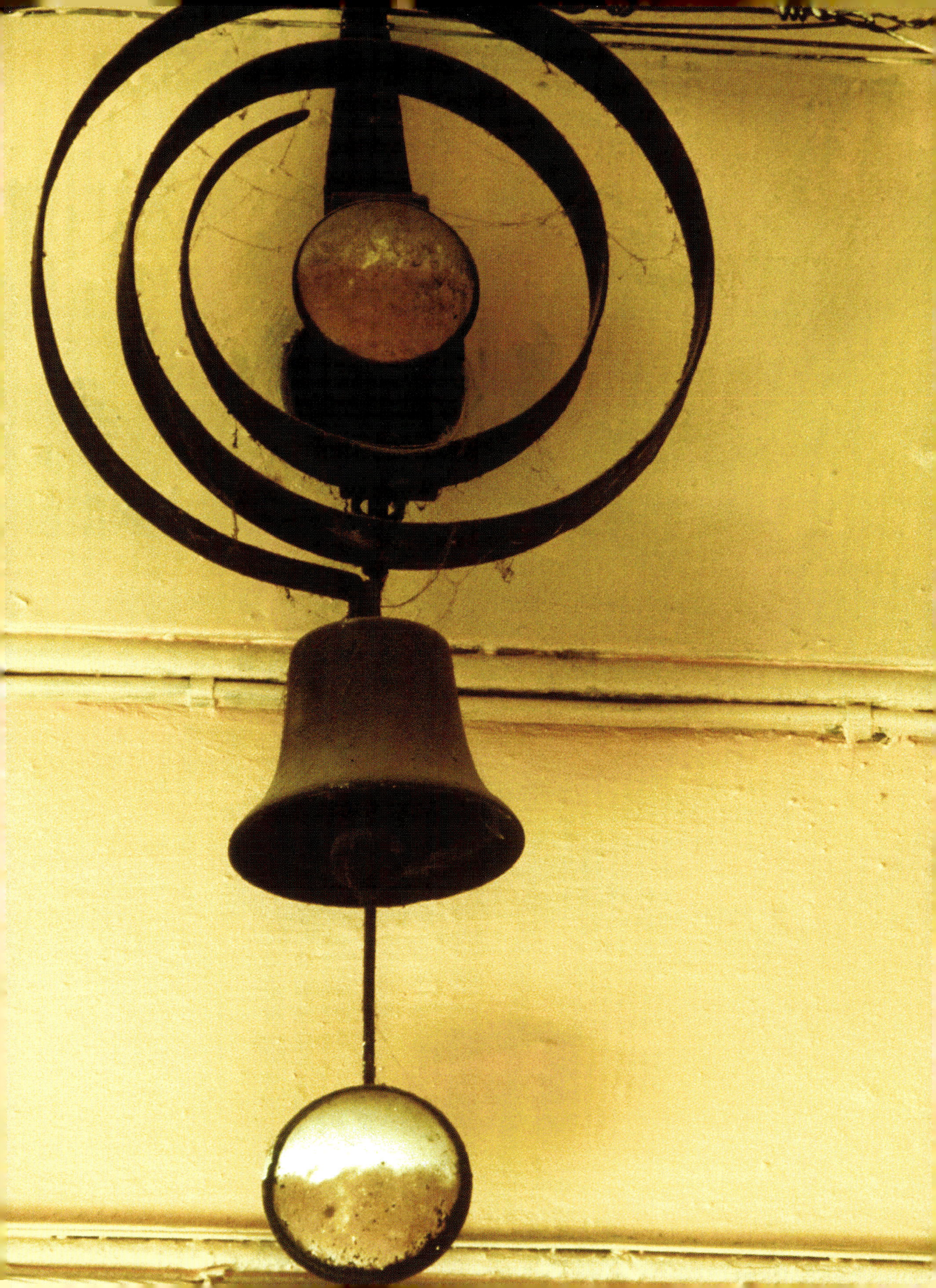

Notes